The Coming Revolution:

Capitalism in the 21st Century

The Coming Revolution:

Capitalism in the 21st Century

Ben Reynolds

Winchester, UK
Washington, USA

First published by Zero Books, 2018
Zero Books is an imprint of John Hunt Publishing Ltd., No. 3 East St., Alresford,
Hampshire SO24 9EE, UK
office1@jhpbooks.net
www.johnhuntpublishing.com
www.zero-books.net

For distributor details and how to order please visit the 'Ordering' section on our website.

Text copyright: Ben Reynolds 2017

ISBN: 978 1 78535 709 1
978 1 78535 710 7 (ebook)
Library of Congress Control Number: 2017940873

A CIP catalogue record for this book is available from the British Library.

Design: Stuart Davies

Printed and bound by CPI Group (UK) Ltd, Croydon, CR0 4YY, UK

We operate a distinctive and ethical publishing philosophy in
all areas of our business, from our global network of authors to
production and worldwide distribution.

Contents

For the unborn.

Acknowledgments

Writing is usually considered a solitary enterprise, and yet this book would never have come into existence without the support and aid of countless friends and fellow travelers. The writer's voice is merely a recombination of the voices of all those who they had the pleasure or misfortune of encountering in their time on this Earth. To those of you on both sides of this divide, I offer my undying gratitude. There are, however, some who deserve special mention for the assistance they offered in the creation of this particular work.

First, this book could not have been written without the love and care of Neal and Cara, my parents, my sister, Dylan, and my partner, Adriana. Nor could it have come to fruition without the support and love of my friends. I owe a great deal to conversations with and comments from John Baltes, John Lombardini, Patrick Higgins, Ari Lindenbaum, Hassan Ould Moctar, Vera Mey, Alex Berry, Asia Beevi Ebrahim, Alex Pino, Amanda Raffaele, Daniel Singer, Adam Mounts and many others who I've doubtless forgotten. I am incredibly grateful for the edits and comments of James Lewis, Drew Staples, Zack Quaratella, Cara Bachenheimer and the editorial staff at Zero Books. Jake Douglas deserves a special mention not only for his extensive edits and suggestions, but also for making three of the figures used in the book. And last, but of course not least, I thank all of my comrades in New York and around the globe, whose indomitable spirit convinces me that we really can change the world.

Introduction

Radical advances in automation, robotics, and computer technology have thrown millions out of work and will only continue to do so in the years to come. At the same time, cheap, individually accessible machines will wrestle for primacy with both gleaming, highly automated factories and sweatshops alike, ultimately eroding the dominance of industrial production. Economic growth is slowing down and, short of massive capital destruction on the scale of a world war, it is not going to speed up again. The pressures fueling today's global unrest will not go away and are only going to get worse as wages stagnate in many countries, solid employment becomes harder to find, and cuts to social benefits continue. Competing radical and reactionary ideologies will clash as political consensus crumbles and the world's peoples search for answers to these challenges. In its opening decades, the 21st century will be one of war and revolution. By the end of the 21st century, capitalism will be consigned to the history books. Despite the seeming darkness of our era, our future is filled with incredible possibility. If working people organize themselves to take power in their own communities, we can create a world of freedom, beauty and abundance, where poverty and tyranny are merely distant memories for our grandchildren.

These may seem like bold and perhaps reckless predictions — after all, the universe seems to love thwarting our expectations — but I feel perfectly comfortable putting them forward. I drew all of these predictions from events that are already happening, and that we can understand with a little bit of study and careful thought. In the pages that follow, I explain how fundamental, long-term changes in the way that we produce goods are already changing the world we live in and will continue to do so. I show how the present economic crisis has its roots in a 50-year process that began with capitalism's response to its last epic crisis. I link the current struggles of working people with stagnant living standards, high unemployment and underemployment, and continuous cuts to welfare programs to both of these processes, showing why our desperate attempts to fight for a decent life seem like struggling against a rising tide. Throughout this entire book, I follow a simple method: tracing seemingly distant events and trends to their root causes.

The world of the early 21st century may seem far too complex for any ordinary person to understand. When we feel that we simply don't understand what's happening around us, we often feel paralyzed and powerless to change anything. I wrote this book so that people like myself—working people, students, everyday activists and so on—can learn the answers to a series of difficult and often confusing questions: Why are rents rising so quickly and why are poor people like me being pushed out of my neighborhood? Why is life in my neighborhood and city so hard for the people around me? Why is it so difficult to find a decent job? Why does it seem like unions are declining? Why is the economy so bad?

I wrote this book so that anyone who picks it up and makes an honest effort to read it should be able to understand it. Because this is not a book for university professors, I have avoided using uncommon words and phrases as much as possible, and have defined words that may be new to the reader wherever they first appear. I have added a glossary of these terms at the end of the book that you can flip to if you need to see what something means while reading. I have tried to keep the book concise and direct, to make it as short as possible while still covering everything that needs to be covered. I try not to define words more than once or spend longer than necessary explaining an idea.

Many of the statements that I make in this book may seem strange, strong or radical. I do not apologize for this; it is my job as an author to provoke you to think about things differently. I can only promise you that I have done my best to interpret the evidence that I have gathered correctly and that I have written exactly what I think. I see no point in using cute phrases or careful wording so that I can sell more books, secure tenure at a university or ensure that I don't get fired from my job. In short, I promise to be completely honest with you. All I ask in return is that you keep an open mind.

Ben Reynolds, 13 September 2016

Part I

The Production Process

The bourgeoisie cannot exist without constantly revolutionizing the instruments of production, and thereby the relations of production, and with them the whole relations of society.

Karl Marx, *The Communist Manifesto*

Chapter 1

The Printing Press

A single technological leap, however grand it may be in itself, foretells a much larger social revolution. This is the historical lesson that this book seeks to impart. The printing press was not just a radical innovation in the production of text. It was a forewarning of an entire industrial society in waiting, the outlines of which could be understood from the printing houses themselves. What the printing press was to industrialism, the personal computer and the Internet are to an entire system of production that has only begun to emerge today. This new system promises to shake the foundations of our society. But we must not get ahead of ourselves. As with any story, we must begin at the beginning.

Sometime before 1450, a German man named Johannes Gutenberg invented a printing press that worked with moveable type. So, at least, the traditional story goes. Between 1450 and 1455 presses were established in Germany and put into operation, each turning out hundreds of books. By 1471 the printing press had spread to Cologne, Paris, Rome and Seville. By 1480 the empire of the press stretched from Krakow in the east to Lübeck in the north, Naples in the south and Salamanca in the west. The first press in the Americas was established in 1539 in Mexico City, and Goa in India received its first printing press by 1557. In the span of a century, mass production was underway in cities and towns separated by 9000 miles (14,400 kilometers) of land and sea.[1]

Text was the first globally mass-produced product and the printing press was the means of its manufacture.[2] Prior to the invention of the printing press, book production was an extremely labor intensive and expensive process. In the early Middle Ages, scribes were almost completely confined to monasteries and abbeys, and the production and transfer of written knowledge was limited to the priestly class. The rise of the first universities in cities like Bologna and Paris from the 11th to the 13th century created an additional, though limited, market for the written word. Universities employed their own scriveners to produce the manuscripts demanded by scholars.

In the hundreds of years preceding the press, the production of manuscripts scarcely changed. Copyists laboriously copied text from an exemplary manuscript onto sheets of parchment or paper in their own hand, with great variations in style and handwriting between copyists. The manuscript was passed to a rubricator, who would highlight particular passages or headings for emphasis. An illuminator would then add any necessary images or artistic flourishes, depending on the quality of work demanded.[3] Finally, a stationer or leather-worker would assemble and bind the manuscript. Each of these professions had its own guild to regulate work and was often organized in separate workshops with separate production lines.[4]

The invention of the printing press changed everything. Moveable type made it possible to reuse and recombine impressions of letters and numbers, allowing for the standardization and simplification of scripts. The design of the press meant identical pages could be produced in rapid succession. Even the earliest commercial presses could turn out a page every 15 seconds. Compositors produced a "form"—a blueprint for several pages—by arranging pre-made characters into lines held together by a wooden frame. The form was then set in the bed of the printing press and inked. Next, the printer laid the paper sheet over the inked form and pressed a plate firmly over the paper to impress the type. The printer then lifted the inked page from the printing press and hung it to dry with thousands of other pages. Finally, a binder bound the pages and the book was ready for distribution.

The creation of books, which had been extraordinarily labor intensive, became a machine-aided process. As a result, the cost of books dropped dramatically. In England, for example, a printed folio cost only 2 per cent of the price of an average manuscript prior to the advent of printing.[5] As the market for printed books developed, it became increasingly easy for members of the learned professions to amass substantial libraries, though books were still a luxury item for some time.

It is hard to overstate the immense increase in production printing made possible. "A man born in 1453, the year of the fall of Constantinople, could look back from his fiftieth year on a lifetime in which about eight million books had been printed, more perhaps than all the scribes of Europe had produced since Constantine founded his city in A.D. 330."[6] Other estimates suggest that around 20 million books were printed before 1500. Historians conservatively estimate that between 150 and 200 million books were printed in the 16th century alone. These numbers dwarfed the possibilities offered by the technology of manuscript production. "Once set up in type, a text could be reproduced in an almost infinite number of copies; there were no technical difficulties about producing large editions even with the earliest, or almost the earliest, presses."[7] The main limitation to producing printed books was developing a market capable of absorbing this remarkable output.

The printing press necessitated a larger market than that supplied by university towns and local clergymen. Publishers and printers did not want to absorb the costs of unsold books, and tried to erect a network of outlets where their products could be sold as quickly as possible. Books were dispatched across Europe from their printing shops in relatively small shipments, as most towns could not absorb them in any large number. Printed books had the additional constraint of being heavy, delicate products. Because of their weight and the danger of being exposed to the elements, transportation costs were quite high. Transport by boat was significantly cheaper then overland, and publishing houses positioned near ports and waterways had an advantage over their landlocked competitors. The book trade and its distribution networks were thus heavily influenced by the natural limits of geography.[8]

While a printing press was relatively inexpensive by itself, setting up a successful printing operation required resources that far outstripped those possessed by most printers, who were largely craftsmen. The raw materials—typesets and paper—and labor required for a single edition cost more than it took to equip a printing shop. Financiers stepped in to provide the necessary capital.[9] These early capitalists loaned money and equipment to printers in exchange for a substantial share of the profits, and took a large role in selecting books for publication, and arranging their sale and distribution. The publishers were able to gain effective control over the means of production in the world of printing simply by virtue of the large amount of money they required, and the largest among them set up their own printing shops to turn out new works.[10]

States financially supported printing enterprises by granting privileges and monopolies to certain publishers, particularly larger ones, and by offering favorable contracts to print certain books. State intervention spurred the centralization of capital and encouraged booksellers to join together into syndicates. This was a matter of political policy as much as it was a means of ensuring financial stability. Reducing the number of printers made it easier for the state "to reconcile printers to becoming docile instruments of policy."[11] The fewer the people who had control of the means of producing books, the easier it would theoretically be to control the spread of dangerous ideas and information. This did not work particularly well in practice. Insurgent printers consistently defied state control by printing heretical tracts. They exploited lax regulations in states just across the border from their intended markets. Protestant printers operating in Geneva exported their books to Catholic-dominated France, helping to fuel the religious wars of the 16th century. A couple of centuries later, freethinking printers in Amsterdam smuggled the works of the philosophers into French salons. The French Revolution toppled the monarchy due in no small part to the ideological war waged by Enlightenment authors against the aristocracy.

Inside the printing house, new social classes began to form. Printing houses produced a class division between the printers and their financial backers on one hand, and the laboring apprentices and journeymen on the other. Printers were concerned primarily with securing the greatest possible profit from their efforts, which drove them to demand long workdays and to maximize the amount of unpaid labor—apprentices—they employed. The printing houses transformed journeyman printers into wage laborers with little hope of one day becoming master printers unless they married into a successful printing family. Journeymen constantly fought to protect themselves from competing sources of labor, like apprentices and foreign workers, and abusive conditions, organizing themselves in brotherhoods and associations within towns and larger printing establishments. Lucien Febvre and Henri-Jean Martin wrote that "Even in the 16th century they organised strikes which sound quite modern and, in support of their claims, wrote manifestos which the Syndicalists of 300 years later would not have disavowed... In the 19th century, numerous printers were to be found in the ranks of the first Socialists." They demanded increased wages, reduced production targets and a shorter working day.[12]

The journeymen occupied a position somewhere in between the ranks of the artisans and a yet-to-be-born industrial proletariat. Journeymen were wage laborers with nothing but their labor power to sell. They engaged in forms of struggle that would only become common in other professions in the 19th century. Printing required working habits that resembled those of the factory much more than those of handcraft production. Compositors had to master a series of movements, to the point that they became almost automatic. As Febvre and Martin argue, "This type of manual rhythm had not previously been required in the manufacturing processes of the 15th century."[13]

The larger the capital invested, and the size of the printing shop, the more the work of printing resembled a factory organized along industrial lines. A publisher like Christophe Plantin in Amsterdam could operate more than 20 presses and employ dozens of workmen by the late 16th century. The pursuit of profit drove large publishers to increasingly rationalize production and specialize the tasks assigned to workers. But large printing houses were a rarity for centuries after the invention of printing and many were still operated by single families.

Apprentices often lodged with their masters. Journeymen in these smaller outfits had to work in a much wider capacity, serving in various roles as production demanded. The production process of the printing house developed to the extent that available capital and the size of local populations would allow, but most stopped short of properly industrial organization. The world of the press took the shape of a future yet to come: the world of industrial production.

Endnotes

1   Febvre, L. and Martin, H.J. (1976) *The Coming of the Book: The Impact of Printing, 1450–1800.* (London: Verso) pp. 178–9, 208, 212.

2   There are examples of mass production, like the shipbuilding of the Venetian Arsenal, that precede the advent of the printing press. However, each of these examples was geographically limited by the forces required to sustain production on such a scale. This includes the earlier-version

printing press developed in China in the 11th century, which also spread to Korea. The nature of the Chinese written language – which is logographic and does not have an alphabet – probably made the cost of casting movable type prohibitive. The Korean language is alphabet-based and a famous text known as the "Jikji" was printed as early as 1377. The Sino-Korean press, unfortunately, did not become generally used.

3 I Illuminators sometimes used block printing for the production of shorter, cheaper works or impressions in larger manuscripts. This method, which had been in use for centuries and was still employed until the late 1400s, was comparatively inefficient, as the wooden blocks wore down easily with each impression and took a very long time to create.

4 "In the age of scribes, book making had occurred under the diverse auspices represented by stationers and lay copyists in university towns; illuminators and miniaturists trained in special ateliers; goldsmiths and leather workers belonging to special guilds; monks and lay brothers gathered in scriptoria; royal clerks and papal secretaries working in chanceries and courts; preachers compiling books of sermons on their own; humanist poets serving as their own scribes." Eisenstein, E. (2012) *The Printing Revolution in Early Modern Europe* (Cambridge: Cambridge University Press) p. 27.

5 Bennett, H.S. (1950) "Notes on English Retail Book-prices, 1480–1560." *Library*. pp. 172–8.

6 Clapham, M. (1957) "Printing," *A History of Technology, vol. 3, From the Renaissance to the Industrial Revolution*. ed. Singer, C., Holmyard, E.G., Hall, A.R. and Williams, T. (Oxford: Oxford University Press) p. 37.

7 Febvre, L. and Martin, H.J. *The Coming of the Book: The Impact of Printing, 1450–1800*. pp. 249, 262, 216.

8 Ibid. pp. 216–23.

9   *Capital* is money, tools, buildings and so on put to work to produce a surplus. In its simplest form, capital is money used to make more money. Because someone needs to labor in order to turn money into more money, a pile of money is not capital. Capital is the social relationship that allows its owner to make a surplus out of the things that they own.

10 The *means of production* are the collection of tools, machines, buildings and raw materials needed to produce a good.

11 I use Murray Bookchin's definition of the state. Per Bookchin, the state is "a professional body composed of bureaucrats, police, military, legislators, and the like, that exists as a coercive apparatus, clearly distinct from and above the people." As Friedrich Engels argued, the state is a product of society with class divisions, or class society. A revolution that did away with class divisions would also do away with the state and as such the idea of a "people's state" is incoherent. Febvre, L. and Martin, H.J. *The Coming of the Book: The Impact of Printing, 1450–1800.* p. 127; Bookchin, M. (1991) "Libertarian Municipalism: An Introduction" in *Social Ecology Project's Readings in Libertarian Municipalism.* Available at: http://theanarchistlibrary.org/library/murray-bookchin-libertarian-municipalism-an-overview [accessed 10 May 2017]; Engels, F. (1884) *Origin of the Family, Private Property, and the State,* trans. West, A. and Baggins, Z. B., p. 92. Available at: https://www.marxists.org/archive/marx/works/download/pdf/origin_family.pdf [accessed 10 May 2017].

12 Febvre, L. and Martin, H.J. *The Coming of the Book: The Impact of Printing, 1450–1800.* pp. 128–35.

13 Ibid. p. 61.

Chapter 2

Industrial Production

All of the elements that would come to characterize modern mass production and the industrial economy can be found in the development of the printing press. First and foremost, the printing press was the first generalized example of machine-aided mass production in the Western world. Printing houses revolutionized the production of text and images, allowing for the production of substantial amounts of material, with a significantly decreased amount of labor. This radical increase in productivity caused the price of printed texts to drop rapidly. Printing houses also needed a large outlay of funding for their continued operation, much of which was supplied by merchants and other early financiers. Ultimately, the explosion of production created by the printing press made it necessary to establish new distribution networks to overcome the limitations of local markets. Thus, the printing press established the *industrial production paradigm.*

A production paradigm is a general model of the process employed for the production of goods. Production paradigms differ from individual schemes, blueprints, and shop layouts by being general and abstract. While manuscript production followed its own logic and structure, it was simply one example of a much larger paradigm that we can call the *artisanal production paradigm.* Artisanal production relies on specialized groupings of skilled workers organized according to trade. In manuscript production, copyists, illuminators, goldsmiths, leatherworkers, monks and clerks each had their own role to play in creating a single manuscript. These workers employed relatively simple tools, and the value of their products highly depended on the skill and expertise of individuals. Artisans often owned their own tools, as it was not particularly expensive to acquire them. Artisanal production largely serviced the demands of local markets. Importantly, artisanal production was quite labor intensive. As a result, the development of the artisanal production paradigm was coextensive, with the growth of the large sedentary populations needed to sustain a stratified division of labor.

Any production process that falls under a production paradigm will largely follow its general rules. Producing manuscripts and gunsmithing were two very different technical processes, but both can be understood as examples of the artisanal production paradigm. By understanding a production paradigm, we can predict how future production processes will work, and how existing processes and industries are likely to develop. We could have predicted, for example, that a society that needed to produce more manuscripts would have to invest more labor rather than labor-saving capital to do so. We could have predicted that artisan gunsmithing would look like other artisanal professions. Gunsmiths, for instance, could have been expected to mostly control the conditions of their own work. These are not particularly important or shocking predictions today. We already know how artisan production works. But we can apply these insights to understand our own world and newly emerging technologies. We can use these general principles to predict how the production of goods will change in the future.

A production paradigm is the technical foundation of a *mode of production*. A mode of production is the dominant system that a society uses to produce the goods it needs to sustain itself. A mode of production is made up of productive forces—the tools and raw materials required, the kind of labor needed, the production paradigm—and social relations. The industrial production paradigm, for its part, is the technical foundation of industrial capitalism. But while a production paradigm may have certain tendencies, it does not determine the social relations that actually characterize a given society. Technical aspects of production are always socially integrated. A factory can be run collectively by the workers or it can be run for the benefit of capitalist shareholders. Neither of these outcomes is predetermined; each is the result of a chain of historical events that can be analyzed and understood. The way that a production paradigm is integrated into a society depends on the politics of that society – its class composition, its values and its power relations. There were relatively few people in early modern Europe with the resources necessary to set up a printing house or an early factory. The merchant classes would establish early industrial production lines and employ the poor as wage laborers. But this outcome was a product of the class relations of the time. If the peasants had vanquished their feudal overlords in one of their many uprisings, they might have owned the land and held its surpluses in common. Such a society might have established industrial production in a cooperative fashion, managed as a commons in following with the traditions of European peasant society. A production paradigm does not determine the general mode of production. A mode of production is a *social relationship mediated by technology*.

It takes a long time for a production paradigm to develop its full potential. The earliest examples of a production paradigm may be comparatively inefficient or have limited applications. It can be very difficult to recognize at the time that the small, gradual changes taking place have explosive implications. All of the changes in production that we associate with the Industrial Revolution were first embodied in the operations of the early printing houses. It took the development of Watt's steam engine, over 300 years later, for this new production paradigm to finally start spreading throughout the rest of the Western economy. In the 20th century industrial production conquered most of the world, pushing artisanal production and subsistence agriculture to the margins of the global economy. Each and every factory, office and mechanized field can be seen as part of a genetic chain, leading back to the first printers in 16th-century Germany. We can draw some of the general characteristics of industrial production from our earlier sketch of the printing press, adding the wisdom of subsequent centuries:

1. Industrial production is *machine-aided.* These machines range from the moveable type press to the robots of contemporary automated factories. In industrial production, workers work alongside machines, becoming part of a continuous productive machine made up of both human beings and capital. Workers might be needed to skillfully operate a single machine or they may supervise dozens of robots. But a worker may also be needed to do something that machines are currently incapable of doing or their labor may be cheaper to use than a machine. The tendency in industrial production is for increasing amounts of machinery to be substituted for human labor, because this is the most reliable way to produce more goods in a given period of time. The ratio of machines to labor tends to increase constantly.

2. Industrial production is *mass production.* Industrial production attains its incredible efficiency by producing massive numbers of identical copies of a product using specialized machines designed for a more-or-less narrow role. Mass production means that goods tend to become increasingly standardized, whether in size and shape or in the standards of code that they use. Mass production also necessitates the creation of a mass market – a body of consumers, who are both capable and willing to purchase the standardized products on offer. This requires producers to mold tastes and habits to uniform standards, through the use of extensive advertising and the influence of the culture industry.

3. Industrial production is *centralized and capital intensive*. In any factory, materials are imported from a wide geographic area, combined on the floor and exported to a network of clients. The distribution network in industrial production is physical, made up of roads, railways, shipping lanes and airways. To a large extent, the scale of industrial production is determined by the ability of a product to penetrate a wide range of markets. Physically, this means that a lot of effort is spent to ensure that products can be cheaply transported to markets across the world. Politically, it means that legal and social barriers to trade must be eroded. As stated previously, the tendency in industrial production is for greater amounts of capital to be invested to increase the productivity of labor. More productive firms drive their competitors out of business or absorb them. Capital becomes increasingly centralized in fewer hands. Industrial production thus eventually tends to establish monopolies.

Industrial Capitalism

The development of industrial production was perhaps the most profound force shaping and reshaping the socioeconomic structure of modern societies. The incredible expense of the machines and workplace needed barred the vast majority of the population from ever having any chance of owning their own tools. Ruthless competition from large manufacturers and violent expropriation led to the gradual elimination of small proprietors, peasant farmers and other independent producers.[1] The productivity derived from production at a grand scale continuously pushed industry to develop in increasingly centralized forms, eliminating smaller competitors and consolidating capital under the control of ever-larger organizations. Industrial production created a world where the vast majority of the population lives by wage labor, while a small minority lives off the proceeds of ownership.

Capitalism is a system comprised of workers and owners engaged in production for profit. It arose hand in hand with industrialism. One class cannot have a monopoly on the means of production if the means of production consist of little more than a quill and leather skins. Skilled workers, in the preindustrial world, could much more easily acquire their own tools and operate their own shops, though under the strict regulations of guilds and feudal towns. This possibility did not and does not exist for the industrial worker. Financial institutions will not lend workers the capital needed to purchase their own means of production and the state will violently intervene if workers try to use productive capital without the permission of its owners. The industrial worker is dependent on the owners of capital, who derive their "right" to this monopoly from a piece of paper issued by the state.

As Marx argued, this state of affairs was not actually a necessary consequence of industrial production itself. Capitalism was the result of a particular social integration of the industrial production paradigm. For Marx, the destructive and exploitative elements of industrial capitalism coexisted with its progressive and liberatory potential. Capitalist development massively increased the productivity of labor, making it possible to produce an incredible amount of new goods. Capitalism also brought workers together in cooperative enterprises, requiring them to work together and discover their common interests in the production process. Marx believed that increasing centralization and increasing productivity would eventually overwhelm the capitalists themselves, and that society as a whole would take over the management of production in the wake of a revolution led by the working class. Because capitalism created such a powerful and productive economy, it would now be possible to create an egalitarian society with abundant goods and plenty of free time, instead of generalized poverty. This social vision is known simply as communism.

Marx's vision required the full realization, and even the intensification, of the industrial production paradigm. Expensive and centralized capital would be owned and managed by society as a whole, instead of a few rich capitalists. Workers would employ the most sophisticated techniques and machinery, boosting their productivity by further rationalizing the production process. But instead of promoting uneven and unfair development, workers would equally distribute the rewards of their labor and invest in increasing the free time of every member of society. Marx wrote that a communist society would allow its members to "hunt in the morning, fish in the afternoon, rear cattle in the evening, criticise after dinner, just as [they] have a mind, without ever becoming hunter, fisherman, herdsman or critic."[2] Marx was able to envision a future radically different from his own time that still depended on the actual economic developments that he witnessed. Instead of fatalistically accepting the brutal ways that society made use of technology during the Industrial Revolution, he forecast a future that used technology to liberate humanity from toil and suffering.

What Marx could not possibly have foreseen, however, was that a new production paradigm just as revolutionary as industrial production would emerge within capitalism's lifespan. The computing and Internet revolutions are changing the world in ways that we are only beginning to understand. Even as the centralization of capital continues unceasingly, with remarkable developments in robotics and automation, a new paradigm is emerging within the shell of the old. That paradigm is distributed production.

Endnotes

1   For a review of the history of political expropriation, see:

Polanyi, K. (1944) *The Great Transformation* and Marx, K. *Capital*, "Chapter Twenty-Six: The Secret of Primitive Accumulation." Available at: https://www.marxists.org/archive/marx/works/1867-c1/ch26.htm [accessed 10 May 2017]. It should be noted that so-called primitive accumulation is actually a continuous process throughout capitalist development. Capitalists are always looking for untapped sources of land and resources, untapped markets and new pools of cheap labor. These factors are never opened without violent struggle against the existing social structures in a particular area. The wealth that allowed capitalism to arise in Europe and North America was created through the brutal exploitation of slavery and colonialism. To this very day, capital employs state power and mercenary forces to perpetuate imperialism and neocolonialism. "Primitive" accumulation continues in the Canadian government's attempts to dispossess First Nations peoples, in the US's endless wars in the Middle East, and in the struggle between the indigenous peoples of South America and global capital for control of indigenous land and resources.

2   Marx, K. and Engels, F. *The German Ideology*, "Private Property and Communism." Available at: https://www.marxists.org/archive/marx/works/1845/german-ideology/ch01a.htm [accessed 10 May 2017].

Chapter 3

The Computing and Internet Revolutions

The birth of this new production paradigm was the invention of two ultimately codependent technologies: the personal computer and the Internet. Both technologies emerged and spread across the globe within the 20th century, and their use only became widespread in the late 20th and early 21st. In 1935 Alan Turing, a talented mathematician and cryptanalyst, described a machine that could read and write symbols on an infinite length of tape. By following an "instruction table," the Turing Machine would turn symbolic instructions into a desired product. Turing hypothesized that this machine could potentially solve not only mathematical problems, but also problems in any field of knowledge that could be expressed with symbols.[1] Only a decade later, John von Neumann described the invention of a new architecture for computing. Rather than being fed in via tape, programs could be digitally stored in the memory of a computing machine.[2] Taken together, these two concepts formed the intellectual schematic for all subsequent modern computers.

Prior to the invention of the electronic computer, computing was a human task. Clerks known literally as "computers" would follow a set of labor-intensive and mind-numbing instructions for exhausting tasks, like creating navigational tables for sailors. Human computing was tedious and human computers were prone to error. Some remarkable individuals believed that such a task could be performed much better by machines than humans. Charles Babbage, a British mathematician and economist, worked as a supervisor in the process of table making. "Babbage complained about the difficulty of table making, finding it error prone and tedious; and if he found it tedious just supervising the table making, so much the worse for those who did the actual computing."[3] By 1847, he created a machine dubbed the "difference engine" – a hand-cranked mechanism capable of producing error-free calculations. Babbage's device arrived a century early. It required precisely made parts that were exceedingly expensive to produce. The radical implications of his work, however, have become clear with the passage of time.

A century later, modern industrial-scale computers sprung on to the scene thanks to the bloodbath of the Second World War.[4] The first electronic computers were massive, taking up entire floors, and incredibly expensive. Governments and large research institutions built or purchased them to perform long sets of calculations fed into the machines by punch cards. British cryptographers used computers to decipher German codes, German computers were used for aeronautical engineering calculations and the US's own Mark I was used in the development of the atomic bomb. Supporting these machines required a massive amount of funding that only states were capable of supplying. As computing technology became cheaper and more compact in the 1950s and 60s, it eventually spread to modern offices in insurance companies, financial firms and other sectors that relied on complicated calculations. These computers represented the automation of human calculation on an industrial scale.

The introduction of personal computers changed the face of computing for good. Minicomputers were an early result of the shrinking size of computers. These computers were miniature only by the standards of the 1960s; many were the size of a relatively large cabinet. Designed to fit smaller budget and size constraints, minicomputers were still far too expensive for consumers, costing significantly more than the median income of a 1960s American family. Corporations used them in niche roles like controlling other machines or switching telephone lines. The invention of increasingly smaller and cheap microprocessors finally allowed for the creation of computers priced for ordinary consumers. In 1975 the Altair 8800, the world's first true personal computer, was introduced to the market. The Apple I was released soon after, and computer developers continued releasing new and improved products with each passing year. Personal computers, like most products of the information technology revolution, became increasingly cheap, powerful and versatile. A standard Altair 8800 had 256 bytes of random-access memory and required a floppy disk to store information.[5] Forty years later, the average iPhone has one gigabyte of RAM and up to 128 gigabytes of built-in storage. The iPhone has around 4 million times the memory of an Altair and can store over 150,000 times as much information, despite costing less than a seventh of the Altair in real terms. Computers have been widely adopted as a result of these skyrocketing capabilities. A few thousand Altair 8800s were sold in 1975. Two to three million Commodore 64s, another popular early computer, were sold in 1985. In 2015, there were around 2 billion personal computers and 7 billion mobile devices in use, which means there are now more computing devices than there are people on Earth.

The computing revolution began to attain its real potential with the advent of the Internet. The development of the Internet, like the computer, began as a state project. During the Cold War, US military planners and scientists wanted to create an instantaneous communications network that would never fail. The Advanced Research Projects Agency (later known as DARPA) began tinkering with communications between computer systems across the US. Early networks were created to link supercomputers at research universities. By the late 1980s and early 1990s, commercial networks were established and used for corporate information gathering and communication. In his pioneering work, Tim Berners-Lee theorized and created the first working "hyperlinks," allowing documents and information to link to any other information on a network. The modern Internet was born. Private users began to connect their computers to the

Internet. The spread and improvement of Internet technology was incredibly rapid. "In the fall of 1990 there were just 313,000 computers attached to the Internet; five years later the number was approaching 10 million, and by the end of 2000 the number had exceeded 100 million."[6] In 2015, there were an estimated 15 billion devices connected to the Internet.[7]

The Internet has now become a ubiquitous network, offering nearly instant communication between devices across the entire world. The speed of this communication appears to make distance itself collapse, bridging the physical barriers between events in the non-digital world. As Paul Virilio wrote, the Internet is driving "the negation of space" itself, creating a closed world by erasing the distance between people and events.[8] Any simple statement about this development would be completely trite; it defies comprehensive understanding and it has only just begun to shake the foundations of our world.

In the span of less than a century, computers transformed from large, specialized, state-owned machines into personal devices like laptops and phones. Today's computers are used to control factory machinery, coordinate shipping and warehousing operations, pilot airplanes and monitor the communications of dissidents. They are also used for a panoply of different purposes by clever and inventive groups of people. The computer Internet network facilitates commerce, both on legal websites like Amazon and illegal forums like the Silk Road. The network makes a wide amount of knowledge and analytical tools freely available to computer users, from the texts of radical authors to programs that model the effects of climate change. Computers are used to create and distribute texts, images, films and audio. Albums are produced in their entirety with digital programs and posted for free on the Internet. One can find information on surviving in the wilderness, oil painting, bomb making, automobile repair and virtually any other topic of interest online. All of this and much more has been enabled by the personal computer and the

Internet, but this is only just the beginning.

Computing machines existed long before the personal computer, just as the telegraph approximated the communication speeds of the Internet a century prior. But the combination of these two technologies initiated a revolution in the nature of communication and production, the implications of which we have only just begun to realize. Just as the printing press preceded the spread of mass production by centuries, the early products of this new production paradigm have yet to fulfill its true potential.

Endnotes

1 Turing, A. (1937) "On Computable Numbers, with an Application to the Entscheidungs problem," *Proceedings of the London Mathematical Society*. Vol. 42. pp. 230–65. Available at: https://dx.doi.org/10.1112%2Fplms%2Fs2-42.1.230 [accessed 10 May 2017].

2 Neumann, J. (1945) *First Draft of a Report on the EDVAC*.

3 Campbell-Kelly, M., Aspray, W., Ensmenger, N. and Yost, J.R. (2014) *Computer: A History of the Information Machine*. (Boulder: Westview Press) p. 6.

4 This gives us reason to believe Paul Virilio's theory that military logic is at the forefront of modern social organization and development.

5 "MITS Altair 8800", *Old Computers*. Available at: http://oldcomputers.net/altair-8800.html [accessed 10 May 2017].

6 Campbell-Kelly, M. et al. *Computer: A History of the Information Machine*. p. 275.

7 Evans, D. (2011) "The Internet of Things: How the Next Evolution of the Internet is Changing Everything". Available at: http://www.cisco.com/web/about/ac79/docs/innov/IoT_IBSG_0411FINAL.pdf [accessed 10 May 2017].

8 "We're living in the time of the finite world, not a world

about to start... Progress triggered finitude, transportation, the exhaustion of natural resources, speed, real time, etc. Most people think of speed as progress, they believe that speed simply means going faster from one point to another; but they forget that the world is closing in on us and that we're being asphyxiated by our way of life." Virilio, P. and Lotringer, S. (2008) *Pure War*, trans. Mark Polizzotti. (Cambridge: Semiotext(e)) p. 222. See: Virilio, P. and Lotringer, S. *Pure War* and Virilio, P. (1986) *Speed and Politics*, trans. Mark Polizzotti.

Chapter 4

Distributed Production

The integration of personal computers and the Internet has given rise to a radically new production paradigm that will revolutionize the creation of goods. Since the 1990s, electronic communications of all forms have become instantaneous, nearly free to the consumer and completely ubiquitous. One of the principal errors of contemporary economists is the widespread belief that the impacts of this "information technology" revolution have already been exhausted. Economists like Yochai Benkler have focused on the computer Internet network as a means of producing communications, but not as a potential means of producing other traditional commodities.[1] In fact, the computing and Internet revolutions have revealed the possibility of a new form of production: the *distributed production paradigm*.

The general principles of distributed production can be drawn from the computer Internet network:

1. Distributed production is *machine-dominant production*. Although designing texts, images and goods often requires artisan levels of skill and expertise, production and reproduction after the design phase is largely automatic. The labor required to produce a good after it has been designed is minimal, often as little as pushing a button, which collapses the time between design and production. Production is highly automated. The technical characteristics of the means of production are so complicated that they are only fully understood by a tiny fraction of their users, but they are still fully functional in the hands of the average user.

2. Distributed production is *individualized production*.

Personal computers and 3D printers are designed for individual use. While their utility is still directly dependent on the contributions of other members of society on the network, an individual does not immediately need the aid of others to produce what they want, as they would in the case of a factory.[2] Computers are now cheap enough for almost anyone to own and powerful enough to fulfill a wide range of functions. Control of certain kinds of production is directly in the hands of computer owners.[3] The extent to which the individual is capable of producing what they want is limited by the current state of technology, as well as its cost and diffusion. In distributed production, the means of production become cheaper and more accessible over time, in direct opposition to the general trend of industrial production.

3. Distributed production is *decentralized production*. The production of goods—whether individually or in large quantities—occurs at each of the nodes of the production-distribution network. These nodes can be a computer, a phone or a 3D printer. Rather than shipping a product from a factory, distributed production transfers the code to a machine, which creates the product where the user is. The distribution network is electronic, not physical. The transmission of designs and blueprints on the Internet is essentially instantaneous and ubiquitous. The designer of a new product can distribute it instantly to everyone connected to the network at a negligible cost. In this sense, distributed production not only preserves aspects of mass production by allowing for the infinite duplication of codes, but it also allows the user to individually modify the final product.

In the development of computers and the Internet, the prevailing long-term trend is the move from highly specific, capital-intensive applications to cheap and completely generalized products. This chain directly traces the evolution of distributed production from industrial production itself. Unlike industrial mass production, which witnessed the increasing centralization of the ownership of productive capital, distributed production is made possible by the creation of cheaper and more accessible means of production. Functionally, a printing press is similar to a computer with an Internet connection. Both are required to produce and reproduce texts. However, owning a printing press was outside the reach of almost any tradesman without significant financial support. Virtually everyone in the developed world now owns a computer or mobile device that is more useful, and works cheaper and faster than a printing press.[4] This is because the means of production in distributed production have been designed as mass-market consumer goods, unlike the highly specialized and expensive equipment used in industrial manufacturing.

Interestingly enough, we witnessed this progression in multiple industries throughout the 20th century. Telegraphs gave way to the household telephone, and electronics for automating manufacturing became consumer electronics. "In each case, a collectively consumed service—often emerging from an intermediary service within industry—was transformed into a series of individually purchasable commodities, opening up new markets, which in turn became mass markets as costs fell and production increased."[5]

In a similar sense, the technologies that would ultimately allow for distributed production to emerge were developed as a result of the requirements of expanding industrial capitalism. Cybernetics was developed to open new frontiers in industrial automation, like computer-controlled machinery and robotics. Computer networks were put in place to make production more flexible, and increase management's ability to supervise and control the production process. Telecommunications networks allowed capitalists to integrate geographically separate business operations, linking together production and supply chains across countries and continents.

This enabled capital to feasibly seek out the cheapest sources of labor and raw materials globally, opening new frontiers of exploitation in the developing world. Just as crucially, cybernetic technologies enabled new forms of financial activity, from high-frequency stock trading to bundling and selling complex derivatives.[6] These were the exact same technologies that would make the computer Internet network possible. In this sense, distributed production emerged directly at the apex of industrial production and as a somewhat unintended product of its own internal dynamics of technological development.

Where industrial mass production required the concentration and cooperation of large numbers of workers, distributed production individualizes the production process. While an individual worker might tend a particular machine, the standard organization of a factory relied on dozens of individuals working in concert. Fordist production methods required the assembly line worker to focus on an intensely specialized segment of the production process.[7] A worker might have spent their entire shift driving bolts into one section of a car door. Maintaining such a highly differentiated system required the constant supervision of engineers, technicians, and upper managers. In the industrial system, this hierarchical chain continued all the way up a giant pyramid to the chief manager of the firm. Whether this ideal of industrial feudalism was actually necessary for efficient production is a matter of debate, but it certainly was the prevailing trend throughout the history of industrial capitalism.

Cooperation is still required in distributed production, but central control becomes largely unnecessary. Cooperation is often anarchic, appearing as an emergent feature of day-to-day interaction. Projects like the development of Linux, a computer operating system, and Wikipedia, the world's largest encyclopedia, both follow this model. Kevin Carson and Mark Elliot have compared this trend to the natural phenomena of "stigmergy," where a coherent project emerges from the spontaneous and self-directed actions of different individuals.[8]

While specialization and the division of labor can still be productively applied, distributed production allows the individual to oversee and control the entirety of the production process. Distributed production thus places immense power in the hands of individuals.

Compare the symphonic orchestra of the industrial ag — with dozens of master musicians each with their own part to play—to today's digitally produced music. There are surely qualitative differences between the two and a synthesizer is still no replacement for a gifted violinist. But the difference in terms of scale is undeniable. In the 1800s, the creation and performance of a symphony required the combined efforts of dozens of people, a possibility only afforded by the mass concentration of the industrial city. Today, it requires one artist and a computer program.

One of the principal challenges of economic development for most of human history was establishing an adequate transportation network for the distribution and exchange of goods. For this reason, cities tended to develop next to rivers and waterways, where transportation by shipping was easiest. Transportation problems and the natural limits to distribution were perhaps the primary factor limiting the development of printing and other manufacturing enterprises up through the Industrial Revolution. Industrialization produced railroads and steamships to carry mass-produced goods, which were eventually followed by automobiles and aircraft. The development of new means of production necessitated the development of new means of transportation and distribution. As ever greater quantities of goods were being produced in centralized locations, ever greater means to distribute those goods were demanded.

By contrast, distributed production occurs at every "node" of a combined network of production and distribution. Where industrial production distributed goods outward from a central producer, distributed production distributes the "codes" for production across a network. Because this network is electronic, and not composed of highways and waterways, distribution is effectively instantaneous. The Internet is not a network for distributing products, but a network for distributing codes. Computers reproduce products from these schematics. A music file downloaded onto one's computer from the Internet is not music—it is the *code* for music. The computer then translates this code into a usable product. In the case of music, the product is sound. The transmission of texts, images and audio over the Internet is actually the transmission of codes and blueprints that individual machines make use of to create new products.

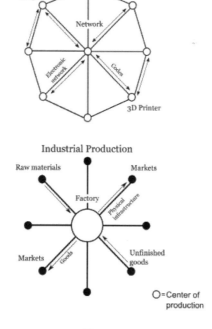

As a distribution network, the Internet preserves many of the benefits of mass production. Information uploaded to the Internet is, absent interference, accessible to anyone at will. The only limit to procuring identical copies of a particular schematic is the physical limitation of bandwidth or the amount of traffic that a network connection can support. Peer-to-peer sharing helps to overcome these limitations by distributing the burden of uploading information across a network of computer systems. *Anyone* with a computer can now mass produce text, audio and images, and distribute it to the entire world.

Some Economic Quirks

The explosive growth of the Internet has accurately been labeled a technological and economic revolution. But information and communications technologies (ICT) have yet to deliver the expansive boost to growth predicted by their most enthusiastic proponents. The burst of the dot-com bubble in 2000 and the crisis of 2008 dampened expectations of a new economic boom on the scale of the Industrial Revolution. Economists like Robert Gordon now argue that the potential economic effects of the Internet revolution have been exhausted, and that productivity and GDP (gross domestic product) growth are flagging in developed nations.[9] As Gordon argues:

What is notable about the [period] of 1996–2004 is not only how short-lived was the productivity revival associated with the invention of e-mail, the internet, the web, and e-commerce, but also how part of this short-lived productivity revival was offset by the beginning of a historic decline in hours [worked] per capita. Everything collapsed after 2004. Productivity growth returned from its temporary 1996–2004 growth rate of 2.54 to a mere 1.33 percent in the nine years ending in 2013.[10]

This rapid decline caused productivity to return to the flagging growth rates that characterized the US from the 1970s onward. This contributes to slowing economic growth on the whole, as productivity increases are the most important factor driving growth. In short, the observable impacts of the ICT revolution in economic statistics have been far less significant than many commentators seem to have expected.

Distributed production thus poses a problem for economists and society as a whole. How is it possible that clearly beneficial and widely used technologies have such a limited impact on the growth of the capitalist economy? Distributed production has a series of traits that tend to be difficult to assimilate under economic models developed during the heyday of industrial capitalism. First and foremost, the "problem" of distributed production is that its benefits tend to be social and not commercial. Because the means of production is often in the hands of the same people who intend to use their products, distributed production does not need to produce goods for sale on the market.

Economists have driven themselves mad trying to estimate the "consumer surplus" derived from free Internet services. All of Google's services, for instance, are provided free of charge to the consumer. (For what it's worth, Google's actual product is its users' information, which advertisers consume.) This is not a benevolent choice that Google makes—it is necessitated by the nature of distributed production. The low entry costs associated with digital services push firms to offer their services at the lowest possible cost. If Google were not providing its services for free, someone else would and Google might simply go out of business.[11] The benefits derived from free email, video hosting and so on do not show up in GDP statistics, since they do not create a direct commercial transaction. Only Google's advertising and data farming revenue creates income that can be distributed into wages and profits, get taxed and finally show up in the economic statistics. Free goods and services, despite being eminently useful, directly add nothing to productivity figures. Utility can easily be derived from goods and services without producing a profit, but production for profit is the purpose of capitalism. I will return to this theme in the next section.

Just as significantly, the codes for goods can be instantly copied for essentially no cost. The supply of these codes is infinite, regardless of the demand. Whatever the initial labor and capital required to design and produce a new product, the value of labor and capital embodied in an individual code approaches zero. Goods that can be instantly reproduced by a computer, such as text and audio, cost basically nothing to create. Unlike land or machinery, making use of a particular code has no effect on anyone else who wants to use it. Other users are free to copy and use what they wish. The natural price of these codes, in the form of software or digital files, is nothing. This is why it makes inherent sense, particularly to young people, that one should not have to pay for things like books, music and movies on the Internet. The free software movement grew based upon this sentiment and it survives to this day despite the aggressive policies of commercial giants like Microsoft.

When the supply of a good is potentially infinite, as is the case with software, barriers must be erected to force people to pay for it. The state creates this barrier with intellectual property laws. By granting a legal monopoly to copyright owners, the state enables these owners to charge rents in exchange for permission to use their codes. Of course, things do not work this smoothly in reality, as the spectacular success of file-sharing sites like The Pirate Bay demonstrates. Even when the state attempts to enforce intellectual property laws, there is often little long-term effect. When the Swedish government shut down The Pirate Bay's servers on 9 December 2014, an anti-piracy firm detected a 6.7 per cent drop in the number of people downloading torrent files it tracked. By 12 December 2014, a mere 3 days later, these numbers had recovered to their pre-raid levels.[12]

Finally, ICT firms require comparatively small investments of capital and labor to attain their astronomical market values. Tech companies employ tiny amounts of labor compared to their industrial-age counterparts. The infamous example of Kodak and Instagram demonstrates this painfully. Kodak—a photography company—employed 145,300 people at its peak, while indirectly creating demand for many thousands more through its supply chain and distribution networks. Just 15 people created Instagram, a popular application used to share photographs. In 2012, Facebook bought Instagram for over $1 billion, a few months after Kodak filed for bankruptcy.[13]

Photography is more popular than ever, facilitated by free and instant sharing on social networks. This popularity generates a tiny fraction of the employment that it once might have and most of those who previously worked in the industry are now totally superfluous in the production process. But even the capital employed by these firms is often comparatively cheap. As Larry Summers points out, WhatsApp—a messaging application—has a greater market value than Sony—an electronics manufacturer and media company—despite requiring close to zero capital investment to get there. Companies like Google and Apple, which historically would be expected to go to the market to finance expansion, are sitting on massive amounts of cash and are fully capable of expanding themselves without outside help.[14]

This trend delivers massive profits to the lucky few capable of cashing in on it—Facebook's public-share offering created hundreds of millionaires and ten billionaires—but nothing to the workers who find themselves unemployed in an era of digital technologies.[15] Tech firms are at the pinnacle of a process that produces surplus capital and surplus labor. This is how growth in the ICT sector, which is widely hailed as the engine of the future capitalist economy, actually works.

From Bytes to Bullets

In the 16th century it would have been considered absurd for someone to predict that all goods, from food to weapons, would eventually be produced with the paradigm seen in printing houses. But they would have been right and they might have been able to understand that Europe's feudal society would be shattered by the spread of the new production paradigm. The potential uses and implications of a new technology are often unclear for decades after it is first conceived. The same goes for production paradigms. If we examine historical examples of technological development, we can identify a general pattern that most inventions follow before being widely adopted:

1. There is an initial invention or breakthrough, which in most cases is not cost effective.
2. The initial inventors and others take up the challenge of improving upon the design, and through a steady stream of continuous experiments and tweaks, they create the first cost-effective versions of the technology.
3. Early adopters who have a particular need for the technology and can afford it make use of these versions.
4. Developers continue to enhance the technology, making it more efficient and driving down its cost
5. Increasing amounts of users adopt the technology, leading to mass adoption and ultimately saturation.

It seems that the period of time in each of these phases tends to decrease on average as history progresses. It took 45 years for the steam-powered loom to overtake handlooms in textile production in England, but only around a decade for personal computers to make minicomputers obsolete. Technological development is a useful metaphor for understanding how production paradigms develop. Around three hundred and fifty years passed between the invention of the printing press and the expansion of the industrial production paradigm to other commodities. Internet use has only been widespread for a couple of decades and distributed production has only been applied en masse to media products: text, images and sound. Thus far, the average person has only encountered distributed production as a communications technology, much as the printing press was the only widespread example of mass production for centuries. But new forms of distributed production are already emerging.

Hints of the future started to emerge alongside early personal computers in the workshops of hobbyists. Japanese manufacturers used cheap semiconductors and computers to create small, flexible machine tools for their extremely successful "lean production" model. These computer-numerical-control (CNC) tools allowed the user to perform a wide range of simple tasks, including manipulating, cutting and drilling objects. Most importantly, the new CNC machine tools were cheap, small and relatively accessible to use.[16] Mechanics, local manufacturers and hobbyists would adopt these machines for their own purposes, enabled by the spread of the personal computer. A computer could now control a cheap, precise, multipurpose tool small enough to sit on one's desk. But although CNC machine tools are accessible in terms of price, they still require a fair amount of skill to use. This means that true mass adoption of these tools has always been unlikely.

We did not have to wait long for more sophisticated forms of the paradigm to arise. Additive manufacturing is beginning to fulfill the potential of distributed production. Traditional industrial manufacturing is subtractive, cutting products from larger unfinished materials or molding and casting products from pre-made forms. While these methods have become quite efficient in large-scale industrial production, modern industrial manufacturing is capital intensive. Additive manufacturing, by contrast, builds a product by layering its component materials from the bottom up. Additive manufacturing is far more flexible than traditional manufacturing, because the same machine can be used to create a wide range of products in different shapes and sizes. 3D printing is the present incarnation of this new technology of production.

3D printing was invented in 1984. It has been used for rapid prototyping and producing specialized parts for decades. 3D printers have only been a consumer product since around 2010. Just as was the case with computers, 3D printers are gradually making the transition from specialized, capital-intensive applications to cheap and generalized applications. Chuck Hull, the inventor of 3D printing, sold his first printer for $100,000 in 1988.[17] The only companies that could afford or even use the technology were airplane and medical equipment manufacturers.[18] In 2015, commercial manufacturers like Makerbot offered models as cheap as $1375 and open-source designs like Rep Rap could be assembled for as little as $300–600. The low costs associated with producing a Rep Rap are partially attributable to the fact that many of the required parts can be 3D printed. Prices will continue to drop and the ones quoted here may seem quaint within a few years of this book's publication.

For a long time 3D printers were only capable of printing in either plastics or metals, which made them unable to create most things that people commonly use. New developments in 3D printing, however, leave reason to believe that these limitations will be short-lived. Developing technologies like continuous composite printing have the capacity to both lower the cost of the raw materials consumed in manufacturing and increase the range of goods that can be produced by a printer.[19] Continuous composite printing allows a 3D printer to work with multiple complementary materials simultaneously, both increasing the strength of the finished product and conserving valuable resources. There are also a wide range of promising applications in fields like medicine.

Scientists have developed a technique to print living human kidneys.[20] Research is underway on printers capable of printing other organic tissues, like artificially produced skin.[21] There are even printers capable of printing edible products, like structures made of chocolate and sugar. On a larger scale, experimental printers are being used to build entire structures. One Chinese company employed large printers using a mixture of cement and construction waste to build ten houses in 24 hours. Owing to the lack of labor required and cheap materials used, each house cost as little as $5000 to produce.[22] Perhaps the most fascinating possibility is the idea of a "molecular printer" or a 3D printer capable of printing goods at the molecular level. Such a printer would build a product out of individual molecules from the ground up, allowing an unprecedented degree of control and customization in the production process. Specialized molecular printers could be used to print medicine and other drugs, and a general-purpose molecular printer could print virtually anything comprised of the molecules it used.[23]

The most advanced printers, like the molecular printer described earlier, seem to fulfill the longstanding human pursuit of the instant gratification of any material desire. These technologies are extraordinarily expensive and far beyond the reach of any contemporary consumer. It will take many decades before they become available to even a portion of the population. But the reality is that it is only a matter of time, though it may be a long while, before advanced printers become accessible to a portion of the world's population. It is conceivable that the logical fulfillment of distributed production—nearly instant production of anything, at will, anywhere in the world—will arrive within the lifetime of children born at the time of this writing.

Today's printers are still expensive, imprecise and of limited utility. As such, they have not been adopted on a wide scale. This will probably not be the case two decades from now. When

41

a single machine can print plastics, carbon fiber, metals, wood composites and circuitry simultaneously, and when this machine costs the equivalent of a contemporary laptop computer, it will be both very useful and very desirable. It is wondrous to think that such a machine is not just a distant possibility, but also an inevitability. The character of our era makes even the most remarkable developments seem banal, but the fulfillment of this vision will have revolutionary implications.

What distinguishes additive manufacturing as a revolutionary concept is its absolutely general character — production is limited only by the available materials and schematics. As stated previously, the general trend in computing and distributed production is the march toward tools of increasingly general utility. The first industrial-scale computers were only useful for complex calculations. Now, a personal computer is a multipurpose tool that can publish essays, create images, videos and music, play games, design products, communicate with most of the world and so on. Additive manufacturing fulfills the promise of the personal computer as a means of production — producing anything at all, on demand, for direct consumption. Skeptics will counter that these kinds of machines will never achieve the efficiency or productive capacity of modern mass production. For example, it is unlikely that large airliners will be manufactured entirely with distributed production, even if they make extensive use of technologies like 3D printing.

However, there is reason to doubt this as a general principle. Contemporary manifestations of the distributed production paradigm have both dramatically increased the volume of goods produced and decreased their prices. Eric Brynjolfsson and Andrew McAfee write that "of the 3.5 trillion photos that have been snapped since the first image of a busy Parisian street in 1838, fully 10 percent were taken in [2014]."[24] Digital cameras allow their users to produce massive numbers of photographs at very little cost. The same can be said of any technology that allows the digitization and instant transfer of information. Why should distributed manufacturing be any different? A 3D-printed product eliminates the costs associated with shipping and distribution, marketing, corporate overheads and taxation. Together, these form a significant portion of the costs of most manufactured products. Designs can simply be copied from products that have already been developed by large firms, evading the costs of research and design. Better yet, inventors and designers can freely share their work with consumers all over the globe. It only takes one good free design to render dozens of designs protected by copyright obsolete. Will most people buy a mass-produced good, when it takes little effort to make a cheaper one in your own home? The millions of people who freely share music and movies with their friends and complete strangers already know the answer to this question.

Opening Shots

It is naive to think that such a radically new production paradigm will be contained by the social structures that developed around industrial capitalism. Distributed production fundamentally erodes one of the basic pillars of capitalism—the monopolistic control of the means of production by an elite class. This is an inherently political development. Those who control capital, control the means by which a society reproduces itself. This is demonstrated by an event of incredible importance: the creation of the printed gun.

In 2012, an organization known as Defense Distributed announced a project to develop the world's first 3D-printed firearm. The project raised over $20,000 via crowdfunding from small donors. Despite having its rented printer confiscated by Stratasys, the printer's manufacturer, Defense Distributed, released the files for the Liberator under a year later.[25] The Liberator is a single-shot pistol made entirely of plastic components. It can be manufactured by any contemporary 3D printer, it is cheap and it can pass through a metal detector unnoticed. As many observers note, the Liberator barely holds a candle to contemporary mass-produced firearms. It can easily malfunction, it is not particularly accurate and its effective range is short. Useful weapons produced via distributed production, it seemed, were years away. Just one year later, Defense Distributed released a cheap CNC mill capable of producing untraceable lower receivers for the AR-15, a modern assault rifle.[26] First, unthinkable; then, a distant possibility; all of a sudden, reality.

Defense Distributed's project inspired further design and testing work by numerous other enthusiasts and radical libertarians. An improved version of the Liberator, made from $25 in plastic, fired eight shots without sustaining damage. A Canadian gunsmith created a rifle called the "Grizzly" based on the Liberator's design. Another inventor shared a five-shot printed revolver called the "Reprringer." In 2014, Yoshitomo Imura was arrested in Japan for producing and possessing 3D-printed handguns. Imura designed a six-shot printed revolver known as the ZigZag. While gun possession is not illegal in Japan, it is extremely restricted and Japan has one of the lowest rates of gun ownership in the developed world. In the description of a video demonstrating the ZigZag, Imura wrote: "Freedom of armaments to all people!!... A gun makes power equal!![sic]"[27]

If political power comes from the barrel of a gun, then the creation of the printed gun marks the point where the control of armed power slipped definitively out of the hands of centralized authority. Of course, people have used all kinds of strategies to acquire weapons when necessary, but this is different. In the foreseeable future, anyone will be able to get their hands on a weapon. This is incredibly threatening to those who presume to hold a monopoly on the use of force. The US State Department quickly issued a legal order under international arms trafficking regulations for Defense Distributed to take down the files. Defense Distributed complied, but the order was practically irrelevant.[28] The files had already been downloaded thousands of times and were immediately uploaded to file-sharing sites, where they are still available to this day.

The Liberator was merely the opening shot in an emerging battle between two production paradigms. Industrial production allows for the comforting illusion that careful regulations and oversight, put in place by the owners of capital and the state, can ensure that production only takes places in ways that reinforce the existing structure of society. These sorts of regulations are actually evaded all the time, but this is explained as an exception to the general rule of rational planning, and widely shared beliefs about what should and should not be done with technology. Distributed production shatters this myth. Now, anyone can produce whatever they want, and restrictions and regulations seem like the helpless flailing of a drowning system. These products will not just be worthless plastic junk, nor will they only be guns. They will be all kinds of different things, from machine parts to water filters, medicines to prosthetic limbs, hammers to sophisticated electronics, and everything in between.

It is easy to understand that this will be incredibly useful—it will help us use our resources more effectively and it will help save lives. But we should not have any illusions about where this process is going. Designs for these goods will skirt around legal protections and intellectual property rights, and they will reduce the demand for many kinds of mass-produced goods. The demand for labor in these industries will also fall and people will lose their jobs as a result. There is no way around this—distributed production cannot be un-invented, just as the printed gun is here to stay. Eroding the primacy of industrial capitalism means that wage labor, which depends on the health of capital, will also be eroded.

Endnotes

1 See: Benkler, Y. (2006) *The Wealth of Networks*. (New Haven: Yale University Press)
2 Of course, this is how things *appear* and not how they actually work. A computer Internet user is still dependent on the collective labor of society to produce electrical power, the computer itself, to maintain the physical network and so on.
3 This is not to repeat the blithe statements of technology enthusiasts that the means of production *in general* are in the hands of the individual. Working-class people still do not own the factories that produce the goods they need, they do not own the land that grows their food and they are still dependent on the owners of capital for their livelihoods. At the moment, distributed production gives the individual the ability to produce certain kinds of media and communications, and little else.
4 The fact that the first product of *both* industrial and distributed production was language, in the form of text, suggests an almost natural course of development. The desire to transmit language seems to act as the technological vanguard of human development.
5 "Misery and Debt: On the Logic and History of Surplus Populations and Surplus Capital," in *Endnotes 2: Misery and the Value Form*. (2010) Available at: http://endnotes.org.uk/en/endnotes-misery-and-debt [accessed 10 May 2017].
6 Cybernetics is the science of controlling and communicating with machines (and human beings). See: Dyer-Witheford, N. (2015) *Cyber-Proletariat*. (Chicago: University of Chicago Press) pp. 33–4. Dyer-Witherford's book, coming out of the autonomist/workerist tradition, focuses on the impact of cybernetic technology in contemporary capitalism on the working class. It is an excellent companion piece

and corrective to this book, which focuses largely on the development of technology and capital.

7   Fordism, named after Henry Ford, is the name for the system of standardized mass production based upon the highly rationalized differentiation of labor functions in the assembly line.

8   See: Carson, K. "The Stigmergic Revolution", *Center for a Stateless Society*. 12 November 2011. Available at: https://c4ss.org/content/8914 [accessed 10 May 2017].

9   The *gross domestic product* is the total value of all of the goods produced in a given economy.

10 Gordon, R. (2014) "The Demise of U.S. Economic Growth: Restatement, Rebuttal, and Reflections" p. 6. Available at: http://www.nber.org/papers/w19895. [accessed 29 May 2017]

11 Some firms are able to avoid this problem by monopolizing certain markets. eBay, for instance, derives its ability to charge a premium for online auctions from its large user base. The value of networks of this sort is dependent on the size of the user base. If vendors found another site that charged less but still had a sufficient number of potential clients, they would probably switch to that site. However, Internet monopolies can be quite persistent.

12 De Looper, C. "The Shutdown of The Pirate Bay Did Nothing: Here's Why," *Tech Times*. 23 December 2014. Available at: http://www.techtimes.com/articles/22670/20141223/shutdown-pirate-bay-nothing-heres-why.htm [accessed 10 May 2017]. "On Dec. 8, one day before the raid on The Pirate Bay, a total of 101.8 million Internet users torrented files being tracked by anti-piracy firm Excipio. These files including movies, music, games and other digital media. For the next three days, the number of users downloading these types of files dropped down to around 95 million, before bouncing right back to 100.2 million on Dec. 12."

13 Brynjolfsson, E. and McAfee, A. (2014) *The Second Machine Age: Work, Progress, and Prosperity in a Time of Brilliant Technologies.* (London: W. W. Norton & Company) p. 61.

14 Weisenthal, J. "Larry Summers Nails The Radical Economic Implications of The Facebook-WhatsApp Mega-Deal", *Business Insider.* 26 February 2014. Available at: http://www.businessinsider.com/larry-summers-on-whatsapp-2014-2 [accessed 10 May 2017]; Summers, L.H. "Reflections on the new 'Secular Stagnation hypothesis'," *VOX.* 30 October 2014. Available at: http://www.voxeu.org/article/larry-summers-secular-stagnation [accessed 10 May 2017]. See also: Roberts, M. "Capitalism: stagnation or hypochondria?" *The Next Recession.* 22 August 2014. Available at: https://thenextrecession.wordpress.com/2014/08/22/capitalism-stagnation-or-hypochondria/ [accessed 10 May 2017].

15 Lynley, M. "Facebook's IPO Will Make These People Millionaires and Billionaires," *Business Insider.* 2 February 2012. Available at: http://www.businessinsider.com/these-people-will-be-fabulously-wealthy-after-facebooks-ipo-2012-2 [accessed 10 May 2017]; Shontell, A. "Meet the 10 Billionaires of the Facebook IPO," *Business Insider.* 18 May 2012. Available at: http://www.businessinsider.com/meet-the-10-billionaires-of-the-facebook-ipo-2012-5 [accessed 10 May 2017].

16 Carson, K. (2010) *The Homebrew Industrial Revolution.* p. 184. Available at: https://dl.dropboxusercontent.com/u/4116166/NewHomeBrew.pdf [accessed 10 May 2017].

17 This is the equivalent of roughly $200,000 in 2015.

18 Davis, A. "Layer-by-Layer: The Evolution of 3-D Printing," *The Institute*, 14 November 2014. Available at: http://theinstitute.ieee.org/tech-history/technology-history/layerbylayer-the-evolution-of-3d-printing. [accessed 29 May 2017]

19 Halterman, T. "A Path to the Future – Continuous Composite

3D Printing," *3D Printer World*, November 12, 2014. Available at: http://www.3dprinterworld.com/article/path-future-con tinuous-composite-3d-printing. [accessed 29 May 2017]

20 Ashley Feinberg. "Scientists Can Now 3D Print Transplantable, Living Kidneys," *Gizmodo*, August 13, 2013. Available at: http://gizmodo.com/scientists-can-now-3d-print-transplantable-living-kidn-1120783047. [accessed 29 May 2017]

21 Sarah Butler. "Medical implants and printable body parts to drive 3D printer growth," *The Guardian*, August 24, 2014. Available at: http://www.theguardian.com/business/2014/aug/24/medical-implants-drive-3d-printer-growth. [accessed 29 May 2017]

22 "3D printers print ten houses in 24 hours," *Xinhua News*. April 25th, 2014. Available at: http://news.xinhuanet.com/english/sci/2014-04/25/c_133290171.htm [accessed 29 May 2017]; Amanda Froelich. "Revolutionary 3D Printer Can Build 10 Houses In 24 Hours For Only $5,000 Each," *techswarm*. September 15th, 2015. Available at: http://www.techswarm.com/2015/09/revolutionary-3d-printer-can-build-10.html?m=1.[accessed 29 May 2017] Workers still have to install the roof, pipes, electrical wiring, windows, and so on.

23 "3D Printer for Small Molecules Opens Access to Customized Chemistry," *HHMI News*. March 12th, 2015. Available at: http://www.hhmi.org/news/3d-printer-small-molecules-opens-access-customized-chemistry. [accessed 29 May 2017]

24 Eric Brynjolfsson and Andrew McAfee. *The Second Machine Age: Work, Progress, and Prosperity in a Time of Brilliant Technologies*. (2014) pp. 126–27.

25 "Liberator – Dawn of the Wiki Weapons," *Defense Distributed*. May 5th, 2013. Available at: https://www.youtube.com/watch?v=drPz6n6UXQY. [accessed 29 May 2017]

26 The receiver is the part of a firearm that houses its working components. Under US law, only the receiver counts as an

actual firearm and only the receiver needs to be registered with a serial number. By allowing individuals to easily mill their own receivers, Defense Distributed exploits a loophole in US law that allows for the legal production of unregistered guns. See also: "Ghost Gunner," *Defense Distributed*. October 1st, 2014. Available at: https://www. youtube.com/watch?v=xwRtll3jjU4. [accessed 29 May 2017]

27 Andy Greenberg. "How 3-D Printed Guns Evolved Into Serious Weapons in Just One Year," *Wired*. May 15th, 2014. Available at: http://www.wired.com/2014/05/3d-printed-guns/. [accessed 29 May 2017]

28 In legal terms, however, the order may establish the precedent that schematics and ideas—in other words, speech—shared on the Internet can be censored if the US government deems them to be a possible threat to national security.

Chapter 5

Radical Automation

...for if each of the instruments were able to perform its function on command or by anticipation... so that the shuttles would weave themselves and picks play the lyre, master craftsmen would no longer have a need for subordinates, or masters for slaves.

Aristotle, *Politics*[1]

Concealed in a forest near Mount Fuji, Japan, a factory complex churns out avatars of the future. Inside, bright yellow robots are building other robots, from industrial robotic arms to CNC machine tools. The robots work 24 hours a day, creating around 50 other robots in each 24-hour period. Fanuc, the corporation that owns the facility, is extremely secretive, but details about its operations still leak out. In 2003, Fanuc's robots were reportedly capable of running unsupervised for 30 days. When the factory's stocks filled up with finished machines, human workers would arrive in trucks to ship them off to customers. Fanuc achieved the manufacturer's dream of "lights out" production—a factory that could run fully dark because no human beings were required in the production process. "Not only is it lights-out," a Fanuc vice president boasted, "we turn off the air conditioning and heat too." After all, robots do not sweat. While human workers are employed in the process, there are only ever a handful of workers on the factory floor. "One 86,000-square-foot (8,000-square-meter) factory in Oshino, making industrial robots, is staffed by only four people at a time." Fanuc's work drives the automation of production elsewhere. Its robots have been used in automobile manufacturing for quite some time. In recent years, its machines have enabled factory automation in China, where its machine tools are used to shape the cases of smartphones, like Apple's iPhone.[2]

Robots producing robots producing iPhones is a neat little story, but reality is much more complex. In 2011, Foxconn chairman Terry Gou vowed that he would replace the 1 million workers in Foxconn's Chinese factories with 1 million robots within years. Foxconn—an electronics manufacturer that produces smartphones and tablets—was struggling with a wave of worker unrest in its plants and resulting bad press. From 2010 to mid-2012, at least 16 people at Foxconn's factory in Shenzhen committed suicide, some by leaping from factory roofs, and 300 workers at a factory making Xbox consoles threatened mass suicide during a dispute. Foxconn infamously installed nets around its worker dormitories and factories as a suicide prevention measure. Uprisings involving thousands of workers became common.

None of this was surprising. Working conditions in Foxconn's factories are completely inhuman. Workers perform one task thousands of times a day—placing stickers on screens or installing a tiny electronic component—regularly working 60-hour weeks. Some workers reported working for 35 hours straight, for as little as 31 US cents an hour. They are forbidden to speak with one another, they wear identical uniforms and are constantly monitored by a team of security guards. In such an atmosphere of fear and exploitation, it is simultaneously incredible and unsurprising that workers struggle to assert their dignity, whether by halting production or simply refusing to be exploited any longer. These persistent problems made automating the worker out of existence attractive for Foxconn. Per the famous phrase, robots don't go on strike.[3]

But the promised expulsion of the worker has not gone exactly as planned. In 2015, Foxconn had around 50,000 robots, but it still employed over 1 million workers in its factories. Some of Foxconn's factories are supposedly "lights out," but the company has had difficulty matching the skill and dexterity of human hands. In an industry where packing minuscule electronics components into smaller and smaller spaces is an essential task, contemporary robotics still falls short. Foxconn customers, like Apple and Samsung, constantly change the specifications of their products—turning out new models that render their old products obsolete is the center of their business model. Until Foxconn's robots become as flexible as its human workers, it will still need human beings in the production lines. It remains to be seen how long leaping this technical hurdle will take. Labor costs in China are rising and increasingly automated factories are becoming the norm. Terry Gou claims that "Foxconn will probably use robots and automation to complete 70 percent of its assembly line work" by 2018. For now, Foxconn is experimenting with automating other kinds of work out of existence. "Foxbots" are being used to cut noodles and Foxconn's engineers are trying to teach them to cook noodles, as well.[4]

Cybernetic and computing technologies are responsible for more than the rise of a new production paradigm. Cybernetics has been employed remarkably in virtually every area of production in the 20th and 21st centuries.[5] Industrial robots assemble planes and automobiles, computer programs coordinate shipping and trade stocks, and self-operating harvesters reap corn and wheat fields. Computers were initially designed as a tool for automation and they continue to perform very well in this regard. Understanding just how well they will perform is absolutely central for anyone who is interested in how goods are produced in our society, from the worker to the revolutionary.

Automation is the replacement of human work with that of self-governing machines. While human and animal bodies remained the motive power of production—for the first 100,000 years of human history—there was comparatively little that could be automated. Fishing traps and long lines saved a great deal of work over using simpler hand lines, but they still had to be regularly checked and tended, and would not produce a catch without constant human supervision.

The prospects for automation changed with the invention of the steam engine, which unleashed the energy trapped in coal. A steam engine could work reliably and virtually without ceasing if it was given the proper care. Engineers during the early Industrial Revolution immediately went to work putting this newly unleashed energy to use. Edmund Cartwright invented the power loom, which could be driven by water or steam, in 1785. The machine was not a commercial success and the first factory to employ the looms at Manchester burned down. But a subsequent chain of small inventions and improvements made the looms increasingly efficient. By 1830, power looms overtook handlooms as the dominant tool used to produce textiles in the UK. By the end of 19th century, weaving a yard of cloth took only 2 percent of the human labor it took on a handloom at the start of the century.[6] But this innovation also drove handloom weavers out of work, leading to reduced wages and great suffering for a period of time.

While the dispossession and suffering endured by the weavers was real, most eventually found work elsewhere, as economists are quick to point out. During the Industrial Revolution, displaced workers like the weavers were absorbed by other industries, often with great speed. Dozens of new products were being turned out of new factories and the markets for these goods were constantly expanding—first in Europe and the US, and then in the rest of the world. The potential uses of labor appeared virtually limitless and some argued it was inconceivable that labor could ever really be permanently replaced in any industrial sector.

Many economists today will argue as a matter of faith that automation can never produce an overall decline in the demand for labor. Arguing otherwise leads one to be accused of endorsing the Luddite Fallacy, supposedly disproved by the great scions of economics. As James Bessen blithely writes, "[l]essons from the Industrial Revolution... suggest that today's Information Revolution could yet yield similar gains [in wages and employment]."[7] As we will see, the assumptions of this model are no longer valid. Before we begin to learn why, it is also worth noting that this argument is simply wrong even at first glance. The amount of hours that each manufacturing worker labored per week declined continuously from the beginning of the Industrial Revolution up until the post-World War II era.

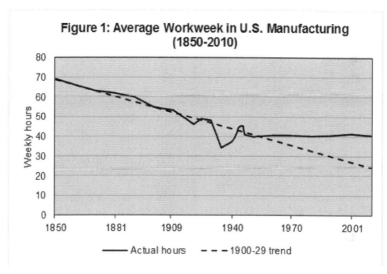

Figure 1: Average Workweek in U.S. Manufacturing (1850-2010)

This means that, for the *entirety of the industrial working class*, the hours of labor demanded per worker decreased reliably over 100 years. The constant expansion of new industries and the opening of new markets helped to prevent widespread structural unemployment. More significant in this regard, however, was the constant agitation of an organized working class for higher wages, better working conditions and a reduction of the length in the workday. Industrial society made major adjustments to accommodate the effects of rising productivity. As seen above, the most important one of those adjustment mechanisms—the reduction of labor hours—halted after the Second World War.

Radical automation is a long-term decline in the demand for hours of labor per worker caused by the introduction of labor-saving machinery. Radical automation can occur in a particular firm, in an industry, in an entire sector and in an entire economy. Automation does not always lead to a decline in the demand for labor. History shows that there are specific structural causes of radical automation. First, a market's ability to consume a particular product or group of products eventually reaches its limits. More importantly, capital eventually becomes so productive that it is no longer profitable to employ additional labor in the production process at virtually any cost. In the US, radical automation crept from sector to sector throughout the 20th century. The US is an advanced capitalist economy and it has been at the forefront of automation in many fields. The development of the US is not a perfect proxy for the course that today's developing countries are likely to follow; nor is its history identical to that of other developed nations. Nevertheless, it is an instructive case study of how radical automation works and can thus provide a template that will help us to understand the likely course of radical automation in the 21st century.

Seed and Steel

At the dawn of the 19th century, the US was a predominantly agricultural society. In large parts of the American South, plantations based on slave labor produced cash crops like cotton and tobacco. In the North, Northwest and parts of the South, smaller farms worked by families and hired hands produced crops for market and for their own consumption. In some areas, like rural Vermont, forms of subsistence agriculture persisted for decades after the American War of Independence.[8] In 1800, the largest US city – New York – only had a population of 60,000.[9] A trip across the nation would have revealed a country dominated by farmland, and uncultivated areas punctuated by a few small cities and towns. This was a society in transition and change would arrive quickly.

From its humble beginnings onwards, agriculture was always a labor-intensive process. Indeed, it is likely that more work was needed to produce food with agriculture than with many forms of hunting and gathering.[10] The Industrial Revolution changed this dramatically. By the mid-1800s, inventors began to apply mechanical innovation to agriculture. In 1833 and 1834 respectively, Obed Hussey and Cyrus McCormick began selling reaping machines for grain crops. A steady stream of improvements on their initial designs followed and by the mid-1850s, large numbers of farmers began to adopt the machines. Instead of cutting their grain by hand with a scythe, farmers could use a horse-driven machine to cut and bundle their harvest.[11] Machines of this sort were particularly valuable to US farmers, as labor was often scarce in rural areas. Output grew, and the number of farms and farmers continued to expand throughout the century.

The Homestead Act of 1862 opened land previously used by Native Americans in the West to settlement and farming. From 1870 to 1890 the number of US farms increased by 80 per cent. Output continued to expand, leading up to the depression of 1893, when crop prices collapsed. Many farmers went out of business and farms grew larger as they were consolidated.

In 1892, John Froelich invented the first gasoline-powered tractor. Again, tweaks and improvements continued for some time. In 1917 Ford introduced the Fordson, which was to become the Model T of tractors. Tractors started replacing horses on farms, as they were more efficient and allowed large areas of land to be cultivated with fewer hands. Buoyed by high crop prices and expanding foreign markets, farmers produced significant surpluses. By 1921, US farmers were chronically overproducing crops and prices entered a collapse that lasted for two decades. Deep in debt from their investments of the preceding decade, farmers routinely faced bankruptcy and the loss of their land. This was the atmosphere John Steinbeck captured in *The Grapes of Wrath*, a portrait of a few Oklahoma farmers among tens of thousands migrating to find work.[12]

The US government intervened with a series of legislative acts in 1922, 1929 and 1933, establishing a comprehensive price-setting and subsidy system. Crop prices were given federally mandated floors to guarantee profits, and overproduction was discouraged by paying farmers not to grow crops and to destroy their existing stocks. Still, the mechanization and rationalization of production continued.

During World War II, when the labor supply was tight, combine harvesters hitched to tractors began to enter use, which self-propelled combines replaced in the 1950s.[13] In the decades after World War II, chemical fertilizers and genetic modification continued to boost production, further reducing the need for farm labor. By 2000, tractors could basically drive themselves, thanks to improvements in computerization and GPS technology.[14]

Radical automation was first observed on a large scale in the mechanization of agriculture. A table from 1899 already detailed the remarkable improvements of machinery over hand methods in farming: planting corn took nine times the labor by hand, planting cotton eight times, planting potatoes a little under fifteen times, and harvesting and baling hay required over three times the labor.[15] These results were recorded even before the use of tractors or combine harvesters. As a result of mechanization and a wide range of changes in technique, farmers produced ever-greater quantities of crops throughout the 19th and 20th centuries. At the same time, the agricultural labor force dwindled.

Employment in agriculture peaked as a percentage of the population at 42.7 per cent in 1890 and in absolute terms in 1910.[16] Since 1910, the total number of people employed in agriculture in the US has been in an uninterrupted decline. In 2012, there

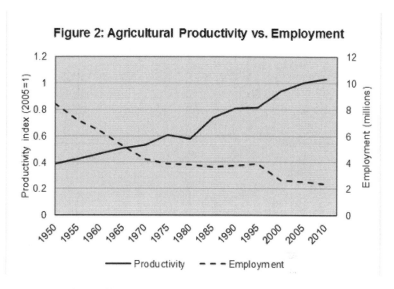

Figure 2: Agricultural Productivity vs. Employment

were around 2 million people employed in agriculture in the US, less than half in total of those employed in 1965, when the US population was only half as large.[17]

The mechanization of agriculture had massive impacts on the shape of US society. The decline in agricultural employment led millions of farmers and farmworkers to migrate to industrial cities in search of work. Black farmers were prominent among the dispossessed. The Great Migration, which saw 6 million black Americans move from the rural South and into Northern, Midwestern and Western cities, was a product of this shift. Urban centers swelled as the rural population declined, a process which continues to this day. In 1900, 39.6 per cent of the US population lived in urban areas. In 2000, that number rose to 79 per cent.[18] Farming ceased being a way of life for the vast majority of the US population. In economic terms, the result of this process was the industrialization of the farm. The ever-greater capital required to extract the maximum product from the soil led to the consolidation of smaller farms. From 1900 to 2005 the number of US farms fell 63 per cent, while average farm size rose 67 per cent.[19]

Farming became an industrial-scale business, dominated by contract production companies and agricultural supply companies. For example, the company Monsanto, which sells genetically modified (GMO) crop seeds, holds about 80 per cent of the market for US corn seeds and 90 per cent of the market for US soybean seeds. Given that GMO seeds are used to produce over 90 per cent of major US crops, this represents almost complete dominance. Thanks to state-guaranteed intellectual property rights and a host of abusive intimidation practices, Monsanto holds a virtually unassailable monopoly atop the pyramid of US agribusiness.[20] Cornered by companies like Monsanto and their contracts with processing companies, most US farmers have no real control over the production process and many do not even own their land. An increasingly productive, automated agricultural system led directly to the expulsion of the farmworker from the production process and extreme centralization of capital, propped up by a state-managed pricing system.

From the Farm to the Factory

There was little time for US workers to breathe after the radical transformation of the farm. By the late 1960s, when agriculture was beginning to move on to bioengineering, radical automation had moved on to the factories. Cybernetics allowed for the creation of increasingly efficient machinery, including CNC machine tools and industrial robotics. The changing nature of production hit the US automobile industry hard. In 1955, four out of every five cars in the world were produced in the US, half of those by Detroit's own General Motors.[21] Detroit embodied the automobile-driven vision of the American dream. In the 1950s, "the Detroit area had the highest median income, and highest rate of home ownership, of any major U.S. city." In 1963, it was estimated that one in six US jobs depended on the auto industry for their existence, either directly or indirectly.[22]

Powerful unions and strong labor demand guaranteed decent wages for autoworkers, which black Americans were eventually able to take advantage of after a long struggle to enter the industry. This dominance did not last. After the oil shock of the 1970s, Japanese automakers began to enter the US-dominated market with smaller cars. Japanese manufacturers like Toyota cut costs by implementing a new production model dubbed "lean production" or "post-Fordism," founded on flexible manufacturing, co-opting and suppressing labor, and the aggressive use of industrial automation.[23]

General Motors, Ford and Chrysler struggled to keep up with Japanese competition. In the late 1960s, General Motors experimented by building a highly automated factory in Lordstown, Ohio, but resistance from rank-and-file workers, including sabotage and wildcat strikes, discouraged the practice.[24] The influx of Japanese cars overcame this reluctance. Through the late 1970s and 1980s, both US and Japanese automakers brought industrial robotics into their plants. In the US, management canceled its post-war bargain with the United Autoworkers union, forcing a series of layoffs and pay cuts. The union leadership, for its part, accepted the cuts in hope of preserving its remaining jobs and the pension system for older workers. The real wages of auto industry production workers peaked in 1977 and started declining afterward.

Over the next decade, those wages fell by almost 12 per cent.[25] Still, Japanese imports soared throughout the 1980s. These changes in the automotive labor force should not be blamed on foreign *labor* competition. By the mid-1980s, foreign automakers began moving some of their plants to the US, particularly to areas with low wages and weak unions. Toyota opened its first US manufacturing facility in 1986.[26]

At the same time that manufacturing workers were being laid off in the US, the Japanese manufacturing sector shed workers, as well. Japanese manufacturing employment declined as a percentage of total employment from a temporary peak in 1973 onward.[27] From 1991 to 2013, the Japanese manufacturing labor force shrank by around 33 per cent.[28] The rest of US manufacturing mirrored the general trends of the auto industry.

Automation in the core of the industrial sector continued unceasingly. Manufacturing employment declined from a high of nearly 40 per cent of the labor force during World War II to less than 8.7 per cent in 2015.[29] In absolute terms, US manufacturing employment peaked at 19.5 million people in 1979. At the time of this writing, only 12.3 million people work in industrial jobs.[30] At the same time, US manufacturing output increased continuously. The US is not producing fewer manufactured goods. In fact, it is producing more manufactured goods than ever before. It just employs fewer and fewer people in the process.

Falling manufacturing employment shaped the development of US society throughout the second half of the 20th century. As the US lost its global monopoly on manufacturing, and as cybernetics and machinery made workers more and more productive, the status of the industrial worker declined. In 1963, James Lee Boggs wrote that:

> [t]he working class is growing, as Marx predicted, but it is not the old working class which the radicals persist in believing will create the revolution and establish control over production. That old working class is the vanishing herd. There are only 12 million of these production workers left in American industry, out of a total work force of 68 million.[31]

His contemporaries on the Ad Hoc Committee on the Triple Revolution (of which Boggs was a member) complained of persistent, excessive unemployment and the formation of a class of permanently superfluous workers.[32] Automation struck black Americans the hardest, as they were at the bottom of the labor hierarchy. Black Americans were the last group to gain access to industrial employment and they were also often the first to be forced out. So-called unskilled workers in the assembly line watched themselves become superfluous, replaced by machines that did not slow down, stop or go on strike. Jobs that once provided a modest share of the country's wealth to workers were ruthlessly eliminated. In US industrial cities like Baltimore, St. Louis, Oakland and Detroit, the stream of waged work dried up. The results of "de-industrialization" were frightening. Take Baltimore, Maryland as an example. Once a hub of steel production and shipping, the city's official unemployment rate hovers at almost twice that of the State of Maryland as a whole.[33] In 2013, its unemployment rate for black men between the ages of 20 and 24 was an astonishing 37 per cent. By comparison, the official unemployment rate of Greece in 2013—a country in total economic free fall—was 27.5 per cent.[34] There are around 16,000 abandoned buildings in the city, which also has a homeless population of 30,000.[35] Nearly 24 per cent of the city's population lives below the poverty line. Public health is equally dismal. The average life expectancy of some poor neighborhoods is 20 years lower than that of wealthy suburbs just a few miles away.[36]

In such a depressed economy, people do what they must to survive, often turning to criminalized activities in the informal economy. Owing to its aggressive and structurally racist police force, Baltimore "holds the highest percentage of its population in jail when compared to the other 19 largest jails in the country."[37] These are the conditions that produced the 2015 Baltimore uprising, sparked by the police murder of Freddie Gray, all of which can be traced directly to the legacy of de-industrialization and systemic racism.

A part of the journalistic and political classes devotes its time to expounding upon the "culture of poverty" that is supposedly responsible for the decline in the status of the black working class. Teeming with thinly veiled racism, this body of literature stands as a monument to the extreme lengths that some will go to in apologizing for and rationalizing the failings of capitalism.[38] Of course, there is nothing particular to black culture that has anything to do with the causes of poverty.

As the process of de-industrialization began to impact the white working class from upstate New York to Appalachia, even reactionaries like Charles Murray were forced to admit that they observed exactly the same effects: changing family structures, persistent high levels of unemployment, rising disability claims and mass incarceration.[39] Today, one can find panicked diatribes about the white "culture of poverty" that echo the racial anxieties and anti-immigrant screeds of yesteryear's professional bigots.[40] As it turned out, the plight of the black worker was nothing less than a vision of the future for a large segment of the entire working class, whites included.

Developed economies still have not dealt with the consequences of de-industrialization—the simultaneous rise in industrial productivity alongside an absolute decline in industrial employment. To be sure, the rise of low-to-middle wage service jobs absorbed the majority of the workers displaced by industrial automation. But a tour of the industrial centers of the US, and much of the rest of the developed world, reveals a pattern of wreckage and decay. In Detroit, Michigan, seemingly endless blocks of houses lie abandoned alongside the ruins of former auto plants. Facing municipal bankruptcy, the city shut off the water supply to many of its residents, while real estate speculators bought up land in droves.

In 2014, *Newsweek* dubs Wilmington, Delaware—the former site of shipyards, steel foundries and auto plants—"Murder Town USA."[41] The poverty rates in some of the city's neighborhoods range from 41 to 77 per cent, but the city center is a financial hub owing to Delaware's early elimination of usury laws in the 1980s.[42]

But capitalism is a global system and the belt of superfluous labor stretches across the world. The conditions that hold for these US cities are equally valid in Bristol, UK, or the banlieues on the outskirts of Paris, France. These desperate conditions have forced the dispossessed to take to the streets with increasing frequency, as the present system offers little hope for redress. But even as poverty and rage explode into protests and riots across the world, a new specter looms on the horizon.

Into the 21st Century

One might hope for some respite from this storm, but steady progress in the development of robotics, cybernetics and computer systems reveals that the replacement of human labor will continue far into the 21st century. In 1973, US sociologist Daniel Bell argued that advances in industrial efficiency and automation would produce a post-industrial society, where the vast majority of jobs would be found in the service and public sectors. Bell's prediction was based on the observation that the productivity of industrial work rose much faster than the productivity of service-sector jobs.

To a certain extent, Bell was right. In 2012, 79.9 per cent of US employment was in the service sector—a sprawling category including retail, transportation and logistics, information technology services, finance, business services, education, healthcare, hotels and restaurants, and government employees— as opposed to the goods-producing sectors.[43] Bell's work was the foundation of an entire line of thought hailing the rise of a new "post-industrial" or "information" economy, where comfortable service jobs and technical work would replace the hard labor of the industrial era. Bell was wrong, however, to suspect that services had an inherent "ceiling of productivity"—namely: that they could not be automated.[44] With each passing year, we find that there is comparatively little that *cannot* be automated.

In 2010, Google announced that it was developing a self-driving car. Using GPS technology, programmed road maps and an array of sensors, Google's driverless vehicles are capable of navigating complex city streets and traffic without causing accidents. In 2015, *Reuters* reported that Google was in discussions with General Motors, Ford, Toyota, Daimler and Volkswagen about manufacturing self-driving cars for the market.[45] Numerous other companies are investing in creating autonomous vehicles.

The potential benefits of a self-driving car are obvious. The majority of traffic jams and traffic accidents are caused by human error, which could be reliably eliminated by taking human hands off the steering wheel. Self-driving cars could be programmed to drive more efficiently, to reduce their energy consumption and emissions. Both of these are undeniably good things. But cheap, effective, ubiquitous self-driving vehicles will be the end of the millions of jobs currently provided by the global transportation industry. Truck drivers, bus drivers, taxi drivers and many more will find themselves being replaced by machines that do not sleep or make mistakes.

In the US, the transportation and logistics industry is one of the largest employers, responsible for around 3 per cent of total employment, or 4.4 million jobs in 2012. The largest individual components of this sector are truck drivers and bus drivers.[46] Uber, one of the largest global taxi services, has vowed to transition to a fleet comprised only of self-driving cars over the coming decades. Speaking indirectly to Uber's current employees, CEO Travis Kalanick callously stated that "the world isn't always great."[47] For their part, most commercial airplanes are already functionally autonomous—they fly using autopilot programs, and can take off and land without supervision.[48] The main barriers to full automation, in their case, are state regulations and a lack of trust from passengers.

What about the other part of the global logistics network—warehousing and supply-chain management? New technologies like RFID chips and advanced software are making it easier than ever to track and manage all kinds of goods.[49] Just as significantly, robotics threatens to make much of the human labor that goes into warehousing—moving boxes and pallets, packing goods and so on—obsolete.

In 2012, Amazon—one of the world's largest warehouse operators—acquired Kiva, a robotics developer. Kiva's bright orange robots are used to move shelves full of products, a role traditionally performed by human warehouse workers. In late 2014, Amazon was already putting these robots to work in a state-of-the-art fulfillment facility. Developers are currently working on robotic arms capable of picking items out and packaging them for shipping. By combining these technologies with conveyor belt systems, sophisticated software and automated transportation networks, the logistics industry will ultimately be capable of expelling much of its human workforce from the process altogether.[50]

Radicals have identified organizing the logistics labor force as a key priority, given that the logistics and transportation system is a vital choke-point in an increasingly complex international system of production. Most of this workforce is already part-time or employed short-term, an effect of the growing use of precarious labor. But it will be increasingly difficult to bring the strength of organized labor to bear when robots are becoming more and more capable of performing this work, and where automation can be used as a weapon against working-class struggle.[51]

Retail and the food service industries are not immune to automation, either. The favorite examples of this trend, even among those who are otherwise deaf and blind to technological change, are the ATM, the self-service checkout lane and the automated parking lot pay station. These, however, are only early hints of where we are headed. A US company called Momentum Machines has developed an automated machine that produces, cooks and delivers finished burgers on a conveyor belt. The machine forms the burgers immediately before cooking them, cooks them reliably and uniformly, and freshly prepares toppings like tomatoes and pickles, before sending them directly to an employee or a customer. It can produce a burger every 10 seconds. The company claims that its next generation machine will be able to make custom meat grinds for every customer, and that its products are capable of creating sandwiches, salads and other foods.[52]

Briggo, another US company, created an automated barista system capable of creating anything one might normally order in a coffee shop. The system is reliable, precise and flexible. Users can order their drinks remotely over the Internet, specifying minute details, and pick up their drink when it is ready. The machine learns the customer's drink preferences over time, so that a network of the machines would remember their usual order wherever the customer went.[53]

A Japanese sushi chain is ahead of the curve. In Kura's 262 restaurants, robots help produce sushi, while waiters have been totally eliminated by conveyor belts.

Customers order using touch panel screens, and when they are finished dining they place the empty dishes in a slot near their table. The system automatically tabulates the bill and then cleans the plates and whisks them back to the kitchen. Rather than employing store managers at each location, Kura uses centralized facilities where managers are able to remotely monitor nearly every aspect of restaurant operations.[54]

Altogether, machines such as these could reliably eliminate a substantial portion of the workforce in chain and fast-food restaurants. In 2013, 3.6 million people were employed in fast-food restaurants in the US, while the restaurant industry as a whole employed 13.1 million.[55]

The possibilities in retail are slightly more limited, for now, but they are still significant, as Martin Ford points out. For starters, online retailers like Amazon and eBay have already wreaked havoc on many local retailers, like bookstores, by offering cheaper products and a greater selection. Amazon is experimenting with drones that will enable it to deliver products on the same day that they are ordered, eliminating one of brick-and-mortar retail's few advantages over its Internet competitors.

As we have already seen, these Internet firms are also at the forefront of eliminating labor from their warehousing and logistics operations, where jobs theoretically would have been gained as other locations went out of business. Additionally, kiosks and vending machines like RedBox, in addition to online services like Netflix, destroyed Blockbuster, a national video rental chain that employed 60,000 people at its peak. These businesses employ fewer people, and cut down on maintenance and delivery labor, with sophisticated monitoring systems. Finally, large retailers like Walmart are experimenting with using robots as a tool to track store inventories and potentially restock shelves.[56]

Many of the job categories discussed consist largely of poorly paid, part-time and precarious work, but these are areas responsible for the bulk of US job growth in recent years, particularly in the wake of the 2008 crisis.[57] What about the temple of white-collar work, the corporate office? In the 1980s and 1990s, the rise of computing and communications technologies led to a wave of corporate restructuring. Authors like Jeremy Rifkin wrote of waves of layoffs and the formation of support groups for out-of-work middle managers.[58] From 1996 to 2004, corporations registered a spike in productivity gains, presumably as a result of their investments. Computers were substituted for a number of jobs, including bookkeepers, telephone operators and customer service representatives. In principle, many kinds of white-collar work are actually easier to automate than "low-skilled" manual labor. AI researchers call this Moravec's paradox, "the discovery by artificial intelligence and robotics researchers that, contrary to traditional assumptions, high-level reasoning requires very little computation, but low-level sensorimotor skills require enormous computational resources."[59]

Today, the process continues. Text and data-mining software is used in law firms and corporate offices, to the detriment of paid researchers, who once performed the same tasks. Machine learning and artificial intelligence have become quite sophisticated. Automation engineers can now teach programs how to perform a task by showing them a starting position and a correct series of solutions, which allows the program to figure out how to correctly get from A to B. Automated programs of this sort are used in all kinds of applications, from detecting credit card fraud to testing software and websites for vulnerabilities.

Considering that a great deal of office work actually consists of doing repetitive tasks, like working with spreadsheets or producing formulaic reports, the barriers to automation in the field are not particularly high. This is tough news for the middle-class, white-collar worker. Software is cheaper than robotics and office workers are more expensive than low-wage service employees. As a result, middle-income professions have been hollowing out over the past two decades, while job growth largely comes from low wage areas and a few growing high-wage categories.[60]

One of the more dramatic examples of automation is in the financial services industry. From 1999 onward, computers began playing the stock market. By 2009, high-frequency trading accounted for 60–73 per cent of all US equity trading, though it declined to 51 per cent by 2012.[61] High-frequency trading uses computer algorithms that make lightning-fast trades based on a particular model or observed behavior. These algorithms might be designed to rip off pension funds, for example, or compete with other trading algorithms for fractions of a cent worth of profit. This has enabled the stock market to be manipulated and rigged in a spectacular fashion.

Recently, the Swiss Bank UBS was charged with secretly helping high-frequency traders to exploit investors inside its private stock market. Barclays misled investors about the presence of high-frequency traders in its own private market, facilitating their fleecing. Michael Lewis accurately describes the contemporary US stock market as "fully automated, spectacularly fragmented, and complicated beyond belief."[62] The New York Stock Exchange is now a TV set designed to simulate a more reassuring image of clamoring human voices driving the rise and fall of the financial markets. As the owners of capital, financiers are probably not about to automate themselves out of existence. Nevertheless, finance offers an advanced example of the ability of cybernetic technologies to replace formerly human activities.

What of education and healthcare, two sectors that are likely to continue expanding for some time? There are obvious reasons that these professions are resistant to automation. In healthcare, doctors and nurses are required to provide a high level of personalized care, combining technical knowledge with physical dexterity. In education, quality is heavily dependent on the personalized attention that a teacher can offer. To date, developing well-rounded, emotionally developed human beings is not a province of robots and computers. Neither of these facts mean that these sectors are wholly resistant to automation.

IBM's Watson, a supercomputer, is being used to provide care and diagnostics for cancer patients. Over time, it is likely that more computer systems will be used to compile and analyze medical records, using their knowledge to provide accurate diagnoses. In 2000, the first robot-assisted surgeries were approved by the Food and Drug Administration.[63] In education, massive open online courses (MOOCs) are being rolled out using the Internet as a platform. MOOCs are free, open to anyone who wants to sign up, and available over the Internet as a series of lectures, readings and assignments. The courses have tiny completion rates and are often criticized for being ineffective publicity stunts.[64] But if one cynically believes that quality of education is irrelevant, as most corporate education "reformers" seem to, then it is not hard to imagine how MOOCs and similar online courses might be used to erode the status and security of professors and teachers.

The preceding discussion is by no means exhaustive.[65] It merely shows that many of the commonly supposed limits to automation are limits of the imagination, not of science or technology. In this brief survey, I deliberately chose to confine my examples to technologies that already exist and already work. A famous study by Carl Benedikt Frey and Michael Osborne, based on similar analysis, suggests that 47 per cent of US jobs are at high risk of being automated in the next couple of decades. Now that we have seen that a segment of every industry in the service sector is susceptible to automation, these figures do not seem unreasonable. The important question now is the same question one might have asked about any of the technologies developed during the productivity revolutions in agriculture and manufacturing: When is capital going to start putting these to use?

The Dynamics of Automation

As we saw before, the question is not whether automation can or will replace human labor, but when. There are relatively simple and concrete answers to this question. From the perspective of a capitalist, human workers are neither special nor indispensable, nor uniquely desirable. Labor is an input like anything else. Capital functions as a substitute for labor. At base, the equation is simple: if it is cheaper to use labor in a particular application, the capitalist will employ more labor, and if it is cheaper to use capital, the capitalist will employ more capital. What matters overall are the factors that make labor and capital cheap or expensive.

The first hurdle in introducing automation is whether or not technology exists that can perform a particular task. One cannot substitute tractors for horses if tractors do not exist. The second hurdle is how well a technology performs the task for which it is intended. As we have seen, early inventions are typically inefficient and costly. They may break often, they may be clunky or they may be difficult to use. This is a normal part of the process of technological development. As the invention becomes cheaper, more efficient and more reliable, the chance of adoption becomes more likely. There is typically an inflection point at which the adoption of a particular technology becomes widespread. It took a little over 20 years after initial invention for the McCormick reaper to start becoming popular in US farming. But after that point, adoption was relatively rapid.

The other side of this equation is the cost of labor. There is a greater incentive to automate production where labor is more expensive. Agricultural machinery was in high demand in many areas of the rural US for a long time owing to a chronic scarcity of workers. Sophisticated automation is not in particularly high demand in areas of the developing world that still support labor-intensive manufacturing, because labor in those countries is extremely cheap. Again, there is an inflection point at which it simply becomes uneconomic to employ labor over machinery in a particular job. There is no demand for workers to push plows in the US because tractors and combines are so much more efficient that one generally could not make a profit using anything else to grow corn. If a machine can do a job for less than the absolute minimum compensation necessary for a person to survive in a given society, or the minimum wage, that job is not going to be performed by humans.

The cost of labor is also affected, of course, by the actions of working-class people. Unlike robots, workers make demands and struggle to assert their dignity. By organizing themselves into unions, bargaining with their employers for higher wages and benefits, and demanding shorter workdays and better conditions, workers raise the cost of labor in the eyes of the capitalist. Capitalists, for their part, use automation as a weapon against the working class, to drive down wages, break up unions and limit the worker's ability to control the production process. As we saw with Foxconn, attempts or threats to automate a profession often directly follow the decision of the workers in that profession to organize and agitate for better conditions. After fast-food workers in the US began organizing for a $15 USD minimum wage, McDonald's started leaking news that it was looking at using automated burger cooking machinery in its restaurants.

Workers do not always lose these battles outright. The International Longshore and Warehouse Union (ILWU), which represents workers in ports on the Pacific coast of the US, is often held up as an example of victorious labor organizing in the face of automation. In 1960, the ILWU signed a contract that allowed the use of container shipping over labor-intensive methods in exchange for higher wages, benefits and pensions. It was able to do this as a result of organizing all of the West Coast's ports under one union contract, in addition to the fact that ports occupy a crucial position in global trade that cannot be moved or outsourced. Today, some union longshoremen make over $100,000 a year without a high school-degree, owing to having actually shared in the benefits of rising productivity. But this contract came at a cost—some workers were laid off and the ILWU gave up the right to represent part-time dockworkers, who make up a large share of the workforce and do not earn nearly as much.[66] In a world of globalized trade, capital and labor, winning victories like these is quite difficult.

Capitalist investment, whether in labor or capital, is driven by the belief that a profit can be made producing a particular commodity. To make a profit, commodities have to be sold. A capitalist may invest more labor or more capital because markets are expanding, or because they predict that producing cheaper commodities will expand the potential market for their products. They may also invest in order to grab a greater share of existing markets from their competitors by producing cheaper or better products, or they may do the same in a defensive fashion because their competitors are doing it. Competition for markets speeds up the pace of automation, because competing firms have to find ways to drive their costs down. We saw this process at work in the competitive struggle between Japanese and US automakers.

The relationship between automation and employment is simple, as well. If the demand for a commodity expands equal to or faster than the rate at which automation reduces the demand for labor in production, then employment will hold steady or even increase. If this does not happen, then employment will fall. Note that Say's Law, which predicts that lower prices will ceaselessly cause consumer demand to grow and thus offset any reduction in labor demand, has never been observed in any of the sectors historically impacted by radical automation. Despite this fact, one still finds plenty of economists who proudly stick to absurd mathematical models in the face of overwhelming real evidence. As stated above, there is also an inflection point, at which it no longer becomes profitable to employ any labor in a particular production process, which we will examine later in greater detail.

Ultimately, Say's Law predicts that all of these effects will be offset by an increased demand for labor in another sector of the economy. If commodities in one industry become cheaper, then demand will rise elsewhere, in newer industries that will employ displaced workers. Job creation in new industries springs from the fact that these industries require new labor to fulfill demand. A large portion of the labor demand from the creation of a new industry, like automobile manufacturing or biotechnology, comes from an increase in the demand for auxiliary services, like transportation and clerical work. But the automation processes invented for existing industries can be ported into any new industry that develops as a result of new technologies.

When manufacturing, construction, and many clerical and service jobs are already almost fully automated, the employment impact of emerging industries will be equally minimized. Google and Apple do not generate more employment for horses, no matter how large they grow. If automation inevitably creates an equal and opposite demand for labor, where is this demand going to come from? Where are these new uses of labor that we have yet to discover? In which industries will all the new jobs be created? Given that there are no answers to these questions, it is time that we accept reality. A long-term decline in the demand for hours of labor per worker is inevitable. As I will demonstrate in the second section of this book, this reality is already upon us.

Leisure, Abundance and Other Good Ideas

In the midst of the Great Depression, the economist John Maynard Keynes wrote of the rising specter of "technological unemployment"—the growing superfluity of human labor due to the rise of machines. Keynes wrote that:

> We are being afflicted with a new disease of which some readers may not yet have heard the name, but of which they will hear a great deal in the years to come—namely, *technological unemployment*. This means unemployment due to our discovery of means of economising the use of labour outrunning the pace at which we can find new uses for labour. But this is only a temporary phase of maladjustment. All this means in the long run *that mankind is solving its economic problem*.[67]

What did Keynes mean when he invoked mankind's "economic problem"? He went on to write that "for the first time since his creation man will be faced with his real, his permanent problem — how to use his freedom from pressing economic cares, how to occupy the leisure, which science and compound interest will have won for him, to live wisely and agreeably and well."[68] Keynes predicted that the astonishing rise in productivity that he saw around him would deliver not just an abundance of goods, but also *an abundance of free time* to ordinary people. Productivity has indeed risen to astounding levels, but free time has barely budged, a phenomenon exemplified by the US. Recent surveys suggest that the average US workweek is 47 hours. This represents virtually no change since the establishment of the 40-hour week in the Fair Labor Standards Act of 1937.

What happened? First, the Second World War intervened by destroying massive amounts of accumulated capital, allowing for decades of investment in rebuilding the destroyed global economy. Then, this post-War accommodation of limitless, profitable investment alongside rising living standards collapsed. Capitalism began to malfunction and it adapted to survive. It unleashed a decades-long assault on the living standards of the working class, smashed its trade unions, ruthlessly introduced automation and expanded into markets covering the entirety of the globe. The rumblings of instability grew louder and louder. Capitalism struggled to find new uses for labor and new means to accumulate surplus value. It propped itself up with a global expansion of credit, creating debts that could never be repaid. This accommodation collapsed, and the reality of structural unemployment and wage stagnation reappeared.

Today, we live in a world where part of the workforce is chronically overworked, while the other part is chronically underemployed or unemployable. Capital seems to have achieved complete dominance over the worker, as inequality everywhere spikes and a tiny parasitic class gets richer and richer. These rising extremes of inequity and instability seem like the victory of capital, but they are heralds of a fundamental shift—the death of wage labor and the death of capitalism itself. Like Marx, Keynes never suggested that the replacement of human labor is a temporary or reversible problem. But unlike Keynes, Marx knew that a system based on production for profit could not establish a society based on equally shared abundance and free time.[69] Instead, capitalism's development would produce persistent instability and crises as a mere result of its attempt to survive while it laid the foundations of its own destruction. Capitalism is an economic system that lives off labor, even though its continued development makes labor increasingly obsolete. Just as Marx suggested, rising productivity is producing a mass of surplus laborers who cannot be profitably employed in production.

The growth of this surplus labor force is a massive contradiction facing the development of capitalism. Marginalized and permanently consigned to precarious work or unemployment, this growing segment of society stands in complete antagonism to the status quo. Technology continues to metamorphosize in remarkable and destabilizing ways that will expel more labor from the production process. The progress of radical automation, the advent of distributed production and long-term socioeconomic trends will shape the future of human society. In the following chapters we will examine the pressures driving the present development of capitalism and what we can expect to see as the 21st century progresses. These investigations reveal that capitalism is in the midst of a profound and fundamental crisis. Capitalism is dying, but a new world has yet to be born.

Endnotes

1   Aristotle. (2013) *Politics*, trans. Lord, C. (Chicago: University of Chicago Press) Book I, Chapter 4.

2   Null, C. and Caulfield, B. "Fade To Black: The 1980s vision of "lights-out" manufacturing, where robots do all the work, is a dream no more," *Business 2.0*. June 1st, 2003. Available at: http://money.cnn.com/magazines/business2/business2_archive/2003/06/01/343371/. [accessed 29 May 2017]; Pfanner, E. "Japanese Robot Maker Fanuc Reveals Some of Its Secrets," *The Wall Street Journal*. March 27th, 2015. Available at:http://www.wsj.com/articles/japanese-robot-maker-fanuc-reveals-some-of-its-secrets-1427384420. [accessed 29 May 2017]

3   Duhigg, C. and Barboza, D. "In China, Human Costs Are Built Into an iPad," *The New York Times*. January 25th, 2012. Available at: http://www.nytimes.com/2012/01/26/business/ieconomy-apples-ipad-and-the-human-costs-for-workers-in-china.html. [accessed 29 May 2017]; Whitney, L. "Apple supplier employee describes working conditions," *CNET*. February 7th, 2012. Available at: http://www.cnet.com/news/apple-supplier-employee-describes-working-conditions/. [accessed 29 May 2017]; Greene, J. "Riots, suicides, and other issues in Foxconn's iPhone factories," *CNET*. September 25th, 2012. Available at: http://www.cnet.com/news/riots-suicides-and-other-issues-in-foxconns-iphone-factories/ [accessed 29 May 2017]; Reisinger, D. "Foxconn worker jumps to death from apartment in Chengdu," *CNET*. June 14th, 2012. Available at: http://www.cnet.com/news/foxconn-worker-jumps-to-death-from-apartment-in-chengdu/. [accessed 29 May 2017]; Zheng, L. "Foxconn Installing Suicide Prevention Nets," *YouTube*. September 22nd, 2013. Available at: https://www.youtube.com/watch?v=Qibxm52y1v8. [accessed 29 May 2017]

4   Luk, L. "Foxconn's Robot Army Yet to Prove Match for Humans," *WSJ Digits*. May 5th, 2015. Available at: http://blogs.wsj.com/digits/2015/05/05/foxconns-robot-army-yet-to-prove-match-for-humans/. [accessed 29 May 2017];

Kan, M. "Foxconn expects robots to take over more factory work," *PCWorld*. February 27th, 2015. Available at: http://www.pcworld.com/article/2890032/foxconn-expects-robots-to-take-over-more-factory-work.html. [accessed 29 May 2017]

5   The term "cybernetics" comes from the Greek word *kybernētēs*, meaning governor or pilot. The word was coined by Norbert Wiener, the founder of the modern science and a remarkable humanist. See: Wiener, N. (1948) *Cybernetics: Or Control and Communication in the Animal and the Machine.* (Cambridge: MIT Press) and Wiener, N. (1954) *The Human Use of Human Beings.* (London: Perseus Books Group)

6   Bessen, J. "Will robots steal our jobs? The humble loom suggests not," *The Washington Post*. January 25th, 2014. Available at: https://www.washingtonpost.com/news/the-switch/wp/2014/01/25/what-the-humble-loom-can-teach-us-about-robots-and-automation/. [accessed 29 May 2017]

7   Ibid.

8   Gilmore, W. (1989) *Reading Becomes a Necessity of Life: Material and Cultural Life in Rural New England, 1780–1835.* (Knoxville: University of Tennessee Press)

9   U.S. Bureau of the Census. "Table 3. Population of the 33 Urban Places: 1800" Available at: http://www.census.gov/population/www/documentation/twps0027/tab03.txt. [accessed 29 May 2017]

10 Diamond, J. "The Worst Mistake in the History of the Human Race," *Discover Magazine*. May 1st, 1999. Available at: http://discovermagazine.com/1987/may/02-the-worst-mistake-in-the-history-of-the-human-race. [accessed 29 May 2017] "For instance, the average time devoted each week to obtaining food is only 12 to 19 hours for one group of Bushmen, 14 hours or less for the Hadza nomads of Tanzania. One Bushman, when asked why he hadn't emulated neighboring tribes by adopting agriculture, replied, 'Why should we,

when there are so many mongongo nuts in the world?'"

11 Olmstead, A. (June 1975) "The Mechanization of Reaping and Mowing in American Agriculture, 1833–1870," *The Journal of Economic History*, Vol. 35, No. 2. pp. 327–52. Available at: htt p://www.colorado.edu/ibs/eb/alston/econ8534/SectionVI/ Olmstead,_The_Mechanization_of_REaping_and_Mowing_ in_American_Agriculture,_1833-1870.pdf. [accessed 29 May 2017]

12 Ikerd, J. (2010) "Corporatization of American Agriculture," Small Farm Today Magazine. Available at: http://web. missouri.edu/ikerdj/papers/SFT-Corporatization%20of%20 Am%20Ag%20%287-10%29.htm. [accessed 29 May 2017]; Fitzgerald, D. (2003) *Every Farm a Factory: The Industrial Ideal in American Agriculture* pp. 17–21. Available at: http:// yalepress.yale.edu/yupbooks/pdf/0300088132.pdf. [accessed 29 May 2017]

13 Blank, S. (2008) *The Economics of American Agriculture: Evolution and Global Development*. (New York: Taylor and Francis) p. 137.

14 Peterson, A. "Google didn't lead the self-driving vehicle revolution. John Deere did." *The Washington Post*. June 22nd, 2015. Available at: https://www.washingtonpost.com/ news/the-switch/wp/2015/06/22/google-didnt-lead-the- selfdriving-vehicle-revolution-john-deere-did. [accessed 31 May 2017]

15 Luxemburg, R. (1951) *The Accumulation of Capital*, trans. Agnes Schwarzchild. (London: Routledge) p. 404.

16 Lebergott, S. (1966) "Labor Force and Employment, 1800– 1960," *Output, Employment, and Productivity in the United States after 1800*. (Cambridge: National Bureau of Economic Research) Table 1 and Table 2.

17 Schuh, G.E. "Structural Changes in the Farm Labor Market," *Purdue Agricultural Experiment Station, Journal Paper 2944, Project 1107*. Available at: http://bit.ly/2eJxgLT. [accessed 31

May 2017]

18 US Census Bureau. (2012) "United States Summary: 2010."
    pp. 20–6.

19 Dimitri, C., Effland, A., and Conklin, N. (2005) "The 20th
    Century Transformation of U.S. Agriculture and Farm
    Policy," *US Department of Agriculture*.p. 2.

20 Mitchell, D. "Why Monsanto always wins," *Fortune*. June
    26th, 2014. Available at: http://fortune.com/2014/06/26/
    monsantogmo-crops/. [accessed 31 May 2017];Barlett,
    D. and Steele, J. "Monsanto's Harvest of Fear," *Vanity
    Fair*. May 2008. Available at: http://www.vanityfair.com/
    news/2008/05/monsanto200805. [accessed 31 May 2017]

21 Schifferes, S. "The decline of Detroit," *BBC News*. February
    19th, 2007. Available at: http://news.bbc.co.uk/2/hi/business
    /6346299.stm. [accessed 31 May 2017]

22 Boggs, J.L. (1963) *The American Revolution: Pages From a
    Negro Worker's Notebook*. (New York: Monthly Review
    Press) Chapter 2: The Challenge of Automation. Available
    at: http://www.historyisaweapon.com/defcon1/amreboggs.
    html#DIV8. [accessed 31 May 2017]

23 While the Japanese "kaizen" system called on workers to
    contribute by constantly improving the production process,
    it often dealt with resistant workers and labor organizers by
    literally taking them outside and beating them.

24 A wildcat strike is taken without the authorization of union
    leadership. Nick Dyer-Witheford. *Cyber-Proletariat*. p. 49.

25 Paul S. Davies. (1993) "Factors Influencing Employment
    in the U.S. Automobile Industry," *The Park Place Economist*,
    Vol. 1, No. 1. p. 47.

26 "Company History," *Toyota Corporate News*. Available at:
    http://corporatenews.pressroom.toyota.com/corporate/
    company+history/. [accessed 31 May 2017]

27 US Bureau of Labor Statistics, "Percent of Employment in
    Manufacturing in Japan," retrieved from FRED, Federal

Reserve Bank of St. Louis September 24, 2015. Available at: https://research.stlouisfed.org/fred2/series/JPNPEFANA/.

28 Levinson, M. "U.S. Manufacturing in International Perspective," *Congressional Research Service.* March 17th 2015. Available at: https://fas.org/sgp/crs/misc/R42135.pdf. [accessed 31 May 2017] p. 11.

29 US Bureau of Labor Statistics. "All Employees: Manufacturing/All Employees: Total Nonfarm Payrolls," retrieved from FRED, Federal Reserve Bank of St. Louis September 24, 2015. Available at: https://research.stlouisfed. org/fred2/graph/?g=eCo.

30 US Bureau of Labor Statistics. "All Employees: Manufacturing," retrieved from FRED, Federal Reserve Bank of St. Louis September 24, 2015. Available at: https:// research.stlouisfed.org/fred2/series/MANEMP/.

31 Boggs, J.L. *The American Revolution: Pages From a Negro Worker's Notebook.* Chapter 1: The Rise and Fall of the Union. Available at: http://www.historyisaweapon.com/defcon1/ amreboggs.html#DIV7. [accessed 31 May 2017]

32 Ad Hoc Committee on the Triple Revolution. (1964) Available at: https://www.marxists.org/history/etol/newspape/isr/vol 25/no03/adhoc.html. [accessed 31 May 2017]

33 Maryland Department of Labor, Licensing, and Regulation. "Local Area Unemployment Statistics," accessed September 24th, 2015. Available at: http://www.dllr.state.md.us/lmi/ laus/.

34 "Unemployment rate by sex and age groups - monthly average, %," *Eurostat,* accessed September 24th, 2015. Available at: http://appsso.eurostat.ec.europa.eu/nui/show. do.

35 Semuels, A. "Could Baltimore's 16,000 Vacant Houses Shelter the City's Homeless?" *The Atlantic.* October 20th, 2014. Available at: http://www.theatlantic.com/business/ archive/2014/10/can-homeless-people-move-into-

baltimores-abandoned-houses/381647/. [accessed 31 May 2017]

36 Malter, J. "Baltimore's economy in black and white," *CNN Money*. April 29th, 2015. Available at: http://money. cnn.com/2015/04/29/news/economy/baltimore-economy/. [accessed 31 May 2017]

37 "Baltimore Behind Bars: How to Reduce the Jail Population, Save Money and Improve Public Safety," *Justice Policy Institute*. June 2010. Available at: http://www.justicepolicy. org/images/upload/10-06_rep_baltbehindbars_md-ps-ac-rd. pdf. [accessed 31 May 2017] p. 4.

38 Birch, J. and Heideman, P. "The Poverty of Culture," *Jacobin*. September 16th, 2014. Available at: https://www.jacobinmag. com/2014/09/the-poverty-of-culture/. [accessed 31 May 2017]

39 Harwood, M. "Why Read Christopher Lasch?" *The American Conservative*. July 28th, 2015. Available at: http:// www.theamericanconservative.com/articles/why-read-christopher-lasch/. [accessed 31 May 2017]

40 See: Dreher, R. "The Virus of Poverty Culture," *The American Conservative*. July 30th, 2014. Available at: http://www. theamericanconservative.com/dreher/the-virus-of-poverty-culture/. [accessed 31 May 2017]

41 Jones, A. "Murder Town USA (aka Wilmington, Delaware)," *Newsweek*. December 9th, 2014. Available at: http://www. newsweek.com/2014/12/19/wilmington-delaware-murder-crime-290232.html. [accessed 31 May 2017]

42 University of Delaware Center for Community Research and Service. "An Overview of Poverty in Delaware." February 2014. Available at: http://c.ymcdn.com/sites/ www.delawaregrantmakers.org/resource/resmgr/Docs/ Overview_of_Poverty_in_Delaw.pdf. [accessed 31 May 2017]

43 Bureau of Labor Statistics. "Employment by major industry

sector," accessed September 25th, 2015. Available at: http://
www.bls.gov/emp/ep_table_201.htm.

44 Bell, D. (1973) *The Coming of Post-Industrial Society*. (New
York: Basic Books) p. 155.

45 Nelson, G. "Google in talks with OEMs, suppliers to build
self-driving cars," *Automotive News*. January 14th, 2015.
Available at: http://www.autonews.com/article/20150114/
OEM09/150119815/google-in-talks-with-oems-suppliers-to-
build-self-driving-cars. [accessed 31 May 2017]

46 Bureau of Labor Statistics. "Employment by major industry
sector." Bureau of Labor Statistics. "Industries at a Glance:
Transportation and Warehousing," accessed September 25th,
2015. Available at: http://www.bls.gov/iag/tgs/iag48-49.htm.

47 Del Ray, J. "Uber CEO: Self-Driving Cars Are the Future,
Drivers Are Not," *recode*. May 28th, 2014. Available at: http://
recode.net/2014/05/28/uber-ceo-self-driving-cars-are-the-
future-drivers-are-not-2/. [accessed 31 May 2017]; Wood, A.
"The future of self-driving cars: CNBC Explains," *CNBC*. June
17th, 2015. Available at: http://www.cnbc.com/2015/06/17/
ubers-self-driving-car-future-vs-california-decision-today.
html. [accessed 31 May 2017]

48 Markoff, J. "Planes Without Pilots," *The New York Times*. April
6th, 2015. Available at: http://www.nytimes.com/2015/04/07/
science/planes-without-pilots.html. [accessed 31 May 2017]

49 Malone, R. (June 2005) "Inside the Automated Warehouse,"
Inbound Logistics. Available at: http://www.inboundlogistics.
com/cms/article/inside-the-automated-warehouse/.
[accessed 31 May 2017]

50 Tobe, F. "Competing robotic warehouse systems," *The
Robot Report*. April 30th, 2015. Available at: http://www.
therobotreport.com/news/goods-to-man-robotic-systems.
[accessed 31 May 2017]; designboom. "15,000 amazon
kiva robots drives eighth generation fulfillment center,"
Vimeo. December 2nd, 2014. Available at: https://vimeo.

com/113374910. [accessed 31 May 2017]

51 See: Allen, J. "Studying Logistics," *Jacobin*. February 12th, 2015. Available at: https://www.jacobinmag.com/2015/02/logistics-industry-organizing-labor/. [accessed 31 May 2017]

52 Love, D. "Here's The Burger-Flipping Robot That Could Put Fast-Food Workers Out Of A Job," *Business Insider*. August 11th, 2014. Available at: http://www.businessinsider.com/momentum-machines-burger-robot-2014-8. [accessed 31 May 2017]; "Momentum Machines," Available at: http://momentummachines.com/. [accessed 31 May 2017]

53 Mims, C. "An army of robot baristas could mean the end of Starbucks as we know it," *Quartz*. October 17th, 2013. Available at: http://qz.com/134661/briggo-coffee-army-of-robot-baristas-could-mean-the-end-of-starbucks-as-we-know-it/. [accessed 31 May 2017]; Briggo Coffee. "Briggo Coffee Experience," *Vimeo*. Available at: https://vimeo.com/77993254. [accessed 31 May 2017]

54 Ford, M. "Robots are coming for your job: Amazon, McDonald's, and the next wave of dangerous capitalist 'disruption'," *Salon*. May 10th, 2015. Available at: http://www.salon.com/2015/05/10/robots_are_coming_for_your_job_amazon_mcdonalds_and_the_next_wave_of_dangerous_capitalist_disruption/. [accessed 31 May 2017]

55 "Number of employees in the United States fast food restaurant industry from 2004 to 2018," *Statista*. Accessed September 25th, 2015. Available at: http://www.statista.com/statistics/196630/number-of-employees-in-us-fast-food-restaurants-since-2002/ and http://www.statista.com/statistics/203365/projected-restaurant-industry-employment-in-the-us-since-2001/.

56 Ford, M. "Robots are coming for your job: Amazon, McDonald's, and the next wave of dangerous capitalist 'disruption,'" *Salon*.

57 Lowrey, A. "Recovery Has Created Far More Low-Wage

Jobs Than Better-Paid Ones," *The New York Times*. April 27th, 2014. Available at: http://www.nytimes.com/2014/04/28/business/economy/recovery-has-created-far-more-low-wage-jobsthan-better-paid-ones.html. [accessed 31 May 2017]

58 Rifkin, J. (1996) *The End of Work: The Decline of the Global Labor Force and the Dawn of the Post-Market Era*. (New York City: G.P. Putnam's Sons)

59 "Moravec's Paradox," *Wikipedia*. Available at: https://en.wikipedia.org/wiki/Moravec's_paradox. [accessed 31 May 2017]

60 Benedikt Frey, C. and Osborne, M. "The Future of Employment: How Susceptible Are Jobs to Computerization?" *Oxford Martin School*. Available at: http://www.oxfordmartin.ox.ac.uk/downloads/academic/The_Future_of_Employment.pdf. [accessed 31 May 2017]

61 "Declining U.S. High-Frequency Trading," *The New York Times*. October 15th, 2012. Available at: http://www.nytimes.com/interactive/2012/10/15/business/Declining-US-High-Frequency-Trading.html. [accessed 31 May 2017]

62 Lewis, M. "Michael Lewis Reflects on His Book *Flash Boys*, a Year After It Shook Wall Street to Its Core," *Vanity Fair*. April 2015. Available at: http://www.vanityfair.com/news/2015/03/michael-lewis-flash-boys-one-year-later. [accessed 31 May 2017]

63 Benedikt Frey, C. and Osborne, M. "The Future of Employment: How Susceptible Are Jobs to Computerization?" *Oxford Martin School*. p. 17; "Robotic Surgery," *Mayo Clinic*. Available at: http://www.mayoclinic.org/tests-procedures/robotic-surgery/basics/definition/prc-20013988. [accessed 31 May 2017]

64 Pappano, L. "The Year of the MOOC," *The New York Times*. November 2nd, 2012. Available at: http://www.nytimes.com/2012/11/04/education/edlife/massive-open-

onlinecourses-are-multiplying-at-a-rapid-pace.html. [accessed 31 May 2017]

65 A clever and convincing version of the preceding discussion has been produced by CGP Grey, a popular YouTuber. See: "Humans Need Not Apply," *YouTube*. August 13th, 2014. Available at: https://www.youtube.com/watch?v=7Pq-S557 XQU. [accessed 31 May 2017]

66 Kirkham, C. and Khouri, A. "How longshoremen command $100K salaries in era of globalization and automation," *Los Angeles Times*. March 1st, 2015. Available at: http://www. latimes.com/business/la-fi-dockworker-pay-20150301-story. html. [accessed 31 May 2017]

67 Keynes, J.M. [accessed 31 May 2017] "Economic Possibilites for Our Grandchildren." p. 3. Available at: http://www.econ. yale.edu/smith/econ116a/keynes1.pdf. [accessed 31 May 2017]

68 Ibid. p. 5.

69 I owe many thanks to Jehu Eaves for bringing up this comparison. See: Eaves, J. "Why Keynes predicted a 15 hour workweek, but Marx did not," *The Real Movement*. September 16th, 2015. Available at: https://therealmovement. wordpress.com/2015/09/16/why-keynes-predicted-a-15-hour-workweek-but-marx-did-not/. [accessed 31 May 2017]

Part II

Capitalism in the 21st Century

The way up and the way down is one and the same.

Heraclitus

Chapter 6

On Value

A revaluation of all values: this question mark, so black, so
huge that it casts a shadow over the man who puts it down...
Friedrich Nietzsche, *Twilight of the Idols*

A theory of value is the foundation upon which all economic
theories are built. Theories of value try to explain why goods
are worth something and why people exchange them with one
another. Ultimately, a theory of value helps to explain how
economic systems work on a grand scale. Dueling economic
theories of value inform our expectations about how capitalism
develops. Depending on whether you agree with one theory of
value or another, you will probably believe that capitalism is an
economic system that either tends toward stability or collapse.
In other words, you might believe that capitalism is either: 1.
An economic system that can and will exist indefinitely; or 2. A
stage of development that precedes the next economic system.
Given that this is one of the central questions facing humanity,
it is critical to understand what economic "value" is and what
assumptions produce the models used by today's dueling
groups of economists.

Value does not exist outside of history. Value only exists
to the extent that a society creates it in its social relationships
and in its language. Without human observers, a tree has
no "utility," "exchange value," or "price." It is simply a tree.
(Whether a tree exists if it isn't observed is beyond the scope of
this book.) The study of value, in this book, is the study of the
relationships between people and goods in an economic system
of production for exchange and profit. It is the study of value in
a capitalist society, based on Marx's description of the dynamics

of capitalism.[1] If you have not had the chance to study economics, I hope this chapter will provide a simple, useful introduction to the field.

Use and Exchange Value

Any discussion of value must begin with the distinction between use value and exchange value. Use value is simply the fact that a particular thing is useful to someone. In this sense, use value is subjective, particular and impossible to measure. Different things are more or less useful to different people depending on the situation. For instance, I might find a chocolate bar more useful than a bar of gold. Someone else may have a use for a book by Ayn Rand, whereas I have no use for it whatsoever. There is no way of quantifying these facts or comparing them to one another.[2] There is no way to numerically measure the use value of a cow relative to a gun. As Keynes wrote, "two incommensurable collections of miscellaneous objects cannot in themselves provide the material for a quantitative analysis."[3] (In plain language: you can't just turn a bunch of different, random objects into numbers.) We are used to thinking of the value of things in terms of how much money they cost, but what really matters to most people are the subjective judgments that go into making up what we call "use value." For example, you might be able to sell your dog to someone for $200, but you probably wouldn't. To you, your dog is a priceless loyal friend. To someone else, it's just another dog.

The study of value in economics is the study of exchange value. From this point on, when I use the word "value," this is what I mean unless otherwise specified. As the name suggests, *exchange value* is a relative measure of which commodities will exchange for a particular commodity. A *commodity* is a good that has exchange value. We might say that the value of a pound of flour is equal to a dozen eggs or that the value of a dozen eggs is equal to a fraction of an ounce of gold.

It is crucial to understand that this "value" is not a timeless quality embodied in all products throughout history. The widespread production of commodities with exchange value is only possible in a society where the practice of buying and selling goods has colonized daily life. Throughout the majority of human history, this was not the case. Trade between tribal and ethnic groups was often a highly ritualized process connected to intermarriage and reciprocal practices of gift giving.[4] Until the development of capitalism, the daily use and circulation of goods in most societies was governed by a complex series of social norms. In the Iroquois nations, for instance, goods were stockpiled in longhouses and distributed directly by women's councils.[5] Trading, buying and selling, and exchange simply did not take place within the social group. Today, when it is common even to buy one's food at a supermarket, it may strike us as strange that value is not a transhistorical constant, but it simply isn't.

The fact that some commodity exchanges for some amount of another commodity tells us very little about why these two commodities can be exchanged. If a commodity is going to be purchased, someone must demand it because they either need or want it. Aside from this basic fact, the connection between use value and exchange value is quite shaky. There are plenty of things that have use value but no exchange value, like the air or a good that someone makes for their own consumption. There are commodities that have exchange value that are not really useful, like ballistic missiles. Even a rough estimate of the ratio of use value to exchange value is unstable. Over time, it is possible for two units of a commodity to embody less exchange value than one unit of that commodity in the past. This is confusing, because everyone knows that you get more use out of two apples than one. In terms of exchange value, two apples are much less valuable in 2015 than they were in 1800. They buy a lot less and they take less labor to produce.

This leads us to the issue of comparing fundamentally different things. Different kinds of goods are not equal. An apple is not an orange. They can only become equal through a relationship to something else that they share in common. While goods do not share such a quality, commodities do, and that quality is labor. Labor, in our sense, is different from work. Work is a human activity involving effort, ranging anywhere from farming to cutting hair to writing code. These are inherently different activities with different criteria of quality and success. Farming, cutting hair and coding are only similar in that they are human activities that require some amount of skill and time to complete.

Work has been around since the dawn of humanity. On the other hand, labor is a relatively recent social construct. *Labor* is work that has become measured in terms of hours. It is abstract, because it is bought and sold in quantities. Unlike work, all forms of labor are comparable, because are they are measured in terms of "labor hours." In a capitalist economy, labor is an input like a machine or a building. One applies a certain amount of labor hours to produce a certain amount of commodities. Just as a capitalist purchases and uses a certain amount of car parts to make a new car, they also purchase the labor hours they need to put that car together on the assembly line.

The distinction between work and labor mirrors the distinction between use and exchange value. A laborer performs work—picking tomatoes or stocking shelves—at the same time that they labor. One face of the activity is actually useful (work), while the other is an abstract quantity spent to produce exchange value (labor). Work and labor are two faces of the same thing, but while work has been with humanity for thousands of years, labor has not. Labor can only exist in a society where widespread production for exchange exists, in a society where people buy and sell commodities on the market. This only happens on a large scale, where the means of production are taken out of the hands of society as a whole and placed in a few private hands. Labor only exists in a society where work itself has become a commodity that can be sold on the market, like iron and bushels of wheat.

The labor theory of value thus does not suggest that labor is the foundation of all possible forms of value in every society throughout history. It is not a theory of metaphysics. The *labor theory of value* argues that labor is the source of exchange value under capitalism.[6] The values of commodities are determined by the inputs of labor required on average for their production. The value of labor power, like any commodity, is relative to that of other commodities. It is equal to that of the entire group of commodities needed to sustain the laborer. The value of labor, like anything else, is a social category that depends on the level of development of a particular society, the political strength of organized labor and so on. So-called skilled labor is just the average value of labor power multiplied. The labor power of a US lawyer costs many times that of a Chinese assembly line worker. This does not mean that a lawyer produces more useful things than an assembly line worker—it just means that lawyers have the social power to command a greater share of the goods produced by society as a whole.

Capital adds the other share of value to a commodity. *Capital* is dead labor used in the production of exchange value. On the one hand, capital is the physical product of past labor. It might be a simple tool, a complicated machine or a building. On the other hand, capital is also a process. These forms of dead labor have to be employed in the production of exchange value to become capital, otherwise they are just things. Productive assets only become capital in a society where they can be used to produce value. A pile of money isn't capital. Money, buildings and so on become capital when they are being used to make more money. This is what it means when we say that capital is "circulating."

It must constantly move from the world of production to the world of exchange and back again. The ideal form of capital is money, which is used to buy labor and things, and set them to work producing more money.

The value of a commodity does not increase because someone works unnecessarily hard to produce something that can be made with half the labor. The *average* living and dead labor required to produce a commodity (including labor power) sets its value. Firms that produce a commodity with less labor than average can thus exchange it for more than the value contained in that particular commodity, while less productive firms are forced to do the opposite. More productive firms accumulate more value and less productive firms either adapt or go out of business. Eventually, what was once a substantial technological improvement becomes generally adopted and the average value of the commodity drops to a lower level.

This model of "simple commodity exchange" — in other words, bartering wheat for iron — is only a theoretical exercise that helps us to understand how exchange value actually works. As David Graeber points out, nowhere in precapitalist history do we find examples of a barter economy, where most producers exchange one commodity for another, contrary to the fairy tales presented in modern economics textbooks.[7] Commodity exchange needs a way of representing the values embodied in different commodities. This abstract means must itself be a commodity, otherwise it would not have labor value. Money is this abstraction. The values of commodities express themselves in terms of money, which provides a uniform standard that relates all possible commodities to each other. This is why we say that an orange is worth $2, rather than two apples or two eggs.

But as we said, money can only serve in this role because it has exchange value — because it was produced with labor.[8] When Marx wrote *Capital*, money actually was a commodity:

gold. Precious metals needed to be mined from the earth and required labor to be produced. Banknotes and currency had to be exchangeable for actual money (gold). Currency was an abstraction from money (gold), which represented labor values. This is no longer the case. On 15 August 1971, US President Richard Nixon ended the convertibility of dollars for gold in the midst of an economic crisis. Up until that point, the world's leading central banks anchored the value of their currencies to gold. After this point, the dollar and the rest of the world's currencies would "float" — their price would have no relation to abstract labor. These currencies were dubbed "fiat" currency, from the biblical "fiat lux" — let there be light. From then on, the state could say *let there be money.*

At this point you might say that this proves that labor theory is wrong. After all, it takes labor to produce commodities, but it does not take labor to produce fiat currency. We shouldn't be able to trade something for nothing. But labor theory as described by Marx does not simply state that things exchange at their labor-determined values. That was the theory described by Marx's classical predecessors like Adam Smith and David Ricardo. Marx intended to demonstrate how a system of production for exchange based on labor values would inevitably collapse. As we will see later, the collapse of the gold standard coincided with a massive crisis of capitalism: the shuddering end of decades of rapid growth in the 1960s. The fact that we now exchange commodities for fiat currency, which has no value in the terms of labor theory, does not invalidate labor theory. It reveals that capitalism has been in an extraordinarily precarious position since the crisis of the 1970s. We will return to this issue in the following chapter, when we examine this crisis in greater detail.

This problem leads us to an important question: What is the relationship between exchange value and the price of commodities in a capitalist economy? (A price is just the actual monetary value given to a product.) This may be the most misunderstood point in the entire canon of radical economics.[9] The so-called transformation problem is a critique of the labor theory of value on the grounds that it is difficult (or impossible) to consistently transform labor values into prices. The critique, forwarded by Eugen Böhm von Bawerk, among others, is a complete misunderstanding of the purpose of labor theory. In Volume III of *Capital*, Marx shows that the values embodied in particular commodities *do not* correspond proportionally to their prices.

Marx's model of capitalism moves from the general (a model of capitalism as a whole) to the particular (prices of production for individual firms). The general amount of value produced in the economy is divided between various firms based on fluctuations in supply and demand, competition, monopolization and so on. While prices tend to fluctuate around their abstract labor values, individual commodities are virtually never sold at their value. Instead, they are sold above and below their values in a pattern that, when added together, comprises the general levels of value and profit produced in the economy as an undivided unit.

As early as 1847, Marx wrote that prices were determined on a microeconomic scale by the everyday interaction of supply and demand.[10] Böhm von Bawerk criticized Marx's analysis on the grounds that products cannot exchange in proportion to their values if there is such a thing as a general rate of profit.[11] (We will discuss the general rate of profit later.) He was right, but this was exactly the point that Marx was making. The brilliance of Marx's model consisted in showing how an advanced system based on production for exchange would inevitably diverge from the premises of simple commodity production.[12] "The transformation of values into prices of production serves to obscure the basis for determining value itself," as he wrote.[13] Marx did not predict that individual prices would express labor values, but that individual prices would diverge further and further from labor values as capitalism developed. Nixon revealed the prescience of this prediction when he severed the connection between the price of currency and the labor value embodied in gold. The purpose of labor theory is not to allow us to predict the prices of individual commodities, but to understand how a system of value production inevitably collapses.[14]

An analogy with science might be helpful here. The general theory of relativity allows us to predict the effects of gravity on a very large scale, that of planets and stars. It helps us understand why light curves around large bodies and why the passage of time slows as one travels closer to the speed of light. The general theory of relativity is not that useful for describing small-scale physics, like the motion and position of subatomic particles, which is why we have quantum mechanics. Both models allow us to understand phenomena at a certain scale. This relationship is similar to the relationship between labor theory and modern microeconomics. Microeconomics can tell you all about how prices are formed through the interaction of supply and demand. But, as the past decades have shown, microeconomics tells us very little about the long-term dynamics of capitalism or the origins of crises. Like the general theory of relativity, labor theory helps us to understand how a capitalist economy functions on a grand scale.

As a brief aside, the popular assertion that information is the real source of value in contemporary capitalism is the result of confusing value with price.[15] There are things that have a price but no value, and information is one of them. No matter the amount of labor required to produce an initial piece of information, the labor cost of reproducing that information (a code, blueprint, schematic, etc.) infinitely is essentially zero. In the terms of microeconomics, the supply of information is limitless no matter how high demand rises. Information is a "non-rival" good and a good that requires no labor to reproduce. By a granting a legal monopoly on a kind of information to a company, the state allows that company to sell its products at a price that exceeds their value. The rise of the "information economy," where patents and intellectual property can account for the majority of the price of a commodity, shows how far prices come to diverge from exchange value as capitalism develops.

Now that I have subjected you to a long discussion of the relevant differences between use and exchange value, you may be curious why this actually matters. If there is no meaningful distinction between use and exchange value (for example, if the source of value is use value, or "marginal utility"), then rising productivity will produce an increasing amount of wealth indefinitely without major contradictions. If there is a contradiction between use and exchange value, then rising productivity will create rising unemployment, a succession of crises and the ultimate collapse of production for profit. If the preceding analysis is correct, then the contradiction between use value and exchange value is the foundational contradiction of capitalism.

A mode of production is a social relation mediated by technology. New technologies like automation and distributed production appear to displace the worker and condemn her to a precarious existence, but this is simply not true. The founding element of capitalist social relations is the "law of value," or the requirement to produce ever-rising quantities of exchange value to the detriment of all other considerations. It is the law of value itself that creates rising unemployment, persistent crises and the destruction of our planet's ecological wellbeing. To understand why, we first have to investigate the driving goal of capitalism: the production of surplus value.

Surplus Value

Assume, for the purpose of argument, that an entire economy is just one large company. This company produces commodities, sells them on the world market and divides the revenue earned among its employees. This particular company buys its raw materials, machinery and so on at their value, and sells its products at their value, as well. The company pays its workers fairly—each receives exactly their share of the value they contribute to each product with their work. This company does not turn a profit. Where could it possibly earn one? Since it sells its products at their value, it can only sell them at the price determined by the value of the inputs. It pays the same price for capital as its competitors. All of the remaining value is added by the living labor of the company's employees. Maybe it earns a little more, or less, based on normal fluctuations in the market for its products. But over the long run this company will only break even.

This problem—"Where does profit come from?"—is the reason that the concept of "surplus value" is so important. Contrary to what one might expect, neoclassical economics— today's dominant economic paradigm—has no consistent theory about the source of profit. According to a sample of introductory economics textbooks, profits are either a result of entrepreneurial labor, residual income claimed by firm owners, the reward to innovation, the reward for risk-taking or a rent charged by the owners of scarce capital.[16] Aside from the last explanation, none of these provides a consistent theory of the profit rate, and even the last fails to identify a mechanism that produces profits. Why should entrepreneurship or the management of a firm be considered separate from labor income, since it consists of labor? If entrepreneurial labor is the source of profits, why do profits accrue to shareholders who perform no labor whatsoever? What causes profits to accrue to owners as a "residual income"? If profits are a reward for innovation, why do owners claim profits instead of a firm's research and development team? If profit is a reward for risk, why is there an inverse historical relationship between the rate of profit and the rate of business failures? Instead of asking these questions, much of mainstream economics simply accepts the existence of profits beforehand and proceeds to other points of analysis. This is fine if one accepts the distinction offered in the previous section between the relative merits of microeconomics and labor theory. If not, the neoclassical model faces the fact that it cannot explain the source of profits, which are the engine of the entire capitalist system.

Capitalism is a system of production for profit. Capitalists do not invest money in an enterprise because they are struck by a whim to do so. They invest to make money. Capitalists make money by investing in firms that produce a surplus of value over and above the value they initially invest. They pocket this surplus value as profit. This is actually quite bizarre, since a system theoretically based on the exchange of commodities of equal value should not actually produce a surplus at all. If two apples exchange for two oranges based on their labor values, and you and I make this exchange, neither of us receives a profit. After all, we simply exchanged things of equal value and ended up with exactly the same value we initially possessed.

As we saw earlier, the values of commodities are determined by the average amount of labor required for their production. This total labor consists of two parts, living labor and capital. Capital alone cannot produce surplus value. If all the ore in the world could magically be turned into steel, without any additional labor, then the average labor contained in steel would simply equal that contained in unfinished ore. Its value would not increase one iota. If a totally automated process, from the mine to the point of sale, could produce steel and bring it to market, the value of that steel would be exactly equal to the value of the labor previously embodied in each of the machines used in the process. In production, the value of dead labor is transferred to the new commodity, but it does not produce extra value.[17] What transfers this value is the same thing that produces surplus value: living labor.

Labor power is unique among all commodities, because the cost of labor power can be lower than the value that labor adds to a commodity. As we said, labor power exchanges for the commodities necessary to support the worker—food, transportation, housing and so on. If it takes an average of 4 hours of labor to supply these commodities and the laborer can be made to work for 8 hours, then the capitalist receives the product of those extra 4 hours for free.

The source of surplus value is the fact that workers can be made to work for longer than what is necessary to support them. In simple terms, the cost of labor is less to the capitalist than the value that labor produces.[18] This uneven exchange is only possible because capitalists have a monopoly on the means of production, guaranteed by all the force of the state. Otherwise, there would be no surplus to accrue to capitalists, as it would flow directly to the workers themselves. Surplus value, then, is just an unpaid cost. It comes from the unpaid hours of a working person's life that a capitalist extracts for private benefit. Surplus value is a cost borne by society as a whole, turned into the private profit of an elite class.

The value embodied in a commodity can be broken down into three categories. The value of a commodity (V) is equal to the value of capital (c) required to produce it, plus the exchange value of the required labor power (v), plus the surplus value (s) added by the worker. This can be represented by a simple equation: $V = c + v + s$. This equation is equally valid for the total value of everything produced in an economy. The total value produced in an economy is equal to the value of the capital invested, the value of the commodities consumed by workers and the total surplus value. Of course, this surplus is not supposed to just sit around. It has to be reinvested as more capital and pull more labor into production, in a circular process intended to produce more and more surplus value. Money must be put to use producing value so that it can be turned into more money.

The *rate of profit* is the ratio of the amount of surplus value produced to investment in wages and capital. As capitalists generally try to make as much money as possible, investment flows between different industries and sectors in search of higher rates of profit. Although the rate of profit produced in each firm and industry varies greatly, the interaction and competition between these bodies roughly tends to equalize their gains around an average rate. This average is the *general rate of profit*. This general rate is the rate of surplus value produced by a capitalist economy as an undivided unit.[19]

Some things are initially obvious when we look at this basic model. There is a direct inverse relationship between wages and profits (which is true of any economic model). If all else holds equal, profits go up when wages go down. For a capitalist, lowering the ratio of the cost of labor power to the value it produces is the key to producing more profit. This ratio is known as the *rate of exploitation* or the relationship between the value produced by the worker and what they receive in exchange for their labor.

The simplest way to raise this rate is by lengthening the working day without increasing wages. By raising the workday to 10 hours from 8 hours, and holding the value of wages at 4 hours, the capitalist receives an extra 2 hours of work for free. The capitalist can even raise wages a bit, by offering an hour's worth of overtime pay, and still receive 1 more hour of work for free.

But workers are not machines that can simply be cranked to churn out more labor. From the struggles of the journeyman printers of the 17th century to those of the trade unions of the late 1800s, reducing the length of the workday was the battle cry of organized labor. The conflict around the workday embodied the struggle between leisure and prosperity and private profit, a struggle created by the nature of surplus value.[20]

Given that workers resist the extension of the workday and

that there are only so many hours in a day, capitalists have to find other ways to increase the production of surplus value. They can do this by increasing the ratio of surplus value to wages while holding labor hours constant. The most reliable way to do this is to make labor more productive. If a worker can produce the equivalent value of their wages in less time, then the resulting gain in surplus time can be used for the benefit of the capitalist. There are all kinds of ways that this can happen: workers can become more skilled through training and education, the division of labor and extent of cooperation can be extended, work can be sped up and intensified, and capitalists can invest in productive machinery.

Of course, producing more commodities with less labor time ultimately reduces the value of those commodities. This does not necessarily reduce the rate of exploitation. Let us imagine that two workers are set to work producing a total of 24 cars in 8 hours. Now assume that the working day is divided into 4 hours of surplus time and 4 hours of paid time. If one worker can produce 24 cars in 8 hours owing to improved machinery, then the capitalist can do away with some of their labor costs. If wages hold steady, the remaining worker will earn the equivalent of 2 hours of their labor while contributing 6 hours of surplus value. The living labor needed to produce 24 cars, however, drops from 16 hours to 8, and those 24 cars now contain 6 rather than 8 hours of surplus labor. To arrive at this remarkable outcome, the capitalist invested a sum of capital in labor-saving machinery. Although they initially make more money selling cars above their value (as an early adopter of this technology), they raised the ratio of their investment to surplus value, and lowered their rate of profit.[21]

The other way that the ratio of surplus value to wages can be raised is through dispossession. In this extreme case, capitalists can hold the length of the working day constant while reducing the value of wages directly. As Keynes wrote, however, workers generally resist a reduction in their wages denominated in currency.[22] If the owner of a company walks onto the shop floor and announces that they are slashing wages from $15 an hour to $10, there will likely be hell to pay. Aside from special circumstances where they do not fear riots, factory occupations, unionization campaigns and so on, capitalists generally avoid such a blunt tool. It is much harder, on the other hand, to tell when the real value of wages falls as a result of a decline in the purchasing power of currency. If $15 an hour buys less tomorrow than it did today, we only discover this gradually over time, as prices constantly fluctuate. *Inflation*, a fall in the value of currency relative to commodities, reduces the value of real wages as long as currency wages do not rise faster and can thus increase the rate of exploitation.

Once surplus value has been produced, it has to be *realized* through sale on the market. It does a capitalist no good to have a bunch of surplus cars sitting around outside a factory. These commodities have to be exchanged for money, which can be used to buy everything else that one needs to produce more surplus value—labor, machinery, buildings, land and so on. Capitalists, of course, can only produce commodities for which there is demand if they want to make a profit. This demand is not measured in use values. Even if thousands of people are starving in one's own country, one cannot make money producing food to feed them if they have no money to buy it. Capitalists are concerned with effective demand or the ability of consumers to exchange money for the commodities they desire. This is why one often sees food being exported from countries that are suffering from malnutrition, hunger and famine. In order to buy commodities, one needs money. In order to get money, those who are not born rich have to labor, or sell the products of their labor, or mortgage their land. This necessity draws increasing amounts of labor, resources and land into the capitalist vortex of value production.

In the centuries preceding the Industrial Revolution, the productivity of the average person barely increased from year to year. The annual growth in GDP per capita in the UK from 1300 to 1750 probably hovered between 0 per cent and 0.25 per cent.[23] This means that it would have taken at least 280 years for the value of the UK's output to double. Compare this to an economy that doubles in a little over 20 years, as is the case in an economy that grows at a rate of 3 per cent per year, the standard growth target in developed economies after World War II.[24] Agricultural economies were not totally stagnant, but they did not possess the technology to radically improve the amount of goods they could produce. It was quite difficult to accumulate capital and it took a long amount of time to do so. Surpluses could be extracted by exploiting the labor of slaves and peasants, charging rents for land and levying taxes, but the value that this created was relatively small in modern terms. The incredible technologies of the Industrial Revolution changed this. As labor became evermore productive, the ability to extract greater quantities of surplus value, and thus accumulate evermore capital, increased. This cycle is what we know simply as "capitalism."

Capitalism is a social machine that sucks the life out of human beings, transforming their toil into value. All of today's great owners of capital, from wealthy dynasties to multinational corporations to nation states, can trace the descent of their fortunes to a long history of exploitation. Slavery produced the cotton used in the textile factories of the US and the UK through the greater part of the 19th century, and the labor of workers transformed that cotton into clothing. Steel and oil magnates extracted the natural wealth of iron, coal and petroleum from the soil, expropriating its value for the benefit of a few great owners. Colonial and imperialist ventures spanning the entire world murdered countless millions in the pursuit of markets, raw materials and cheap labor. Today, the conditions in the factories that produce iPhones are so miserable that workers throw themselves from the rooftops to escape. Perhaps the most telling fact of all is that Wall Street was a slave market before it became the center of the global trade in all forms of unpaid labor. The catalog of misery created by the ruthless pursuit of surplus value is too long to fit in any book, but it is the actual history of the wealth of modern society—the wealth produced by capitalism.

Accumulation

Accumulated capital is accumulated surplus value. In a capitalist economy, the process of accumulation must continue without end. This has nothing to do with the fact that greedy capitalists simply "want" to make more money. If accumulation were to halt, the capitalist system would be struck by a sudden massive crisis. Masses of workers would lose their jobs, as they would no longer be needed to drive the expansion of capital. The rate of profit would fall to zero, rendering the mass of surplus capital worthless, as it could no longer be invested profitably. The financial system, which depends on the expectation of future profits, would seize up. Altogether, the capitalist system would come to a shuddering stop.

Profits are the engine that keeps capitalism going and they cannot be done away with in a capitalist economy. The complex network of exchanges required to produce a commodity divides the total surplus into a slew of different categories: industrial profits, financial profits, interest, rents for land and buildings, rents for access to raw materials, taxes and so on. A portion of this surplus is consumed by the owners of capital and by the state, and a portion of it remains to be reinvested.

Investment appears as simple as spending money with the purpose of making more money. Everything from an interest-paying bank account to a stock that pays dividends appears to work this way. But capital does not multiply on its own. It has to be used to produce more value. So capitalists send their money around the globe in search of new sources of labor, opportunities to invest in assets and machinery, raw materials that can be extracted, and land. This process, year in and year out, builds up an increasingly large stock of capital. Capital tends to accumulate faster than it gets worn out, faster than it is replaced by new technologies and, ultimately, faster than new uses for it can be found. The law of value, which can accept no end to its own expansion, pushes capital accumulation to its limits.

Even more than capital expands by moving into underdeveloped regions, it expands by developing the productivity of labor. We saw in the first section what this looks like. Labor is continuously reorganized into the forms best suited to producing value, and a rising tide of machinery and new technologies multiplies the productive capacity of the worker.[25] As the world market expands and the pace of technological change accelerates, the compulsion to make labor more efficient becomes unavoidable. Each firm is engaged in a constant struggle to lower the cost of labor, so that it can compete as effectively as possible.

To the individual capitalist, the rationale is simple. Labor is a cost like anything else and profits will rise if costs can be reduced. If the capitalist gets ahead of the competition, they reap large rewards, as they can sell their commodities far above their cost of production. If they fall behind, they face falling prices and eventual bankruptcy. It is both rational and necessary for every individual firm to continue raising the productivity of labor. If we rise above the fray and examine a capitalist society from above, what we see is an endless stream of investment being plowed into getting labor to squeeze more commodities out of less time.

This process is inherently contradictory. On the one hand, the purpose of investment is to make a profit. On the other hand, investment increases the ratio of capital to labor over the long run, causing the rate of profit to ultimately fall. This contradiction is known as the *tendency of the rate of profit to fall*.[26] As only labor produces surplus value, investing more capital decreases the ratio of surplus value to investment. When this happens in one industry, it could produce a decline in that industry's observed rate of profit, or it might cause the distribution of surplus value between different industries to change. When this happens across an entire economy, the general rate of profit must fall.[27]

Falling profits reduce the possible outlets for profitably investing the surplus capital produced as a result of accumulation. This acts as a break on investment, simultaneously reducing the demand for commodities and the demand for labor. Firms, industries and even entire nations scramble to compete for a falling rate of surplus value. Those that cannot successfully compete go out of business, throwing their workers into unemployment.

Throughout this process, a portion of the surplus capital will be diverted into speculative financial ventures where profits are nominally higher. Money will pour into real estate, financial instruments like derivatives and insurance packages, and the stock market. The prices of these assets come to depend more and more on the assumption that others will be willing to buy them at a higher price, whether or not they produce value. This is how bubbles form. Finally, a shock—like a war or catastrophe, rising oil prices, the collapse of a major firm or foreclosures in the real estate market—triggers what we know as "the crisis." The inflated values of assets fall dramatically, financial institutions call in their debts, companies go out of business and unemployment skyrockets. All of these events are merely the ultimate result of a long-term decline in the rate of profit.[28]

This is a complex process with counter-tendencies that temporarily balance its effects. An increase in the intensity or productive power of labor not caused by investment in capital— for example, by speeding up or rationalizing production—

can increase the production of surplus value. If the value of wages falls, either owing to competition in the labor force or a because a cheaper way of providing subsistence can be found (such as barracks housing for migrant laborers), then the rate of profit increases. If the means of production (raw materials, machinery, etc.) become cheaper, then the cost of investing capital will fall relative to surplus value produced. The depreciation or devaluation of invested capital, owing to wear and tear or technological obsolescence, also reduces the value of the investment and counteracts the general tendency toward overaccumulation. If new industries arise, particularly with a high ratio of living to dead labor, then this can also provide an outlet for profitable investment and employment. Finally, access to underdeveloped markets, cheap labor and cheap raw materials through colonialism, imperialism and other coercive means of reducing barriers to trade, can raise the rate of profit. Cheap capital, cheap labor and uneven exchange are the pillars of capitalist accumulation, as the imperialist ventures of the world's developed countries demonstrate convincingly.[29] All of these counteracting influences can keep profits high for quite some time, but they cannot support them forever.

I urge stubborn economists, who often scoff at this idea, to take note that Keynes' own macroeconomic theory reaches a roughly identical conclusion, though with a different mechanism: "Not only is the marginal propensity to consume weaker in a wealthy community, but, owing to its accumulation of capital being already larger, the opportunities for investment are less attractive unless the rate of interest falls at a sufficiently rapid rate..."[30] In simple terms: Keynes himself argues that the general rate of profit falls as capital accumulates in a community. Indeed, in *The General Theory* Keynes suggests that proper state management of a capitalist economy can only postpone this inevitability.

A crisis of capitalism is not only an expression of its internal contradictions, but it also contains the means for temporarily resolving them and postponing the final reckoning until a later date. By throwing workers into unemployment, capital produces competition between workers who are willing to work for less and the workers who are still employed. As a result of this competition, capitalists can reduce the real value of wages. "Times are hard," the capitalist reminds their employees, "and cuts will have to be made." A crisis also prompts the devaluation of capital. Capital gradually loses value as it becomes obsolete, but capital can rapidly lose its value by falling out of use in the production process. If a crisis causes a factory to be closed, dismantled and sold for scrap, then the value of that capital is partially wiped out. When an entire company goes under, its assets are typically broken up and sold off. The physical destruction of capital is a much more direct way of solving the overaccumulation problem. If a war or natural disaster wipes out a significant portion of the accumulated capital in a society, then the way is opened to renewed investment.

Finally, the state can consume surplus capital and surplus labor in a method that does not directly produce surplus value. By engaging in deficit spending, states are required to borrow capital by issuing bonds. They can then use this borrowed capital to employ surplus labor by pursuing infrastructure projects (which do not produce value, as they are not produced for exchange), building weapons, employing a massive police force and so on. It does not matter whether these state expenditures are useful. It simply matters that they consume the accumulated capital in a manner that does not produce more capital, which would only add to the overaccumulation problem.

Of course, deficit spending solves the problem of surplus capital by guaranteeing its owners a return on their investment. Interest rates serve as a guaranteed minimum rate of return to capital if it cannot be invested elsewhere. This process is only sustainable over the very long run if the state's income grows faster than its debt. Eventually, someone has to pay up or the surplus capital will be revealed as precisely what it is: capital that can no longer be used in the production of value.[31]

The best example of all three of these solutions is total war. The Great Depression ended as a result of the massive consumption and destruction of capital and surplus labor caused by the Second World War. World War II prompted massive deficit spending to support the armed forces of the combatant states, absorbing a huge portion of unused industrial capacity in the production of weapons. These products were then wiped out after use—bombs don't get reinvested—taking with them a massive share of the industrial capacity and accumulated capital of the entire world. States exercised central control over wages and collective bargaining during the War, typically holding them down for its duration. After the War, states inflated a significant portion of their debts out of existence by holding down interest rates, effectively confiscating the value lent to them by bond purchasers during the War. The exit to the worst crisis of overaccumulation that the world had seen was provided only by a war unmatched in human history in terms of its destruction and waste of human life.

The root cause of capitalism's crises is the development of capitalism itself. As discussed here, falling profits are not the result of some intangible law of nature; they can be traced to technological development and the ever-increasing investment of capital it requires. At the very same time that the owners of capital are forced to invest more with smaller returns, the rise in productivity resulting from their investment throw more workers out of work. By reducing the demand for labor, capitalist investment actually reduces the ability of a portion of society to consume the commodities being produced. Crises thus seem to be a crisis of "overproduction" or "underconsumption" when both are simply two sides of the same coin: the natural development of capitalism.

But, as Marx wrote, the crises themselves are the means with which capital overcomes barriers to its further development. A crisis initiates all kinds of compensating mechanisms to restore the possibility of profitable investment: real wages are reduced, existing capital is devalued and the state consumes or destroys as much capital as possible, productively or otherwise. The question, then, is whether or not these means of adaptation have their own limits. If they do, then capitalism cannot persist without end.

The Collapse of Commodity Production

In a segment of his notes called "The Fragment on Machines," Marx wrote that the development of technology would push capital beyond the premises of the law of value. As automated machinery became increasingly productive, he argued, direct labor would occupy an increasingly unimportant role in production. Ultimately, surplus labor would no longer be required in the development of wealth and could no longer be applied to produce value. At this point, labor time could no longer serve as the measure of value. Production based on exchange value would break down and the law of value would collapse. By expelling labor from the production process, capital was not building a foundation for its continued development. It was creating "the material conditions to blow this foundation sky high."[32]

This was a remarkable prediction. Marx argued that capitalism would collapse as a result of its own internal development. As the amount of living labor embodied in commodities approached zero, the law of value would no longer be able to function. The collapse of commodity production did not depend on a revolution of the working class. It was as inevitable as the progress of automation and the development of technology itself. As implausible as this may sound in our own time, when the first "lights out" factories have already been developed, one can imagine how shocking this prediction would have been in the middle of the 19th century.

This was a time before electric lighting, gas-powered engines, airplanes, industrial robotics and the Internet. Even now one might write this prediction off as a bizarre product of following labor theory to its logical extremes. But Marx was right. The foundations of commodity production began to crack in the early 20th century. These cracks appeared exactly where labor theory would have predicted: American agriculture.

With the development of highly mechanized agriculture in the late 19th and early 20th centuries, agricultural commodities required a tiny amount of labor to produce. For example, the labor needed to produce 1 acre of wheat in the US fell from 61 hours in 1830 to 3 hours and 19 minutes in 1896. At the same time, the amount of capital required to operate a farm successfully continued to increase, causing producers to rely more on credit. After the end of the First World War, farmers in the US were chronically overproducing crops. Even before the onset of the Great Depression in 1929, the prices of major commodity crops like wheat were already falling around the world. These prices dropped sharply in the months before the stock market crash in October 1929.

The Great Depression did no favors to farmers. Prices fell even more and overproduction was virtually constant. Global prices for wheat fell over 75 per cent from their highs in 1925 to their lows in 1939, the beginning of the Second World War. With prices so low, production for profit in US agriculture became increasingly unstable. Farmers could no longer make a profit by selling their crops on the market and many were already seriously in debt. Many went out of business, selling their land to pay off their debts. Even droughts and poor harvests in the 1930s could not cause a long-term rise in agricultural commodity prices.[33] Chronic overproduction was here to stay.

In response to collapsing prices, the US government (and

many others around the world) built a comprehensive system designed to limit production and guarantee profits to farmers. The Agricultural Marketing Act of 1929 allowed the state to buy and stockpile the surpluses of farmers at a guaranteed rate of profit, but even this was insufficient to halt overproduction and falling prices. The Agricultural Adjustment Act of 1933 went further. Under the Act, the government would pay farmers to reduce production by letting their fields lie unused.[34] Stockpiled surplus crops were destroyed, burned or plowed over and millions of animals were slaughtered.

While both Acts were ultimately revised and replaced, they functioned as a system to raise prices artificially above the values of agricultural commodities. Instead of encouraging investment, the state intervened to curtail production. None of these methods was capable of returning crop prices to levels that could independently sustain production for profit, but they did manage to keep agricultural production afloat by transferring profits from other sectors through taxation and borrowing. World War II acted as a significant support to crop prices after their historic decline to 1939 lows, but the system of price supports and subsidies was never abandoned.

To this day, the US government and US agribusiness go to great lengths to prop up this system. Agricultural exports have long been the primary means of disposing of US surpluses. The North American Free Trade Agreement (NAFTA) of 1994 allowed cheap US crops to flood the Mexican market, crushing small Mexican farmers. Around 2 million farmers have been pushed off their land since NAFTA's implementation. As a direct result, millions of displaced farmers and agricultural laborers migrated to the US in search of work.[35]

Equally important is the suppression of potential competition from other countries. The FBI and companies like Monsanto work to ensure that genetically modified seeds and fertilizers remain in the hands of US capital. China, for instance, is currently incapable of growing enough food to feed its own population. It imports 94 per cent of its corn from the US. As a result, the Chinese government and Chinese firms are desperate to increase their ability to produce more crops with already-scarce water and arable land. Chinese firms try to smuggle US seed varieties out of the country for testing and reverse engineering, which the FBI combats in the name of protecting intellectual property rights.[36] Of course, maintaining China's dependence on the US for its food supply is as much a geopolitical weapon as it is a means to suppress potential competition from other agricultural producers.

One might expect the massive demand of foreign markets to reliably support US agricultural prices, but it does not. From 1996 to 2006, the cost of producing corn was higher than its sale price, meaning that virtually every ear of US corn sold during that period was sold at a loss. The production of the staple crop of the US was unprofitable for an entire decade. From 2006 to 2014, corn could finally be sold at a profit. Rising demand as a result of droughts, crop failures and bio-fuel production boosted prices. But by 2014 and 2015, corn production again headed into unprofitable territory.[37]

It should be obvious that decades-long periods of unprofitable production can only be supported by a system that transfers surplus value from industries where production for profit is still possible. These bizarre compensation structures create equally bizarre practical results. In 2015, for example, US dairy farmers produced so much milk that they were forced to dump hundreds of tons of it into the ground.[38] There was simply nowhere that could be found to buy it all.

History shows us what happens when capital starts to reach the limits of absolute overaccumulation. Industries become so productive that the value embodied in commodities falls precipitously, all while the capital investment firms need to compete rises. Profits drop and further investment only worsens overproduction, causing a steep decline in the rate of profit. The amazing thing about this example is that it was not a digitized piece of information but a physical commodity that first demonstrated this possibility. US agriculture became so productive that it could no longer carry on the production of exchange value. An industry that could easily feed everyone in the country teetered on the verge of collapse while people were going hungry in the streets. The state chose to manage this problem by destroying produce outright.

There are few clearer examples of the pure irrationality of a system based on production for profit, or the extremes to which the elite will go to preserve such a system. More importantly, it demonstrates that Marx's remarkable prediction was right. The collapse of production for exchange value is not just a theoretical possibility. We can already observe it happening. An agricultural system that sacrificed everything from environmental standards to food quality and safety in the search for profits can no longer sustain production for profit on an independent basis. US agriculture has to be subsidized permanently or it will be unable to operate in a capitalist market.

The natural response to the problem of falling profits caused by overaccumulation is to form a monopoly that can limit production and set prices. This can be achieved either by a cascade of failures and mergers until one or a few players control an entire market, or by state regulations that establish monopoly prices. In the case of US agriculture, the latter was politically more palatable; though the industry's continued development pushes it toward the former.

Monopolization does not cause the production of surplus value to rise, but it allows a firm or industry to secure a larger portion of the total surplus product of society. The problem with this response today is that the very premise of monopoly production is undermined by the rise of distributed production. Any industry that finds itself competing with a form of distributed production will no longer have the option of adaptation through monopolization. Instead, that industry will flail wildly as prices fall back toward their values and as its entire business model disintegrates in slow motion.

The collapse of viable production for profit in agriculture was not an existential threat to capitalism. Investment could be directed into other value-producing sectors, like manufacturing and the service industries. But if these industries approach the heights of productivity seen in modern agriculture, then there is no reason to believe that commodity production will not collapse there, as well. As the living labor embodied in the commodities produced by all industries approaches zero, there will be nowhere left to turn for surplus value to subsidize these industries. Labor will no longer be able to serve as the foundation of exchange value and the law of value will crumble. This is the general crisis that capitalism must inevitably approach. If labor theory is correct, then there is an absolute limit to capitalist accumulation.

In an advanced capitalist economy, production encompasses all of society, even though it appears to be private. The production of steel alone is inextricably linked to: the extraction of raw materials like iron and coal; the production of suitable workers through the education system, and religious and family structures; the creation and maintenance of a global system of transportation and communications, comprised of highways, shipping lanes, air transport and electronic networks; the progress of science and technological research; the demand for steel in construction, automobile manufacturing, weapons production and other industries; and the social and political dynamics of contemporary society, including wars, revolutions, famine, migration, economic crises and so on. This is not an exhaustive list.

The individual capitalist looks at their ledgers and sees a certain amount of profit, and contents themselves with the thought that they were responsible for its production. They do not realize that this profit is a mere portion of the total surplus value produced by global capitalism allotted to them through the shifting sands of prices. By merely studying the movement of prices, they condemn themselves to ignorance of the fundamental dynamics behind their successes and failures. They fail to understand that they are a representative of an impermanent system heading for its inevitable demise.

Labor theory and the critique of value give us a way to form a systemic understanding of capitalism. We can tell this model works, because it allows us to predict the course of capitalist development and identify the origins of future crises. The task now is to apply this theory to analyze contemporary capitalism, understand where it is going and identify the limits it faces. Without this analysis, we will be rudderless in a world of unemployment, rising debt, and social and environmental devastation. The ongoing productive revolution should produce a growing mass of unemployed workers alongside reduced outlets for profitable investment, rising state and private debts, and a succession of bubbles and crises caused by the search for profits. Is this model accurate? If we want to tell this story, we must begin with the most spectacular crisis of capitalism since the Great Depression: the crisis of 2008.

Endnotes

1   While I am not a Marxist for certain philosophical reasons, I believe that Marx's analysis of the dynamics of capitalism is the most complete and useful description of the system ever produced. My interpretation of Marx is closest to that of the "critique of value," or *wertkritik*, school. Although it takes many different forms, "redistributionist" Marxism criticizes capitalism on the grounds that it exploits the worker by stealing a large part of the value of their labor.

The critique of value expands upon this by arguing that capitalism's contradictions stem from the very nature of value in a capitalist economy. Where one calls for the worker to receive the product of their labor, the other calls for the abolition of the law of value. See *Marxism and the Critique of Value* for a useful collection of the works of the *wertkritik* school. Larsen, N., Nilges, M., Robinson, J., and Brown, N., ed. (2014) *Marxism and the Critique of Value*, (Chicago: MCM' Publishing) Available at: http://www.mcmprime.com/files/ Marxism-and-the-Critique-of-Value.pdf. [accessed 31 May 2017]

2   Marx, K. *Capital, Volume 1.* "The Commodity." Available at: https://www.marxists.org/archive/marx/works/1867-c1/ commodity.htm. [accessed 31 May 2017]

3   Keynes, of course, went on to attempt exactly the same analysis, like other capitalist economists. There are no "approximate statistical comparisons" that can be derived from things that are not subject to quantification. See: Keynes, J.M. (1936) *The General Theory of Employment, Interest, and Money.* "Chapter 4: The Choice of Units." Available at: https://www.marxists.org/reference/subject/ economics/keynes/general-theory/ch04.htm. [accessed 1 June 2017] Thanks to Guglielmo Carchedi for pointing this out. Carchedi, G. "Zombie Capitalism and the origin of crises." p. 122. Available at: http://marx2010.weebly.com/ uploads/5/4/4/8/5448228/harman_review.pdf. [accessed 1 June 2017]

4   Mauss, M. (1990) *The Gift*, trans. W.D. Halls. (London: Routledge) https://libcom.org/files/Mauss%20-%20The%20 Gift.pdf.

5   Graeber, D. (2011) *Debt: The First 5,000 Years.* (Brooklyn: Melville House) p. 29. Available at: https://libcom.org/ files/__Debt__The_First_5_000_Years.pdf. [accessed 1 June 2017]

6 Marxists who disagree with this reading should see the following: "Political Economy has indeed analysed, however incompletely, value and its magnitude, and has discovered what lies beneath these forms. But it has never once asked the question why labour is represented by the value of its product and labour time by the magnitude of that value. These formulæ, which bear it stamped upon them in unmistakable letters that they belong to a state of society, in which the process of production has the mastery over man, instead of being controlled by him, such formulæ appear to the bourgeois intellect to be as much a self-evident necessity imposed by Nature as productive labour itself." Marx, K. *Capital, Volume 1.* "The Fetishism of Commodities and the Secret Thereof." Available at: https://www.marxists. org/archive/marx/works/1867-c1/ch01.htm#S4. [accessed 1 June 2017]

7 Graeber, D. *Debt: The First 5,000 Years.* p. 29.

8 This distinction holds for all forms of commodity money, from cattle and cowrie shells to silver and gold.

9 This misunderstanding stems from the fact that both Marx's critics and his sympathizers often forget that his work was not a simple description of an economic system akin to that of Smith, Ricardo and Mill, but a *critique* of political economy. Marx did not spend years laboriously working on manuscripts to reify the categories of political economy; he intended to demonstrate their internal contradictions.

10 Marx, K. (1847) *Wage Labour and Capital.* "By what is the price of a commodity determined?" Available at: https://www.marxists.org/archive/marx/works/1847/wage-labour/ch03.htm. [accessed 1 June 2017]

11 Böhm von Bawerk, E. *Karl Marx and the Close of His System.* "Chapter III: The Question of the Contradiction." Available at: https://www.marxists.org/subject/economy/authors/bohm/ch03.htm. (1 June 2017)

12 "Whether the commodities are sold at their values or not, and hence the determination of value itself, is quite immaterial for the individual capitalist. It is, from the very outset, a process that takes place behind his back and is controlled by the force of circumstances independent of himself, because it is not the values, but the divergent prices of production, which form the regulating average prices in every sphere of production. The determination of value as such interests and has a determining effect on the individual capitalist and the capital in each particular sphere of production only in so far as the reduced or increased quantity of labour required to produce commodities, as a consequence of a rise or fall in productiveness of labour, enables him in one instance to make an extra profit, at the prevailing market-prices, and compels him in another to raise the price of his commodities, because more wages, more constant capital, and thus more interest, fall upon each portion of the product, or individual commodity. It interests him only in so far as it raises or lowers the cost of production of commodities for himself, thus only in so far as it makes his position exceptional." Marx, K. (1894) *Capital, Volume III.* "Illusions Created By Competition." Available at: https://www.marxists.org/archive/marx/works/1894-c3/ch50.htm. [accessed 1 June 2017]

13 Ibid. "Formation of a General Rate of Profit (Average Rate of Profit) and Transformation of the Values of Commodities into Prices of Production." Available at: https://www.marxists.org/archive/marx/works/1894-c3/ch09.htm. [accessed 1 June 2017]

14 Jehu Eaves offers a similar solution to the transformation problem. According to Eaves, the value of a product can never be equal to the price of production in a capitalist system. The formula for this value is V = v (labor cost) + c (capital cost) + s (surplus value). Since the surplus value

embodied in the product is received by the capitalist for free, the total value of a product will always be higher than its cost of production, even if these inputs exchange at their values, unless profits equal zero. See: Eaves, J. "Reply to LK: Notes on the historical and monetary implications of the transformation problem," *The Real Movement.* June 14th, 2015. Available at: https://therealmovement.wordpress.com/2015/06/14/reply-to-lk-notes-on-the-historical-and-monetary-implications-of-the-transformation-problem/. [accessed 1 June 2017]

15   For example, see Paul Mason identifying knowledge "as an independent source of profit," or Jürgen Habermas stating that "It is no longer meaningful to calculate the amount of capital investment in research and development on the basis of unskilled (simple) labor power, when scientific-technical progress has become an independent source of surplus-value." Mason, P. (2015) *PostCapitalism.* (London: Allen Lane) p. 137; Habermas, J. (1970) "Technology and Science as 'Ideology,'" *Toward a Rational Society: Student Protest, Science, and Politics*, trans. Jeremy Shapiro (Boston: Beacon Press) p. 104.

16   Naples, M. and Aslanbegui, N. (1996) "What *does* determine the profit rate? The neoclassical theories presented in introductory textbooks," *Cambridge Journal of Economics*, Vol. 20. pp. 53–71. Available at: http://www.researchgate.net/profile/Nahid_Aslanbeigui/publication/5208043_What_Does_Determine_the_Profit_Rate_The_Neoclassical_Theories_Presented_in_Introductory_Textbooks/links/0c9605227cf43a1798000000.pdf. [accessed 1 June 2017]

17   The idea of "machinic" surplus value suggests that the value produced by machines is capable of exceeding the value embodied in them by the labor used to create them. In effect, it argues that an assembly of machines can behave economically like an assembly of men, producing an excess

of the value necessary to sustain their operation. This is misleading in that it confuses value "in general," which does not exist, with exchange value. Even though a radically automated factory could certainly sustain itself and produce a surplus of goods, it could not ultimately produce a *profit*. We cannot confuse the surplus that arises from production with surplus value. "Wealth produced by machines rather than by men is still wealth," but it is not necessarily profit. See, for example: Lazzarato, M. (2014) *Signs and Machines*, trans. Joshua David Jordan. (Cambridge: Semiotext(e)) p. 43. Aside from this nod to Deleuze and Guattari's theory, this is an excellent book that I highly recommend.

18 Marx, K. *Capital, Volume I.* "The Labour-Process and the Process of Producing Surplus-Value." Available at: https://www.marxists.org/archive/marx/works/1867-c1/ch07.htm#S2. [accessed 1 June 2017]

19 Marx, K. *Capital, Volume III.* "Formation of a General Rate of Profit (Average Rate of Profit) and Transformation of the Values of Commodities into Prices of Production." Available at: https://www.marxists.org/archive/marx/works/1894-c3/ch09.htm. (1 June 2017)

20 Marx, K. *Capital, Volume I.* "The Rate of Surplus Value" and "The Working-Day." Available at: https://www.marxists.org/archive/marx/works/1867-c1/ch09.htm and https://www.marxists.org/archive/marx/works/1867-c1/ch10.htm. [accessed 1 June 2017]

21 Ibid. "The Concept of Relative Surplus Value." Available at: https://www.marxists.org/archive/marx/works/1867-c1/ch12.htm. [accessed 1 June 2017]

22 Keynes, J.M. *The General Theory of Employment, Interest, and Money.* "The Postulates of the Classical Economics." Available at: https://www.marxists.org/reference/subject/economics/keynes/general-theory/ch02.htm. [accessed 1 June 2017]

23 Gordon, R. "Is US economic growth over? Faltering innovation confronts the six headwinds," *Vox*. September 11th, 2012. Available at: http://www.voxeu.org/article/us-economic-growth-over. [accessed 1 June 2017]

24 These estimates are based on the simple "rule of 70," which allows one to estimate when a variable undergoing compounding growth will double. To make an estimate, just divide 70 by the average rate of growth of the variable. (Ex: GDP grows in a particular economy at an average rate of 3 per cent per year. 70/3 = 23.33. GDP will double in around 23 years.)

25 When economists say that productivity is rising, they really mean two things: 1. The economy is producing greater amounts of exchange value; and 2. As a secondary effect, more use value is being produced. This is why free goods and services, while obviously productive of the greatest amount of use value for the people at large, do not figure in capitalist productivity figures, as they produce no exchange value.

26 Some economists argue that Okishio's theorem disproves the tendency for the rate of profit to fall. In a 1961 paper, Nobuo Okishio argued that the introduction of cost-saving technologies cannot lead to a fall in the rate of profit. Okishio's model assumed that real wages remain constant (viz. they do not rise), land and other scarce resources do not exist, and that there is no fixed capital. In short, Okishio contended that the introduction of cost-saving technologies could only lower costs and could not produce a fall in the rate of profit. The general introduction of cost-saving technologies produces more *goods* (in use values) for a smaller cost, but this process diminishes the exchange value of these *commodities* relative to the initial investment. The problem with Okishio's theorem is that there is no representation of the cost of investment—all input costs

miraculously fall without any cost incurred to the capitalist. In practical terms, the investor magically gets to educe the value of their investment *after* the cost of investment has already been sunk. See: Bowles, S. (1981) "Technical change and the profit rate: a simple proof of the Okishio theorem," *Cambridge Journal of Economics*, No. 5. pp. 183–86. Available at: http://tuvalu.santafe.edu/~bowles/TechnicalChange1981. pdf. [accessed 1 June 2017]; Kliman, A. (1996) "A Value-theoretic Critique of the Okishio Theorem," in *Marx and Non-Equilibrium Economics*, ed. Alan Freeman and Guglielmo Carchedi. pp. 206–24.

27 "This mode of production produces a progressive relative decrease of the variable capital as compared to the constant capital, and consequently a continuously rising organic composition of the total capital. The immediate result of this is that the rate of surplus-value, at the same, or even a rising, degree of labour exploitation, is represented by a continually falling general rate of profit." Marx, K. *Capital, Volume III.* "The Law As Such." Available at: https://www.marxists. org/archive/marx/works/1894-c3/ch13.htm. [accessed 1 June 2017]

28 It is possible to have speculative bubbles arise that are not produced by a significant decline in the rate of profit, particularly if the gains expected from the asset being invested in are extraordinarily high. This distinction is the difference between a pure "financial crisis" and a "crisis of capitalism."

29 Marx, K. *Capital, Volume III.* "Counteracting Influences." Available at: https://www.marxists.org/archive/marx/ works/1894-c3/ch14.htm. [accessed 1 June 2017]

30 Keynes, J.M. *The General Theory of Employment, Interest, and Money.* "Chapter 3: The Principle of Effective Demand." Available at: https://www.marxists.org/reference/subject/ economics/keynes/general-theory/ch03.htm. [accessed 1

June 2017]

31 If we assume that deficit spending is not used to produce value, and that it is thus not used to produce commodities, then deficit spending on wages (for example, in supporting soldiers) should create inflation. State employees must use their wages to purchase commodities for subsistence, though they produce no value. The value of commodities relative to wages denominated in currency should rise as a result. This means that deficit spending has the secondary effect of producing a reduction in real wages and a rise in the rate of exploitation.

32 Marx, K. (1858) "The Fragment on Machines," in *Grundrisse*. pp. 705–6. Available at: http://thenewobjectivity.com/pdf/marx.pdf. [accessed 1 June 2017]

33 Marchildon, G. (July 2010) "The Impact of the Great Depression on the Global Wheat Trade," prepared for *Unpeaceable Exchange: Trade and Conflict in the Global Economy, 1000–2000.* p. 4, 9–13. Available at: http://history.uwo.ca/Conferences/trade-and-conflict/files/marchildon.pdf. [accessed 1 June 2017]

34 "Agricultural Adjustment Act of 1933," Public Law 73-10, 73rd Congress, H.R. 3835. Available at: https://fraser.stlouisfed.org/scribd/?item_id=457089&filepath=/docs/historical/martin/54_01_19330512.pdf#scribd-open. [accessed 1 June 2017]

35 Carlsen, L. "Under Nafta, Mexico Suffered, and the United States Felt Its Pain," *The New York Times.* November 24th, 2013. Available at: http://www.nytimes.com/roomfordebate/2013/11/24/what-weve-learned-from-nafta/under-nafta-mexico-suffered-and-the-united-states-felt-its-pain. [accessed 1 June 2017]

36 Genoways, T. "Corn Wars," *New Republic.* August 16th, 2015. Available at: http://www.newrepublic.com/article/122441/corn-wars. [accessed 1 June 2017]

37 Jordan, S. "With no sign of increased demand, farmers battle falling corn prices," *Omaha World-Herald*. August 3rd, 2014. Available at: http://www.omaha.com/money/ with-no-sign-of-increased-demand-farmers-battle-falling-corn/article_64285831-2c09-537f-83e2-048fafde7dc8.html. [accessed 1 June 2017]

38 Mulvany, L. "The U.S. Is Producing a Record Amount of Milk and Dumping the Leftovers," *Bloomberg Business*. July 1st, 2015. Available at: http://www.bloomberg.com/ news/articles/2015-07-01/milk-spilled-into-manure-pits-as-supplies-overwhelm-u-s-dairies. [accessed 1 June 2017]

Chapter 7

The Present Crisis

The pre-crisis view of most professional analysts and forecasters was perhaps best summed up in December 2006 by *The Economist*: 'Market capitalism, the engine that runs most of the world economy, seems to be doing its job well.'

Alan Greenspan

The solution to every crisis lays the foundations of the next. There may be no greater proof of this maxim than the outbreak of the Great Recession. At the time of this writing, 7 years have passed since the beginning of the crisis in 2008. Still, the popular understanding of the crisis, fed by the state and the media, depends on a superficial narrative. According to this misleading and incomplete story, banks and financiers behaved irresponsibly, creating bubbles by making poor investment decisions. Regulators either colluded with the bankers or fell asleep at the switch. Governments and individuals "lived beyond their means," supporting their reckless consumption with unsustainable debts.

As painful as the crisis was, this narrative comfortingly suggests that relatively minor adjustments to the financial system can prevent future crises. This is not true. The Great Recession was the product of a long-term structural change in the nature of capitalism. The conditions that created the financial crisis are still with us. If anything, they are worse than ever. In order to understand why, we have to go looking for the real origins of the crisis.

Origins of the Crisis

The period between 1914 and 1945 saw substantial shocks to the global economic order and a massive decline in the value of accumulated capital. As I have argued, the Second World War ended the Great Depression by destroying and devaluing a significant portion of the globe's accumulated wealth. Thomas Piketty estimates that the value of accumulated capital relative to yearly national income fell from between 600 and 700 per cent in 1910 to 200 and 300 per cent in 1950 in the UK, France and Germany. This massive devaluation of capital is unmatched in modern history. Much of this loss of value can be attributed to physical destruction, but most of it stemmed from bankruptcies, political shocks like the Russian Revolution of 1917, and the "euthanization" of owners of public debt. During the Second World War, savers lent their surplus capital en masse to their governments, who repaid them by inflating the value of their bonds out of existence in the War's aftermath.[1]

This period of destruction and devaluation laid the foundations for the "thirty glorious years" of post-War reconstruction and renewed accumulation in the developed world. Capital's slate was cleared. The US assumed the leadership of a global capitalist bloc founded on the Bretton Woods system — an economic order based upon the convertibility of dollars for gold, and international financial institutions like the World Bank and the International Monetary Fund (IMF). With the US exporting capital around the world and the rise of a manufacturing economy centred around automobiles, consumer appliances, airplanes and so on, the way was paved for high rates of economic growth, near full employment and rising living standards.

GDP grew at an average of over 4 per cent per year in the Organization for Economic Co-operation and Development (OECD) — an organization of the world's developed nations — in the 1950s and 1960s.[2] This remarkable expansion allowed for a historic bargain between organized labor and capital. In exchange for abandoning anti-capitalism, and demands for increased worker control of production and reduced labor hours, union leaders secured consistent real-wage increases. From 1948 to 1973, productivity rose 96.7 per cent in the US. The average hourly compensation of production workers rose 91.3 per cent over the same period.[3]

By the late 1960s, the post-War order began to break down. Countries like Germany, Japan and France, whose economies were completely devastated by the War, became economic powers in their own right. Technological changes made both industry and agriculture increasingly productive. The walls of capital accumulation began to close in, particularly in manufacturing. Markets for mass consumption goods, like the automobile, were increasingly saturated. Production required increasing amounts of capital investment and employed less labor relative to capital. Protected by the political strength of organized labor, wages seemed almost impossible to cut.

Estimated US manufacturing profits declined from a peak rate of over 30 per cent in the mid-1960s to around 12 per cent by the mid-1970s. The rate of profit for the entire US economy fell from around 17 per cent to 10 per cent in the same period. Manufacturing profits were around 40 per cent lower on average between 1970 and 1990 in the G7 economies—the US, Germany, Japan, the UK, France, Italy and Canada—than they were between 1950 and 1970. The general rate of profit in the G7 economies fell from an average of 17.6 per cent to 13.3 per cent over the same decades.[4] None of this is particularly surprising in hindsight. As capital accumulated and became increasingly productive, the rate of profit inevitably fell.

The cracks in the post-War order appeared in a dramatic fashion with the collapse of the gold standard. The Bretton Woods system relied on the US government's promise to exchange dollars for gold at a rate of $35 per ounce. Through the 1960s, the US ran higher and higher deficits to pay for the Vietnam War, and its trade balance swung negative as competitors like Japan and Germany muscled into the US market.[5] The value of the dollar fell as a result of this inflationary spending, putting an immense strain on the gold standard. Central banks in other countries, like France and Switzerland, could simply exchange their dollars for gold and instantly increase the value of their holdings. This process depleted the US's gold reserves, which were the ultimate anchor of the dollar's value.

A coalition of central banks led by the US Federal Reserve tried to lower the price of gold by flooding the market with their reserves when prices rose above $35 an ounce, but this arrangement quickly collapsed. Finally, the US Federal Reserve raised interest rates to tighten the money supply, while the US government attempted to reduce its budget deficits to halt inflation. From 1966 to 1968, the US economy had already shown signs of wavering. In 1969, a recession broke out. A decline in the rate of profit, reduced government deficits and higher interest rates produced exactly what they could have been expected to. Nixon's administration faced a clear dilemma. It could either keep monetary and fiscal policy tight, and send the US into a depression while maintaining the gold standard, or it could lower interest rates in an attempt to keep the economy afloat while abandoning the gold standard.[6]

Nixon chose the latter. The Federal Reserve lowered interest rates and inflation started rising again. In 1971, Nixon announced that dollars would no longer be convertible to gold, unilaterally abandoning Bretton Woods. From now on, the values of currencies would be anchored to nothing, though the dollar would still serve as the world's reserve currency. The effect was a massive increase in the value of gold relative to the dollar. By mid-1973, the price of gold was $90.50 an ounce. It rose to $600 an ounce by 1980—an incredible jump from the pre-1971 exchange rate of $35.[7] Nixon tried to tame inflation by instituting wage and price controls—after all, theoretically, holding wages and consumer prices steady should have stopped prices from rising according to Keynesian principles. This did not work. Inflation was not being caused by rising wages, per Keynesian theory, but by a collapse in the value of the dollar and other currencies relative to gold and other commodities.

The end of Bretton Woods barely postponed a systemic crisis. In 1971, oil contracts were stipulated in dollar terms, owing to US political influence in the oil-producing countries like Saudi Arabia and because the dollar's value was expected to be relatively stable. After 1971, the real price of oil fell relative to virtually every commodity on the world market, especially that of gold. From the end of World War II through to 1971, it took between 10 and 15 barrels of oil to purchase 1 ounce of gold. By mid-1973, it took 34 barrels of oil to buy the same ounce. Lamenting this remarkable change, a Kuwaiti oil minister complained, "What is the point of producing more oil and selling it for an unguaranteed paper currency?"

In 1972, the Organization of the Petroleum Exporting Countries (OPEC) raised prices proportionally with the rising price of gold and agreed to index future prices to inflation. In October 1973, however, Western support for Israel during the Arab-Israeli War provoked an oil embargo from Arab oil producers. On 1 January 1974, OPEC hiked the price of oil from $4.31 to $10.11 a barrel. While this kept the price of oil within its historical range relative to gold, it was a massive shock for the global economy.[8]

Stock exchanges were already crashing at the beginning of 1973, but the oil shock only fueled the fire. By the end of 1974, the main stock indexes of the G7 countries lost 43 per cent of their value in real terms. The US market would only recover the value it had attained at the end of 1972 in 1993.[9] Between 1973 and 1975, global GDP growth dropped from 6.6 per cent to 1 per cent.[10] Unemployment in the US peaked at over 9 per cent in 1975.[11] This was the beginning of the era of deindustrialization in the developed nations. Fierce competition between traditional steel producers and emerging producers like Japan, Korea and Brazil created a chain of depressed zones stretching from the Rust Belt of the US to the UK's Midlands and Germany's Ruhr area. Even after the worst of the crisis in the mid-1970s, high unemployment and high inflation existed side by side for the rest of the decade, a new economic reality dubbed "stagflation."

Around the same time that the post-War economic order started falling apart, the legitimacy of the political and social system came into question. The Sixties in the US saw the rise of the anti-war movement, the black power movement, the Young Lords, the American Indian Movement, the New Left, and a cultural revolt against traditional sexual and social morality. In France, spontaneous demonstrations by millions of students and workers in May 1968 led President Charles de Gaulle to flee the country, fearing an imminent revolution. In the same year, militant Japanese students occupied universities and clashed with the police.[12] In 1969, a wave of strikes and factory occupations flooded Italy during the "Hot Autumn."[13] Capitalist societies — and some in the Soviet bloc, like Czechoslovakia in 1968 — faced a prolonged political crisis that was only compounded by the economic troubles of the 1970s. Capitalism had to adapt or die.

As Marx suggested, the development of capitalism led to an acute contradiction. As capital accumulated after World War II and the rate of profit declined, states like the US had to run higher and higher deficits, to support employment and economic growth. But this inflationary spending made it impossible to stay on the gold standard, which linked the price of money to the labor value embodied in gold.[14] In order to continue propping up growth with debt, the state had to sever the stable connection between its currency and labor values. The end of the gold standard abolished the structural limitations that inflation imposed on state deficit spending and it heralded a new era of capitalism. Currency would no longer have any definite link to labor values. Capital seemed to declare that it would no longer rely primarily on the production of value through manufacturing. From now on, capital staked its future on the belief that money could magically transform itself into more money through the manipulation of debt and finance.

The ways that capitalism adapted to this profound crisis laid the foundations for the crisis of 2008. Capital had to abandon its model centred on accumulation through Fordist mass production, the post-war bargain between labor and capital, and protectionism. First, capital in the developed world abandoned the labor-capital bargain. Capitalist states repressed the most radical elements of the leftist social movements, while corporations broke the strength of organized labor through an onslaught of automation, offshoring to low-wage areas and attacking the politically guaranteed rights of labor unions. With these tactics, capitalists were able to hold wages down and cement their control over the production process.[15]

Capital created a true world market by reducing barriers to trade between the developed nations, opening the markets of developing nations through "structural adjustment" programs, and pulling billions of new workers into the production process with the fall of the Soviet Union and China's turn to capitalism. Finally, capital shifted from a mode of accumulation based on industrial profits to one based on finance. Over and above manufacturing, profits stemmed increasingly from FIRE assets: financials, insurance and real estate. Debt, both public and private, became the main tool for supporting increased consumption.

Among workers in the developed world, the onslaught of neoliberalism is the most well-remembered aspect of this historical transition.[16] The US and the UK famously turned to the Right in the early 1980s, electing Ronald Reagan and Margaret Thatcher to lead the assault on organized labor and deregulate markets. In 1981, Reagan fired 13,000 striking air traffic controllers, breaking their union permanently. There were 39 work stoppages by federal government employees between 1962 and 1981, but none after Reagan fired the air traffic controllers.[17]

In 1984, UK coal miners went on strike to protest against the UK government's plan to close 23 pits and lay off 20,000 workers. The government proposal was only an early part of a larger plan to close over 75 pits in the UK's heavily protected coal mining industry. This plan aimed to break the strength of the miner's union. While the strike involved over 140,000 miners at its height, it was ultimately suppressed using police violence, the infiltration of the miner's union by UK spy agencies, a media smear campaign and pre-planned stockpiling of coal reserves.[18] By 1985 the strike was called off and the closures went forward.

In the following years, pit closures and privatizations almost completely destroyed the UK mining industry. These events symbolized a comprehensive struggle over the role of organized labor in the production process. From 1970 to 2003, the percentage of the workforce belonging to labor unions fell in almost every developed country, with the exception of Finland, Sweden, Denmark, Belgium and Spain. This rate was slashed in half in the US, cut by a third in the UK, cut by two fifths in Japan and plummeted three fifths in France.[19]

As dramatic as the neoliberal turn became during the Reagan-Thatcher era, its roots were already present in supposedly left-leaning governments in the 1970s and early 1980s. Thatcher's famous taunt that "there is no alternative" to capitalism was adopted in principle by the social democratic parties well before she came to power. In the mid-1970s, the UK's Labour Party was already advocating for wage freezes in an attempt to battle inflation. It was the democratic president Jimmy Carter, not Ronald Reagan, who appointed Paul Volcker to implement policies aimed at driving the economy into a recession in 1979, creating skyrocketing unemployment as the price of reducing inflation.[20]

After an initial flirtation with leftist reforms, in 1983 France's socialist prime minister, François Mitterand, slashed state expenditures, hiked taxes on workers and consumers, and lowered taxes on businesses, forecasting the austerity measures that would be implemented across Europe after 2008.[21] This general pattern would hold true throughout the 1980s, 1990s and 2000s, with virtually every major left-leaning party in the developed world adopting neoliberal economic policies that were largely indistinguishable from their counterparts on the Right.

As it broke the strength of the working class in the developed world, capitalism expanded into underdeveloped countries in search of cheap labor, raw materials and potential new markets for goods. The IMF and World Bank used their financial leverage to encourage developing nations to abandon protectionism and privatize publicly owned industries. These institutions offered loan packages to many countries in sub-Saharan Africa and Latin America, which were suffering from their own economic crises, in exchange for adopting neoliberal economic reforms.

These combinations of loans and mandatory economic reforms were known as "structural adjustment programs." A review of these programs in sub-Saharan Africa found that countries with structural adjustment programs actually witnessed lower economic growth than those who did not adopt them. Governments were encouraged to sell off their assets at bargain basement prices. At the same time, IMF programs forced African governments to reduce spending on education, healthcare and sanitation. While many of these measures were justified in the name of reducing these countries' debts, "sub-Saharan [Africa's] debt rose as a share of GDP from 58% in 1988 to 70% in 1996."[22] Economic neocolonialism actually hindered development, but it opened previously protected markets to international capital, which was desperately in need of new outlets for investment.

East Asian countries like South Korea, Taiwan, Singapore,

Malaysia, Thailand and China opened themselves to capital as industrial centers with cheap, disciplined labor. East Asian capital was one of the main beneficiaries of the "deindustrialization" process in the West, which saw a global transfer of manufacturing employment from high-wage developed nations to low-wage developing nations. Thanks to its size and careful transition to state-managed capitalism, China became a massive exporter of all kinds of products, finally surpassing the US as the world's largest trading nation in 2013.[23] With the collapse of the Soviet Union and the Warsaw Pact, and India's entry into the global market, the world's labor pool doubled in size from around 1.46 billion workers to 2.93 billion.[24] Naturally, this dramatically increased the ratio of available labor to accumulated capital, and it facilitated the transfer of industry to regions with low wages, poor working conditions and no unions. Over time, real wages in these developing regions rose as workers organized to claim their share of rising wealth. At the same time, real wages in developed nations stagnated and even declined for the poorest segments of the population.

If we adopt a global viewpoint, we see that neoliberalism is not simply an ideology that promotes "the free market" to the detriment of all other considerations. Instead, we see neoliberalism as a coherent strategy of capitalist adaptation in the face of a long-term decline in profits. Neoliberalism simultaneously created an international market for capital and an international pool of labor. For the first time in centuries, the living standards of working people in the developed world and the developing world began to converge. From the 1990s onward, capitalism became a truly global system. Despite these adaptations, which entailed some of the most significant economic changes in world history, all was not well underneath the surface. The world rate of profit rose after the profit crunch of the 1970s, but it never recovered to its post-War heights.[25] GDP growth in the developed world began a steady decline, as well. Faced with the prospect of lower profits from investment in traditional industry, capital poured into the world's stock markets, purchased public and private debts, and invested heavily in real estate.

Financialization is the process where profits increasingly accumulate through financial channels rather than trade and commodity production. While a portion of these profits are tied to investments in value-producing activities, much of the surplus capital gets invested in attempts to turn money *directly* into more money. Instead of claiming a share of surplus value in the form of dividends, investors try to profit from an increase in stock prices. Financial firms create "insurance" packages that represent little more than gigantic gambles, for example, on the rise and fall of oil prices or the value of subprime mortgages. Eventually, financiers bundle these individual gambles into incomprehensibly complex derivatives that can be traded between banks, hedge funds and pension funds.

The most ruthless financiers, like those at Goldman Sachs, go on to bet against some of the very same derivatives that they sell their clients. At the same time, money from all over the world pours into real estate, most dramatically in financial hubs like New York, London and Dubai, on the expectation that prices will rise endlessly. The rise of finance is an attempt to jump from money to more money without ever passing through the production process. The process of financialization, however, is not a mere distortion of the "real" capitalist economy—it is an absolutely necessary outlet for surplus capital that could not otherwise be invested profitably. The falling rate of profit at the end of the post-War boom led directly to the search for fictitious profits. As we saw in 2008, when this bubble bursts the "real" economy comes to a halt, as well.

As economist Greta Krippner has shown, financial profits assumed an increasingly dominant role as a portion of all US profits from the mid-1980s onward. In 1985, financial profits only accounted for around 15 per cent of US profits. By the mid-1990s, profits from FIRE investments surpassed manufacturing as the largest share of corporate profits in the US economy, reaching over 40 per cent of the total before 2008. By contrast, profits from the service industries—the main source of employment in the post-industrial economy—never exceeded 10 per cent.[26]

Banks and hedge funds were not the only actors responsible for the reconstruction of US capitalism. Non-financial firms came to rely on FIRE assets, as well. By the late 1980s, the ratio of profits accruing to these firms from interest, dividends and capital versus their traditional income increased to *five times* the levels seen during the post-War period. The US is not exceptional in this field. The fraction of national income appropriated by rentiers—the owners of financial assets—rose in every single OECD country for which data was available from the 1970s to the 1990s.[27] Remarkably, among non-financial companies the manufacturing sector actually led the trend of financialization.[28] As Christian Marazzi argues, this "is enough to definitively discard the distinction between (industrial) real and financial economies, distinguishing industrial profits from 'fictitious' financial ones."[29] Or, perhaps more accurately, this is enough to discard the idea that the "real" industrial economy would have persisted without the rise of the financial economy.

The growth of financial capitalism entailed the rise of an economy founded on debt-supported consumption. After all, people still had to consume things, even though real wages were basically stagnant. In the US, the ratio of household debt—including mortgages, medical debt, credit card debt and student debt—to household income rose from under 65 per cent in 1980 to almost 125 per cent in 2007.[30] Indebtedness reached extreme heights in the lead-up to the 2008 crisis. As an IMF report stated:

> In advanced economies, during the five years preceding 2007, the ratio of household debt to income rose by an average of

39 percentage points, to 138 percent. In Denmark, Iceland, Ireland, the Netherlands, and Norway, debt peaked at more than 200 percent of household income. A surge in household debt to historic highs also occurred in emerging economies such as Estonia, Hungary, Latvia, and Lithuania. The concurrent boom in both house prices and the stock market meant that household debt relative to assets held broadly stable, which masked households' growing exposure to a sharp fall in asset prices.[31]

At the same time, states took on their own rising debts. From the 1970s onward, advanced economies steadily accumulated debt as they engaged in deficit spending to consume surplus capital. Taken together, state debt in Australia, Canada, France, Germany, Italy, Japan, Korea, the UK and the US increased from just over 30 per cent of GDP in 1974 to almost 100 per cent of GDP by 2009. Of course, there were serious differences within this group. US public debt rose from 32 per cent of GDP in 1981 to 85 per cent of GDP in 2009, while Japan's public debt soared from 12 per cent of GDP in 1970 to 192 per cent of GDP in 2005. State debts in low-income nations, like Bangladesh and Mozambique, spiked from over 30 per cent of GDP in the early 1970s to almost 120 per cent of GDP by the early 1990s. After a wave of sovereign debt crises, restructuring drove these burdens down to around 60 per cent of GDP by 2009, but today in 2015 debts are rising again, particularly in sub-Saharan Africa. As a group, only the emerging economies—Argentina, Brazil, China, India, Indonesia, Mexico, Russia, Saudi Arabia, South Africa and Turkey—managed to keep their sovereign debts in a range of 30–40 per cent of GDP throughout the entire period.[32]

It should be obvious that the economic model described previously is completely unsustainable. A debt is a mortgage taken out on the future. Debts only stop accumulating infinitely if income grows fast enough to pay them off, if they are wiped out by inflation or if they are canceled. For the workers and states of the developed world, none of this happened. Workers were forced to finance their consumption with debt while their wages stagnated, and developed economies propped up employment and output by increasing deficit spending while economic growth was in a long-term decline.

Everyone who owns debts — governments, banks and people — accounts for these assets as if they are all going to be paid off in the future. State bonds, for instance, are a crucial means of disposing of surplus capital, because states guarantee that they will repay what they borrow with interest. After a state disposes of this capital without producing value, it has to fund its debt payments by taxing workers and firms that do produce value. If it cannot actually do this, then it will simply accumulate a rising mountain of debt until it inevitably defaults — or goes through "restructuring," in IMF jargon. In a default, the value of the surplus capital that has been lent to the state is wiped out completely. The default reveals that the problem of capital overaccumulation was never solved; it was merely postponed.

Financial capitalism created attractive new options for accumulation on the back of this rising debt burden. From the late 1990s into the 2000s, real estate prices soared around the world. As surplus capital kept flooding into the real estate market, investors and ordinary homeowners came to believe that real estate prices could never fall. Spurred on by cheap credit, the rise in prices achieved extreme proportions by 2005. *The Economist* called the global housing bubble "the biggest bubble in history." From 1997 to 2005, US housing prices rose 73 per cent, far outstripping population growth and construction costs. In the UK, prices rose 154 per cent, and they soared 244 per cent in South Africa.[33] (This bubble was simply the latest in a series of bubbles based on pure speculation, the most recent being the dot-com bubble, which burst in 2000.)

In the US, households were encouraged to incur substantial

mortgage debts as an investment strategy. As long as real estate prices rose forever, even a massive debt burden could be seen as a sound investment. Government policy deliberately encouraged debt-fueled home-ownership and by the mid-2000s, government-sponsored firms Fannie Mae and Freddie Mac were pressured to buy mortgages with increasingly large chances of default, and bundle them into securities to be sold in financial markets. Fannie and Freddie, however, were a little behind their peers. Private lenders actively sought out borrowers who they knew would be bad credit risks simply to fulfill the demand for mortgage-backed securities in financial markets. They systematically defrauded the US working class, offering mortgages with ballooning interest payments to poor and disenfranchised groups. These "subprime" mortgages fed the booming market for mortgage-backed derivatives.

Never missing an opportunity to profit from a looming bubble, the financiers went all in. Mortgage-backed securities were bought and sold by everyone who had money to spend—hedge funds, pension funds and banks. Sophisticated financial institutions bundled these securities into massive packages known as "collateralized debt obligations" (CDOs) that hid the underlying weaknesses in the actual debts on which they were based. Goldman Sachs, for example, sold CDOs to its clients that it knew were bound to fail as homeowners went into default. It then helped another one of its clients place swaps (a contract that allows one to make money if an asset loses value) on the same CDOs, betting against the success of its own products.[34]

Credit ratings agencies, who are responsible for evaluating the risks of assets, gave these CDOs the lowest possible risk rating: AAA. The Securities and Exchange Commission allowed five banks—Goldman Sachs, Morgan Stanley, Merrill Lynch, Lehman Brothers and Bear Stearns—to acquire unlimited outstanding debts relative to their actual assets. Even this was basically irrelevant in the derivatives market, as derivatives were entirely exempt from regulations. On the eve of the crisis, AIG had placed $3 trillion in bets, with no assets to cover potential losses.[35] By the peak of this orgy of fake value production in 2007, the "value" of the derivatives market was estimated to be three times the size of the global economy.[36]

In 2006, the housing bubble started to lose steam. As real estate prices faltered and then began to fall, the big lie underpinning mortgage debts unraveled. Nothing turned out to be "as safe as houses." When the interest rates on subprime mortgages ballooned to more than two or three times the initial rate, people started to miss their payments. Homeowners could no longer refinance their loans to lower their interest payments, because home values were dropping. By 2007, around 20 per cent of subprime adjustable-rate mortgages were delinquent. In 2009, this number rose to almost 45 per cent.

As people defaulted on their mortgages, the financial assets and derivatives that depended on those mortgages started to lose value. All of a sudden, investors decided that mortgage-backed securities were toxic. Financial institutions holding CDOs tried to pass them off at almost any price, to cover their massive exposure. By 2007, many of these institutions— including Bear Stearns, Morgan Stanley and Goldman Sachs— held tens of billions of dollars in now-worthless securities that far exceeded the total value of their capital.[37] Many of the US's largest commercial and investment banks were now insolvent.

The Great Recession

On 16 March 2008, Bear Stearns finally collapsed. JP Morgan acquired Bear Stearns for $2 a share, or just 7 per cent of its market value days earlier, receiving a $29 billion loan from the Federal Reserve to cover Bearn Stearns' insolvent assets. On 15 September, Lehman Brothers, the fourth largest US investment bank at the time, filed for bankruptcy. The bankruptcy sent shockwaves through the financial system. The US stock market was already dropping as early as October 2007, but Lehman's failure sent the market into free fall. The value of the US stock market fell roughly 50 per cent from its peak in 2007 to its bottom in 2009.[38] Financial capitalism had seen plenty of bubbles before—there were 139 financial crises in the neoliberal period between 1973 and 1997, as opposed to only 38 in the post-war period between 1945 and 1973.[39] This time was different.

The bursting of the housing bubble revealed the fundamental weaknesses of the developed economies, which had been obscured by the rising prices of FIRE assets. Global GDP growth fell from around 5 per cent per year in 2007 to an average of 1.9 per cent between 2008 and 2011. The US averaged only 0.2 per cent annual growth during the same period, while Japan and the EU shed 0.7 per cent and 0.1 per cent of their GDP respectively. The IMF's official unemployment estimates suggest that the number of unemployed people around the globe rose by 30 million from 2007 to 2010.[40] The developed economies accounted for 55 per cent of this increase, despite holding only 15 per cent of the global labor force.[41] Long-term unemployment, the portion of workers unemployed for a year or more, increased in almost every major OECD economy. The long-term unemployment rate doubled from 2007 to 2014 in the US and rose from around 20 per cent to 50 per cent in Spain.[42] Suicide rates jumped globally, particularly in the countries that the Recession hit hardest.[43]

When the financial channels of accumulation collapsed, everything went with them. Industrial output dropped alongside consumption and millions were thrown out of work. The Great Recession was the most significant economic crisis since the Great Depression. States immediately stepped in to stabilize the financial system. The US government implemented the Troubled Asset Relief Program (TARP), paying out $700 billion to insolvent banks like Goldman Sachs and Citigroup to keep them afloat, followed by a $7.7 trillion stream of emergency loans from the

Federal Reserve.

The bailout was pitched as a means of saving the financial system and preventing unnecessary foreclosures, but the Federal Reserve and the Treasury Department abandoned all pretense of debt relief mere days after Congress authorized the program.[44] Millions would lose their homes while bankers continued to earn multimillion-dollar bonuses. EU countries followed suit, committing 1.3 trillion euros to bail out banks on the verge of failure.[45] States comprehensively socialized the losses of the financial system, propping it up at public expense, so that it could continue reaping private profits.

In the decades preceding the Great Recession, developed nations ran up growing debt burdens. When the Recession hit, state revenues fell and many European economies actually shrank in size. Since these governments assumed the burden of bailing out their insolvent banks, their debts increased even more. Ireland's debt-to-GDP ratio rose from 25 per cent in 2007 to almost 120 per cent by 2012. Creditors, including many European banks, started demanding higher interest payments to fund these deficits. The European debt crisis emerged, as Greece, Spain, Portugal, Italy, Ireland, Cyprus and even France faced mounting concerns that they would not be able to pay their debts. By 2011, Ireland, Portugal and Greece had all received bailouts from the eurozone to keep their governments solvent.

Across Europe, governments adopted austerity measures justified in the name of reducing the sovereign debt burden. In Italy and Greece, unelected governments led by economists slashed wages and pensions, raised taxes on workers and cut spending on social services. These austerity measures only worsened the Recession, throwing even more workers into unemployment. From 2008 to 2015, Greece's GDP plummeted 25 per cent. The official unemployment rate sailed up to 27 per cent in 2014.[46] Walking the streets of modern Greece reveals, in the words of a Greek worker, "people looking through the trash to find something to eat... people getting angry over nothing, just starting to fight each other for no reason... There have been many, many suicides. It's terrifying. But now the majority of people are used to it. It's terrifying to accept you are used to your neighbors killing themselves."[47]

If the cause of the crisis was merely the bad behavior by a few financiers or poor regulation, we would expect international financial institutions to introduce new regulations and unwind debt obligations. Instead, creditor institutions like the IMF behaved *as if* the crisis was caused by falling profits and attempted to restore profitability in the countries most heavily affected by the Recession.

In Greece, Italy and Spain, creditor institutions (in alliance with the local elite) forced governments to lower the minimum wage, cut private and public benefits, and increase taxes on working-class citizens. Creditors demanded minimal additional regulation of the financial sector. Capital's crisis of profitability is being balanced on the backs of workers, the elderly, the poor and the disabled. At the time of this writing in 2015, Europe is still reeling from the effects of the Recession. Official unemployment in Europe is still over 10 per cent and youth unemployment is at 21 per cent. In Greece and Spain, youth unemployment is over 50 per cent.[48] Bailouts and austerity have done little to resolve the sovereign debt crisis, other than simply kicking the can down the road. European capitalism remains in the grip of a structural crisis not seen since the 1970s.

The Great Recession entered its third phase in 2015, as growth in emerging economies like China, India, Russia and Brazil began to slow. The deflationary effects of the crisis, creating falling prices for many commodities, hurt developing economies, who relied on exports to the developed world. When the crisis struck the developed world, capital flowed elsewhere in search of profits. Capital poured into the stock markets of the emerging economies and real estate in cities like Shanghai, China, spurred on by cheap credit being pumped into the system by the Federal Reserve, the European Central Bank and the Bank of Japan.

By 2015, capital started to flee these economies, fearing weakness in their export markets and the predicted end of the cheap credit that sustained their asset bubbles. Around $1 trillion dollars flooded out of the emerging markets in a little over a year. International institutions started warning that the slump would drag the global economy into a recession. Considering that the emerging economies accounted for the majority of global economic growth in the wake of the Great Recession, these predictions imply years of turmoil ahead. Compounding already anemic prospects in the developed world, the emerging markets crisis is just the latest stage of a persistent global crisis of capitalism.[49]

At the start of 2017, mainstream economists are sounding cautiously optimistic about the global economy. One gets the impression that this is their version of prayer and that they fear that sounding any concern about the state of the economy might spook global growth back into hiding in some unknown cave. Meanwhile, the "value" of stock markets, particularly in the US, is reaching historic highs. By some measures, US stocks are as overvalued relative to the actual value of the underlying corporations as they were immediately before the Great Depression in 1929. This surge in prices is founded on almost purely hypothetical good news: hypothetical increases in profits and hypothetical rising growth. In fact, growth remains anemic, profits are stagnant, and corporate and private debt is rising beyond already troubling levels. If profits start falling, or if there is a major shock like a trade war or geopolitical event (remember the Oil Crisis of 1973), we can expect this house of cards to collapse quickly, leading to another financial panic and another recession.

The Great Recession was more than a collection of dreadful statistics. It fractured the carefully constructed post-1970s political order, particularly in the developed world. In December 2008, a youth uprising paralyzed Greece after police murdered 15-year-old Alexandros Grigoropoulos. Youths battling the police on streets choked with tear gas and burning vehicles posted pictures on social media captioned: "we are an image from the future."[50] Greece's young radicals were more prescient than anyone might have expected.

Starting in 2010, protests swept the Arab world, set off in large part by unemployment and rising food prices. Protestors toppled the governments of Tunisia, Egypt and Yemen. Libya and Syria descended into civil wars fueled by the intervention of Western powers and their Middle Eastern allies.[51] A revolutionary movement flowered in Bahrain, which survives to this day, despite the repressive intervention of other Gulf states. Protests and riots surged through Europe. Inspired by the Arab revolts, the "movements of the squares" occupied public spaces in Greece and Spain, declaring their opposition to the parties and institutions of the status quo. In the US, the Occupy movement captured popular sympathy by railing against the financial system and capitalism. As years passed and it became increasingly clear that the failures of the system were here to stay, global revolts became common in a fashion not seen in over 40 years. From Turkey to Chile, Brazil to Bosnia, and Mexico to Baltimore, uprisings became inevitable.

As many of these movements lost steam, the general discontent with neoliberal capitalism created a wave of support for leftist anti-establishment parties (in addition to the extra-parliamentary Left) and ultranationalist and fascist parties. On the Right, France's National Front, Greece's Golden Dawn, Hungary's Jobbik, Ukraine's Svoboda and Right Sektor, Denmark's Danish People's Party, the US Tea Party movement and others saw their support shoot up. The crisis allowed left-wing Syriza to gain control of the government in Greece in 2015. Elsewhere, Spain's Podemos, Germany's Die Linke, Ireland's Sinn Féin, and

Portugal's Communist Party and Left Bloc benefited from the same dynamic.

In 2016, the UK voted to exit the EU and the US elected Donald Trump, a right-wing populist allied with white nationalists. Both events were the result of rising anti-immigrant sentiment, anger at political elites, and general anxiety and uncertainty produced by the crisis. Absent a credible alternative to the present system, sizeable portions of the ethnic majorities in developed countries have redirected their rage and frustration at the most powerless individuals in their societies. This incredible feat of psychological acrobatics has been accomplished with substantial assistance from the major media outlets controlled by the wealthy elite. The similarity of the present moment to the 1920s and 1930s is unmistakable: amidst a systemic crisis, reactionary elites forge an alliance with members of the downwardly mobile middle classes on the basis of racial hatred and ultranationalism. We appear poised for another clash of ideologies, with the revolutionary Left and the fascist Right separated merely by a rapidly crumbling, ineffectual center.

The trajectories of both the Left and Right are symbols of a general failure to understand the actual causes of the crisis. The nationalists and fascists blame immigrants, Muslims, Jews, gays and so on for the declining living standards of the nation's "ethnically pure" population. This is pure mystification, designed to manipulate the fears of the people and redirect their attention away from the power of the elite who actually control the fate of the world. On the other hand, the parliamentary Left—Syriza, Podemos, Die Linke and others—presents itself as a better possible manager of a capitalism softened by a social safety net and Keynesian "job creation" policies. Reorienting state social policy, if even that much is allowed by international finance, will not change the fact that capitalism's engine is malfunctioning. The changes we need are fundamental, and they will require struggle beyond parliaments and the ballot box.

The Way Forward

As it struggles with a systemic economic crisis, capitalism again faces a crisis of legitimacy, which shows no signs of abating in the coming years. Capitalism's legitimacy as a system rests on its ability to provide a rising tide of commodities to the people it exploits. Where it cannot, it resorts to repression and naked violence, to which the inhabitants of the US's ghettos and France's banlieus can testify. This is a far less effective means of propping up a social system than the opiates of US television, Japanese cars and Chinese-made cellphones. As living standards stagnate for workers in the developed world, and as capital expels even more labor from the production process, these basic tensions will only intensify.

It comes as no surprise, then, that capitalist economists like Larry Summers—the leader of the Obama administration's 2009 crisis response team—are raising the alarm about the prospect of "secular stagnation." Secular stagnation is a long-term period of low or no economic growth. Summers and others argue that the Great Recession triggered a potentially permanent decline in growth in Europe and the US, similar to that seen in Japan in the 1990s. Their thesis suggests that it will probably be impossible for capitalist economies to balance full employment, substantial growth and financial stability for the foreseeable future. As a Keynesian, Summers suggests more of the same: lower interest rates and state deficit spending.[52]

Much like the crises of 1929 and 1971, the crisis of 2008 has not yet ended. While technical measurements suggest that the developed economics are no longer contracting, they are stuck in a prolonged period of low growth, structural unemployment and reduced opportunities for profitable investment. This, despite 7 years of central banks pumping cheap credit into the global economy and printing money to buy assets directly from commercial banks.[53] These interventions haven't produced growth or employment; instead, they have contributed to the same process of financialization that led to the Great Recession. Of course, since the rich own most of the world's stocks and real estate, pumping up the prices of these assets directly subsidizes their wealth. States and banks have acted, as expected, to prop up millionaires and billionaires at the expense of the vast majority of the working class. Even in the US, a relative "bright spot" in the developed world, real wages have fallen and employment as a percentage of the working-aged population will likely never recover to its pre-crisis levels.

While capitalists struggle to understand the source of the system's instability, labor theory already tells us what the underlying problem is. Capital in the developed world is suffering from a crisis of overaccumulation. There is simply too much dead labor relative to living labor in the value-producing sectors of the economy. Repressing finance would do nothing to create genuinely profitable outlets for investment. US industry operates at just over 75 per cent of capacity and this figure has been in a long-term decline since well before 1970.[54] This means that a quarter of the US industrial sector's productive capacity is lying dormant. The Great Recession wiped out some accumulated value, but not nearly enough to restore growth and profits to stable levels. As Summers himself writes, absent a war on the scale of World War II, it is difficult to imagine how any of this can be expected to change.

Debt and financial speculation are already being revived to their pre-2008 levels. Since capital has not found a new strategy of adaptation, and the underlying conditions have not changed, it is returning to what it knows best. Worldwide, outstanding debts have grown by $57 trillion, far outpacing economic growth. The global debt-to-GDP ratio rose 17 per cent from 2007 to 2015. Household debt increased in most countries, with the notable exceptions of Ireland, Spain, the UK and the US. In the US, a large portion of this "deleveraging" came from people defaulting on their mortgages and being evicted from their homes.[55] Despite this short period of eviction-based "relief," household debt is on the way back up in the US and is now approaching pre-2008 levels.[56]

Meanwhile, the financial system is busy rebuilding the systemic instability that characterized the pre-crisis world. The value of the derivatives market is again at unbelievable heights and financiers are circumventing the token regulations put in place in the aftermath of the crash.[57] Encouraged by state policy, US banks are even larger and more centralized than they were in 2007—the largest simply absorbed the banks that were allowed to fail.[58] "Too big to fail" got even bigger. Whatever the mechanism may ultimately be, the global financial system is headed straight for another crisis. We should expect future crises to be relatively frequent and severe as long as capitalism retains in its current structure.

Capitalism's long-term ability to survive depends on its ability to restore the rate of profit, which relies heavily on economic growth. This is the essence of the so-called secular-stagnation problem. Without growth, the law of constantly expanding value has to come to an end. If we want to get a grasp on capitalism's probable lifespan in the 21st century, we must examine the realistic possibilities for economic growth throughout the global economy. This examination reveals an interesting trend. Growth is slowing down globally, not just in the developed economies. Is capitalism finally reaching its absolute limits?

Endnotes

1   Piketty, T. (2014) *Capital in the Twenty-First Century*, trans. Arthur Goldhammer. (Cambridge: Harvard University Press) pp. 146–9.

2   Marglin, S. (1990) *The Golden Age of Capitalism: Reinterpreting the Postwar Experience.* (Oxford: Oxford University Press) p.

1. Available at: http://bit.ly/1MgZyT2. [accessed 1 June 2017] The founding members of the OECD were Austria, Belgium, Canada, Denmark, France, Germany, Greece, Iceland, Ireland, Italy, Luxembourg, the Netherlands, Norway, Portugal, Spain, Sweden, Switzerland, Turkey, the UK and the US.

3   Mishel, L., Gould, E., and Bivens, J. "Wage Stagnation in Nine Charts," *Economic Policy Institute*. January 6th, 2015. Available at: http://www.epi.org/publication/charting-wage-stagnation/. [accessed 1 June 2017]

4   Brenner, R. (2006) *The Economics of Global Turbulence*. (London: Verso) pp. 5–7. Available at: http://digamo.free.fr/brenner6.pdf. [accessed 1 June 2017] Note that Brenner's work, like most others, can only be seen as an *estimate* of the rate of profit from our perspective. An accurate measurement of the rate of profit would have to measure net profits (surplus value) divided by capital investment and wages. Mainstream economists typically measure the profit rate as net profits divided by capital investment. These figures would also have to be measured in real terms, adjusted for the fluctuations in prices relative to the values of commodities. Whether this adjustment should be made relative to the value of commodity money (gold) or a basket of commodities (a price index) is a matter of possible dispute.

5   A country's *trade balance* is the difference between the value of the goods it exports and the value of the goods it imports.

6   See: Williams, S. "The Industrial Cycle and the Collapse of the Gold Pool in March 1968," *A Critique of Crisis Theory*. Available at: https://critiqueofcrisistheory.wordpress.com/the-five-industrial-cycles-since-1945/the-industrial-cycle-and-the-collapse-of-the-gold-pool-in-march-1968/. [accessed 1 June 2017]

7   Hammes, D. and Wills, D. (Spring 2005) "Black Gold: The

End of Bretton Woods and the Oil-Price Shocks of the 1970s," *The Independent Review*, Vol. 9, No. 4. Available at: https://www.independent.org/pdf/tir/tir_09_4_2_hammes. pdf. [accessed 1 June 2017] p. 504; Graeber, D. *Debt: The First 5,000 Years*. p. 361.

8   Hammes, D. and Wills, D. "Black Gold: The End of Bretton Woods and the Oil-Price Shocks of the 1970s," *The Independent Review*, Vol. 9, No. 4. pp. 501–11.

9   Davis, E.P. (January 2003) "Comparing Bear Markets – 1973 and 2000," *National Institute Economic Review*, Vol. 183, No. 1. Available at: http://ner.sagepub.com/content/183/1/78. full.pdf+html. [accessed 1 June 2017]

10 Tapia, J. (November 2013) "From the Oil Crisis to the Great Recession: Five crises of the world economy." Available at: http://sitemaker.umich.edu/tapia_granados/files/fromthe oilcrisis-2e_nov_2013_final.pdf. [accessed 1 June 2017]

11 Bullock, P and Yaffe, D. (1979) *Inflation, the Crisis and the Post-War Boom*. "The Crisis as it Presents Itself." Available at: https://www.marxists.org/subject/economy/authors/yaf fed/1979/icpwb.htm#partI. [accessed 1 June 2017]

12 See: Oguma, E. "Japan's 1968: A Collective Reaction to Rapid Economic Growth in an Age of Turmoil," trans. Nick Kapur, Samuel Malissa, and Stephen Poland. *The Asia-Pacific Journal*, Vol. 13, Iss. 11, No. 1. March 23rd, 2015. Available at: http:// japanfocus.org/-Oguma-Eiji/4300/article.html. [accessed 1 June 2017]

13 See: "1962–1973: Worker and student struggles in Italy," *Libcom*. March 12th, 2008. Available at: http://libcom.org/ history/1962-1973-worker-student-struggles-italy. [accessed 1 June 2017]

14 Remember that state deficit spending is inflationary when that spending is not directed to value-producing activities. When a government consumes borrowed capital without producing more capital—for example, by building

roads, bombs, etc.—its employees still need to consume commodities to survive. Spending on commodities without the simultaneous production of additional commodities drives up their prices relative to the currency.

15 Western, B. and Healy, K. (1999) "Explaining the OECD Wage Slowdown: Recession or Labour Decline?" *European Sociological Review*, Vol. 15, No. 3. p. 234. Available at: http://kieranhealy.org/files/papers/western-healy99.pdf. [accessed 1 June 2017]

16 Because most of the analysis of neoliberalism comes from the perspective of *either* the developed nations or developing nations, it is often framed as an assault on the post-war accommodation between capital and labor (in developed nations) or a brutal process of opening protected markets to international capital (in developing nations). Both perspectives are incomplete. Neoliberalism allowed capitalism to forge a world market, both by pushing world labor markets toward convergence and by allowing capital to flow freely between nation states.

17 McCartin, J. "The Strike That Busted Unions," *The New York Times*. August 2nd, 2011. Available at: http://www.nytimes.com/2011/08/03/opinion/reagan-vs-patco-the-strike-that-busted-unions.html. [accessed 1 June 2017]

18 See. Deynion, H., ed. (1985) *Digging deeper: Issues in the miners' strike.* Available at: https://libcom.org/files/digging-deeper.pdf. [accessed 1 June 2017]

19 Visser, J. (January 2006) "Union membership statistics in 24 countries," *Monthly Labor Review*. p. 45. Available at: http://www.bls.gov/opub/mlr/2006/01/art3full.pdf. [accessed 1 June 2017]

20 Frase, P. "Liberals for Recession," *Jacobin*. February 28th, 2012. Available at: https://www.jacobinmag.com/2012/02/liberals-for-recession/. [accessed 1 June 2017]

21 Birch, J. "The Many Lives of François Mitterand," *Jacobin*.

August 19th, 2015. Available at: https://www.jacobinmag. com/2015/08/francois-mitterrand-socialist-party-common-program-communist-pcf-1981-elections-austerity/. [accessed 1 June 2017]

22 Naiman, R and Watkins, N. (April 1999) "A Survey of the Impact of IMF Structural Adjustment in Africa: Growth, Social Spending, and Debt Relief," *Center for Economic and Policy Research*. Available at: http://www.cepr.net/ documents/publications/debt_1999_04.htm. [accessed 1 June 2017]

23 Monaghan, A. "China surpasses US as world's largest trading nation," *The Guardian*. January 10th, 2014. Available at: http://www.theguardian.com/business/2014/jan/10/chin a-surpasses-us-world-largest-trading-nation. [accessed 1 June 2017] Note that this follows the pattern of the US' own path in surpassing the UK as the world's political and economic superpower in the late 19th and early 20th centuries.

24 Freeman, R. (Summer-Fall 2008) "The new global labor market," *Focus*, Vol. 26, No. 1. pp. 1–2. Available at: http:// www.irp.wisc.edu/publications/focus/pdfs/foc261.pdf. [accessed 1 June 2017]

25 See: Roberts, M. (2012) "A world rate of profit." Available at: https://thenextrecession.files.wordpress.com/2012/09/a-world-rate-of-profit.pdf. [accessed 1 June 2017]; Maito, E. (2014) "The historical transience of capital: The downward trend in the rate of profit since XIX century." Available at: https://thenextrecession.files.wordpress.com/2014/04/ maito-esteban-the-historical-transience-of-capital-the-downward-trend-in-the-rate of-profit-since-xix-century. pdf. [accessed 1 June 2017]; and Maito, E. (2014) "Piketty against Piketty. The tendency of the rate of profit to fall in United Kingdom and Germany since XIX century confirmed by Piketty's data." Available at: https://mpra.ub.uni-muenchen.de/55839/1/MPRA_paper_55839.pdf. [accessed 1

June 2017] Note, again, that these are simply estimates of the world rate of profit. It appears that Roberts fails to include investment in wages in his model of the rate of profit. Maito seems to make the same mistake in his paper using Piketty's data, which could simply result from refusing to alter Piketty's measurements of the rate of profit. Nevertheless, these concerns and observations were echoed by orthodox economists through the late Seventies and Eighties, which leads me to believe that Roberts' and Maito's presentations of a general trend are probably correct. See: Feldstein, M. and Summers, L. (1977) "Is the Rate of Profit Falling?" *Brookings Papers on Economic Activity.* pp. 211–28. Available at: http://www.brookings.edu/~/media/Projects/BPEA/1977-1/1977a_bpea_feldstein_summers_wachter.PDF. [accessed 1 June 2017]; and Chan-Lee, J. and Sutch, H. (1985) "Profits and Rates of Return in OECD Countries," OECD *Economics Department Working Papers,* No. 20. pp. 127–167. Available at: http://www.oecd.org/eco/growth/35485300.pdf. [accessed 1 June 2017]

26 Krippner, G. (2005) "The financialization of the American economy," *Socio-Economic Review,* Vol. 3. pp. 178–81. Available at: http://cas.umkc.edu/econ/economics/faculty/wray/631Wray/Week%207/Krippner.pdf. [accessed 1 June 2017]

27 Jayadev, A. and Epstein, G. (January 2007) "The Correlates of Rentier Returns in OECD Countries," *Political Economy Research Institute Working Paper Series,* No. 123. Available at: http://www.peri.umass.edu/fileadmin/pdf/working_papers/working_papers_101-150/WP123.pdf. [accessed 1 June 2017]

28 Ibid. pp. 182–187. In line with the general trend, financial profits accruing to non-financial firms became dominated by capital gains and interest instead of dividends.

29 Marazzi, C. (2011) The Violence of Financial Capitalism,

trans. Kristina Lebedeva and Jason Francis McGimsey. (Cambridge: Semiotext(e)) p. 32. Available at: https://selforganizedseminar.files.wordpress.com/2011/08/marazzi_violence_financial.pdf. [accessed 1 June 2017]

30 Harrison, E. "Chart of the day: US household debt-to-income versus debt servicing cost ratios," *Credit Writedowns*. October 12th, 2012. Available at: https://www.creditwritedowns.com/2012/10/us-household-debt-to-income-debt-servicing-cost-ratios.html. [accessed 1 June 2017]

31 International Monetary Fund. (2012) *World Economic Outlook: Growth Resuming, Dangers Remain*. p. 89. Available at: https://www.imf.org/external/pubs/ft/weo/2012/01/pdf/c3.pdf. [accessed 1 June 2017]

32 Ali Abbas, S.M., Belhocine, N., ElGanainy, A., and Horton, M. (May 2011) "Historical Patterns of Public Debt – Evidence From a New Database." Available at: https://www.imf.org/external/np/seminars/eng/2010/eui/pdf/AB.pdf. [accessed 1 June 2017]

33 "The global housing boom: In come the waves," *The Economist*. June 16th, 2005. Available at: http://www.economist.com/node/4079027. [accessed 1 June 2017]

34 Securities and Exchange Commission. "SEC Charges Goldman Sachs With Fraud in Structuring and Marketing of CDO Tied to Subprime Mortgages." April 16th, 2010. Available at: https://www.sec.gov/news/press/2010/2010-59.htm [accessed 1 June 2017]

35 Denning, S. "Lest We Forget: Why We Had A Financial Crisis," *Forbes*. November 22nd, 2011. Available at: http://www.forbes.com/sites/stevedenning/2011/11/22/5086/. [accessed 1 June 2017]

36 "Roger Martin on Fixing the Game," *Thought You Should See This*. November 18th, 2011. Available at: http://www.thoughtyoushouldseethis.com/post/12973350613/roger-martin-on-fixing-the-game. [accessed 1 June 2017]

37 The Financial Crisis Inquiry Commission. (January 2011) *The Financial Crisis Inquiry Report.* pp. 217, 226–7. Available at: http://www.gpo.gov/fdsys/pkg/GPO-FCIC/pdf/GPO-FCIC.pdf. [accessed 1 June 2017]

38 Dwyer, G. (September 2009) "Stock Prices in the Financial Crisis," *Federal Reserve Bank of Atlanta.* Available at: https://www.frbatlanta.org/cenfis/publications/notesfro mthevault/0909.aspx. [accessed 1 June 2017] Note the similarities between the timing of the events in the crisis of the 1970s and the crisis of 2008.

39 Eichengreen, B., and Bordo, M. (January 2002) "Crises Now and Then: What Lessons from the Last Era of Financial Globalization?" *NBER Working Paper,* No. 8716. Available at: http://www.nber.org/papers/w8716.pdf. [accessed 1 June 2017]

40 "Sharp Rise in Unemployment from Global Recession," *IMF Survey Online.* September 2nd, 2010. Available at: http://www.imf.org/external/pubs/ft/survey/so/2010/NEW090210A.htm. [accessed 1 June 2017]

41 United Nations Department of Economic and Social Affairs. (June 2011) "The Great Recession and the jobs crisis," in *The Global Social Crisis.* Available at: http://www.un.org/esa/socdev/rwss/docs/2011/chapter2.pdf. [accessed 1 June 2017]

42 "World Economic Situation and Prospects 2015," *UN Global Economic Outlook 2015.* (2015) Available at: http://www.un.org/en/development/desa/policy/wesp/wesp_archive/2015wesp_chap1.pdf. [accessed 1 June 2017]

43 Chang, S., Stuckler, D., Yip, P., and Gunnell, D. (September 2013) "Impact of 2008 global economic crisis on suicide: time trend study in 54 countries," *BMJ.* Available at: http://www.bmj.com/content/347/bmj.f5239. [accessed 1 June 2017]

44 Taibi, M. "Secrets and Lies of the Bailout," *Rolling Stone.* January 4th, 2013. Available at: http://www.rollingstone.com/politics/news/secret-and-lies-of-the-bailout-20130104.

[accessed 1 June 2017] Even this number underestimates the amount of aid given to the banks. As Taibbi writes, "Companies like AIG, GM and Citigroup, for instance, were given tens of billions of deferred tax assets—allowing them to carry losses from 2008 forward to offset future profits and keep future tax bills down. Official estimates of the bailout's costs do not include such ongoing giveaways. 'This is stuff that's never going to appear on any report,' says Barofsky. Citigroup, all by itself, boasts more than $50 billion in deferred tax credits—which is how the firm managed to pay less in taxes in 2011 (it actually received a $144 million credit) than it paid in compensation that year to its since-ousted dingbat CEO, Vikram Pandit (who pocketed $14.9 million)."

45 Viscusi, G. "EU Nations Commit 1.3 Trillion Euros to Bank Bailouts," *Bloomberg.* October 13th, 2008. Available at: http://www.bloomberg.com/apps/news?pid=newsarchive &sid=abDNqy86viis&refer=home. [accessed 1 June 2017]

46 Kottasova, I. "Here's what Greeks think about their country," *CNN Money.* June 30th, 2015. Available at: http:// money.cnn.com/2015/06/23/news/economy/greece-crisis-gdp/. [accessed 1 June 2017]

47 Forman, E., and Eleftherios, E. "Life Under Austerity," *Jacobin.* July 12th, 2015. Available at: https://www. jacobinmag.com/2015/07/tsipras-syriza-referendum-debt-euro/. [accessed 1 June 2017]

48 "Unemployment Statistics," *Eurostat*, accessed October 11th, 2015. Available at: http://ec.europa.eu/eurostat/statistics-explained/index.php/Unemployment_statistics. [accessed 1 June 2017]

49 Kynge, J. and Romei, V. "Global US dollar recession creates ill wind for emerging markets," *Financial Times.* October 8th, 2015. Available at: http://www.ft.com/intl/cms/s/3/d86944c0-6d14-11e5-aca9-d87542bf8673.html#axzz3oMf0FHz0.

[accessed 1 June 2017]; Morrison, C., and Papadopoullos, C. "IMF: Emerging markets slowdown has pushed global economy to edge of recession," City A.M. October 7th, 2015. Available at: http://www.cityam.com/225986/imf-emergingmarkets-slowdown-has-pushed-global-economy-edgerecession. [accessed 1 June 2017]; "The world should fear an emerging market rout," *Financial Times.* August 19th, 2015. Available at: http://www.ft.com/intl/cms/s/0/f8936a1a-4667-11e5-b3b2-1672f710807b.html#axzz3oMf0FHz0. [accessed 1 June 2017]

50   Schwarz, A.G., Sagris, T., and Void Network ed. (2010) *We are an image of the future: the Greek revolt of December 2008.* Available at: https://libcom.org/library/we-are-imagefuture-greek-revolt-december-2008-g-schwarz-tasos-sagrisvoid-network. [accessed 1 June 2017]

51   In Syria and Libya, Western states and their Middle Eastern allies knowingly funded and funneled arms to reactionary groups in the hopes of toppling uncooperative regimes. This directly led to the rise of ISIS and the empowerment of Jabhat al-Nusra, an affiliate of al-Qaeda. For an excellent analysis of the Syrian civil war, see: Higgins, P. "The War on Syria," *Jacobin.* August 27th, 2015. Available at: https://www.jacobinmag.com/2015/08/syria-civil-war-nato-military-intervention/. [accessed 1 June 2017]

52   Summers, L. "Reflections on the new 'Secular Stagnation hypothesis,'" *VOX.* October 30th, 2014. Available at: http://www.voxeu.org/article/larry-summers-secular-stagnation. [accessed 1 June 2017]

53   For a simple explanation of quantitative easing, see: "What is quantitative easing?" *The Economist.* March 9th, 2015. Available at: http://www.economist.com/blogs/economistexplains/2015/03/economist-explains-5. [accessed 1 June 2017]

54   Board of Governors of the Federal Reserve System.

"CapacityUtilization: Total Industry," retrieved from FRED, Federal Reserve Bank of St. Louis. October 11th, 2015. Available at: https://research.stlouisfed.org/fred2/series/TCU/.

55 Dobbs, R., Lund, S., Woetzel, J., and Mutafchieva, M. (February 2015) "Debt and (not much) deleveraging," *McKinsey Global Institute*. Available at: http://www.mckinsey.com/insights/economic_studies/debt_and_not_much_deleveraging. [accessed 1 June 2017]

56 Cox, J. "It's back with a vengeance: Private debt," *CNBC*. October 12th, 2013. Available at: http://www.cnbc.com/2013/10/11/its-back-with-a-vengeance-private-debt.html. [accessed 1 June 2017]

57 Melendez, E.D. "Wall Street Setting Itself Up For Next Derivatives Crisis, Market Participants Warn," *Huffington Post*. February 14th, 2013. Available at: http://www.huffingtonpost.com/2013/02/14/wall-street-derivatives_n_2681610.html. [accessed 1 June 2017]; Prabha, A. "$700 trillion in global OTC derivatives? Behind the number," *Milken Institute*. March 31st, 2014. Available at: http://www.milkeninstitute.org/blog/view/580. [accessed 1 June 2017]

58 Cox, J. "Too big to fail banks just keep getting bigger," *CNBC*. March 5th, 2015. Available at: http://www.cnbc.com/2015/03/05/too-big-to-fail-banks-just-keep-getting-bigger.html. [accessed 1 June 2017]

Chapter 8

Prospects for Growth

A zero-growth capitalist economy is a logical and exclusionary contradiction. It simply cannot exist.

David Harvey[1]

If capitalism is a system of endlessly expanding value, then economic growth is a practical necessity for its existence. "Self-expanding value" is an abstract idea. What it really means is that capitalism has to put more land, resources and human work into production as it grows in order to keep making profits. When Malcolm X described capitalists as bloodsuckers, he was articulating a literal truth. Capital is like a vampire that needs to suck more life out of the earth to keep producing value. This doesn't mean that it is impossible to have a society without economic growth. Societies without growth actually existed in the past, and they still exist today in indigenous communities based on sustainable forms of agriculture, handcrafts, hunting and gathering. It is even possible to have a modern developed economy with no economic growth.

A capitalist society, however, cannot abide a steady state. In a no-growth capitalist economy, capital overaccumulation would immediately become acute. There would be no possible outlet for investment other than the outright destruction of existing value. Historically, a crisis of overaccumulation results in the massive devaluation of surplus capital, a dramatic fall in the rate of profit and a spike in unemployment. Capitalism has never yet faced such a crisis while long-term economic growth fell to zero. Without growth, there would be no way to maintain profits and employment. Capitalism would collapse.

Economic growth is slowing down, and not just in developed

countries like the US and Japan. Even developing countries like China are revising expected growth downward. Over the coming decades, demographic changes, the end of the "catch up effect" in developing economies and ecological constraints will produce an inevitable decline in GDP growth. Labor theory tells us that profitable investment is constrained as capital accumulates, but this idea is not just a preoccupation of anarchists and Marxists. It is echoed with equal fervor by the "serious people" of mainstream economics, as we saw with Larry Summers. Optimists counter these obvious trends by arguing that advances in information technology and automation will allow us to produce more value than ever before. While a non-capitalist society would widely benefit from these technologies, probably by forgoing further economic growth, the evidence so far contradicts this claim. In the US, recent decades saw a substantial decline in labor hours per person. Automation is not just being used to boost production. It is being used to push people out of the labor force.

A second line of argument might suggest that growth can be maintained indefinitely by "decoupling" growth from material consumption. The rise of the "dematerialized" information economy is offered as an example of how this might work. There are two obvious problems with this thesis. First, an economy based on distributed production would tend to generate less exchange value relative to use value, slowing economic growth. It is easy to see how we all benefit from Wikipedia, but it is not easy to make money from it.

Secondly, the information economy is not at all immaterial. The physical objects that make up the nodes and network of the computer Internet system are produced from metals, minerals and plastic. The actual process of manufacturing these shiny new objects is one of the most destructive industries in human history. The Chinese refinery that produces much of the world's rare earth minerals a critical component in manufacturing computers, iPhones and electric cars—spews out enough toxic waste to produce a 3.5-square-mile artificial lake. One reporter who visited the area described it as "the worst place on earth."[2] As these rare earth minerals make their way up the supply chain, they arrive in factories where conditions are so hellish that workers commit suicide as a form of protest. This is the system of production that allows Western economists to produce mindless chatter on the Internet about the "dematerialized" information economy.

General Trends

Economic growth is the growth in the total value of the commodities that an economy produces. This is why the size of an economy is measured in terms of its "gross domestic product," or GDP. Note that this is not an absolute measurement of the amount of useful things an economy makes. The "value" of a commodity is determined by the average labor time needed to produce it and value itself is a social construct of capitalist societies. As the 21st century progresses, economic growth will slow down. This might have been a startling prediction in the 1990s, but today it is the province of mainstream economists like Thomas Piketty, Larry Summers and Robert Gordon. One doesn't need to understand capitalism's contradictions or the law of value to see why this is happening. Population growth is slowing in many regions, emerging economies are starting to catch up to the developed world and capitalism is running roughshod over the Earth's basic ecological limits.

Demographics are an obvious area where this trend is currently materializing. A larger population means more potential laborers and more potential consumers. Between the birth of Christ and 1700, global population growth probably averaged no more than 0.1–0.2 per cent per year. This seems like a tiny number and it may be by the standards of the past couple centuries. But even a rate as low as 0.1 per cent means that the world's population would have grown to be five times its initial size in 1700 years. Growth from year to year was higher than this, but it was offset by devastating events like epidemics, famines and wars. In one of the worst examples, a wave of epidemic diseases imported by European colonists probably wiped out around 95 per cent of the indigenous population of the Americas. This disaster was compounded by centuries of genocidal war and brutal exploitation. Before 1492, the indigenous population of the Americas was somewhere between 50 and 100 million people. By 1650, only 6 million remained.[3]

From 1700 to 2012, the Earth's population increased more than tenfold from 600 million to 7 billion. On average, this meant an increase of only 0.8 per cent per year. Growth accelerated as the Industrial Revolution unleashed massive productivity and medical advances. Europe grew at a rate of 0.8 per cent per year from 1820 to 1913 before falling back to 0.4 per cent from 1913 to 2012. The population of the Americas grew by 1.9 per cent per year from 1820 to 1913 and 1.7 per cent per year from 1913 to 2012. Population growth in Africa shot up from 0.6% to 2.2% in the same periods in the 20th century. At the same time in Asia, population growth rose from 0.4% to 1.5%.

Still, these rates are declining across the board. Global population growth fell from 1.9 per cent annually in the post-war decades to 1.3 per cent from 1990 to 2012. UN forecasts suggest that demographic growth will fall to around 0.4 per cent per year across the globe by 2030 and finally return to 0.1 per cent by the 2070s.[4] Africa accounts for all of the expected growth in the second half of the 21st century.

Slowing population growth is a good thing for humanity and a good thing for the Earth. It is not such a good thing for capital, which relies on an increasing population to supply more workers and consumers of products. If all else is held equal, a smaller population means that there will be less competition in the labor force, raising wages. It also means that markets for goods will become saturated more quickly. Even "slow" rates of growth translate into massive real increases in the size of the world's population.

The UN estimates that there will be around 9.4 billion people on Earth by 2070. Given that these are long-term predictions, these numbers may vary significantly.[5] Economic development and modern medicine can both bolster and subdue population growth. As a country accumulates more wealth, it can support more people. But women also get access to birth control and norms about family sizes often shift, particularly as a country transitions away from agriculture. Whatever the case, demographic growth is certainly going slower than it was in the roaring 20th century.

At the same time, global economic growth is returning to more normal levels. As Piketty points out, "there is no historical example of a country at the world technological frontier whose growth in per capita output exceeded 1.5 percent over a lengthy period of time."[6] The idea that economic growth "should be" 3–4 per cent is absurd. These rates are only seen in countries where capital has been obliterated by war or in countries whose development was suppressed for centuries by colonialism and imperialism. It is this "catch-up effect" that allows a country to grow at rates as high 4–5 per cent per year or even 7–10 per cent in the case of China.

As capital accumulates and a country approaches the frontiers of development, growth inevitably falls. Piketty optimistically predicts that world GDP growth (combining population growth and per capita output) will average 3.5 per cent from 2012 to 2030 and 3.0 per cent from 2030 to 2040. The developing world will account for most of this growth. He then predicts it will fall to 1.75 per cent by 2050 to 2070, where per capita output in China, Eastern Europe, South America, the Middle East and North Africa catches up to that of the richest countries.[7] This is an optimistic prediction, because it suggests that the wealthiest countries will continue to grow at rate of 1.2 per cent per year throughout the 21st century and that developing nations will face no major hurdles. Given that the effects of climate change and ecological devastation will be felt disproportionately by the developing world, I find this difficult to believe.

As a catalog of trends in economic growth, Piketty's *Capital in the 21st Century* is very useful. However, the central thesis of his book is incorrect. Piketty argues that the world will become more unequal in the 21st century, because the rate of return on capital will exceed the rate of growth. But Piketty states that this rate of return fluctuates around 4–5 per cent over the long run, based on a bizarre measurement of capital that includes residential real estate (which does not produce value). As critics on both the Left and Right point out, Piketty's own data contradicts his argument when you leave out wealth (in other words, real estate) that does not function as capital.[8] As capital accumulates, the rate of profit falls, as we know very well from history. The world will become more unequal in the 21st century, but this is because capitalists are able to appropriate a growing mass of profit even while the overall rate of profit falls, increasingly by engaging in quasi-fraudulent financial speculation. At the same time, wages will stagnate or decline in the developed world absent serious political upheaval.

Indeed, Piketty's own arguments contradict his model. He holds that falling growth rates encourage "rent-seeking" behavior by owners of capital. A rent is income that the owners of an asset can extract owing to its scarcity, artificial or otherwise, without having to produce any value. One can get rents from leasing more fertile agricultural land or charging for access to oil fields. There is no possible explanation for rent-seeking being preferable to producing value other than the fact that falling growth rates cause a fall in the rate of profit.

Finally, continued growth will run up against the limits of the Earth's capacity to sustain the extraordinarily destructive and wasteful capitalist system. Even if growth continues at the rates forecast earlier which are too slow for a "sustainable" socioeconomic bargain, we are certain to overshoot the widely-agreed limit of an increase of 2 degrees Celsius in the temperature of the planet. This would have catastrophic consequences for our civilization, disrupting agriculture, increasing the frequency of natural disasters and creating a stream of refugees fleeing unlivable zones around the equator. We will explore this problem in depth in a later chapter, but it poses an absolute limit to sustainable growth in the 21st century.

The next question is how the changing nature of production will impact growth and development. Automation is something of a wildcard. On the one hand, it has the capability to increase productivity dramatically. If no labor were expelled from the production process, then we might see a massive increase in production across the world, but this is not what is happening. Radical automation expelled labor from the production process in agriculture and industry in the developed world, and it will continue to do so across many sectors of the economy in the future. Producing more commodities with less labor reduces the value of those commodities and it also reduces the overall extraction of surplus value. Economic growth is a measure of value, not a measure of things. Counter-intuitively, radical automation will probably contribute to a general slowdown in economic growth in the 21st century.

Distributed production is another seemingly ambiguous phenomenon. Its rise fuels the tech industry, which reaps huge profits by combining cheap manufacturing labor with an extreme tendency toward monopolization. However, as distributed production continues to expand it will eat away at the revenues of traditional industries.

The music industry is an excellent example of how this may work. The very idea of buying music is gradually being destroyed by the Internet. Album sales, including digital and physical albums, declined 74 per cent from 2000 to 2013. Apple's iTunes initially picked up part of the slack by selling digital singles, but their sales started to fall by 2014. Streaming music on services like Spotify and Pandora gained steam, but the profits from those companies were not nearly enough to offset all of the industry's lost revenue. People have not stopped consuming music; in fact, they are listening to it more than ever. Having the entire library of humanity's musical heritage at our fingertips isn't a boon for the music industry, it is destroying it. The music industry is in an absolute decline, thanks to the wonders of distributed production.[9] Whether this trend will extend to physical commodities simply depends on whether or not distributed production can become flexible, efficient and cheap enough to compete with highly automated industry. I see no reason to believe that this will not happen.

The Developed World

In the US, Europe and Japan, economic growth is likely to remain at the levels seen in the aftermath of 2008. A similar trend emerged when the Japanese asset bubble burst in 1991 after decades of capital investment and productivity increases, followed by extraordinary financial speculation. Economic growth appeared to be going quite well up until 1991, even leading to a panic in the US about Japanese competition, but the financialization of the Japanese economy and its associated bubbles papered over structural weakness. After the bubble burst, Japan entered a prolonged low-growth period called the Lost Decade. During this period, Japanese companies attempted to boost their profits by employing larger numbers of temporary workers who lack benefits and job security. These workers make up a third of the Japanese workforce and around 48 per cent of workers aged 24 or younger are temps. Real wages fell 13 per cent from 1997 to 2010.[10] Still, economic growth was subdued, even when it received a boost from the debt-fueled consumption of the US. This story is probably starting to sound familiar to readers from Europe and the US.

In a capitalist economy, low growth means that there are diminished opportunities for profitable investment. The general fall in real interest rates across the developed world is solid proof that this is actually happening. "Techno-optimists" like Eric Brynjolfsson and Andrew McAfee argue that we are just around the corner from miraculous innovations that will send economic growth soaring, like self-driving cars and sophisticated robots. As Robert Gordon points out, it is difficult to believe that these inventions will be as significant as steam engines, railroads, electricity, the internal combustion engine, air conditioning, refrigerators, airplanes and flush toilets.[11] Even if the 21st century sees significant technological changes, and it certainly will, there is no reason to believe that these changes will reverse the general trend of capital overaccumulating relative to living labor. Instead, they are going to make this problem much worse.

Depending on the service sector to miraculously boost growth is an equally dubious idea. If by growth one means that we will see the increasing commodification of everyday life then, yes, this is already happening. Japan is a bit of a pioneer in this field, including "rent-a-girlfriend" services that simulate romantic relationships. Riding the subways in New York, one already sees plenty of advertisements for online services that allow the wealthy to outsource their menial chores to people who need the money.[12] Wherever these innovations ultimately take us, the non-financial service sector has never been a primary source of profit in an advanced capitalist society like the US. The rise of ill-paid, insecure, part-time work—precarious labor—will not allow capitalism to extricate itself from its current predicament. It is a symptom of the problem, not a solution, as the Japanese experience demonstrates quite well.

Economic growth in the developed world is going to follow

a much more modest path in the 21st century. We already know how capital will adapt to this problem. First, it will attempt (as it is currently doing) to further erode the living standards of workers by slashing wages, benefits and job security. This will be justified by raising the specter of international competition. What this trope really suggests is that more profitable investment is available in the developing world, so that workers should prostrate themselves in front of capital for the "privilege" of having a paying job. Secondly, capital will continue to engage in reckless speculative activities fueled by a supply of cheap credit. This is just an attempt to turn surplus capital into more capital without having to go through the difficulties of producing value. Thirdly, capital will use its international mobility to flow into areas where profitable investment is possible—in other words, where it is guaranteed by the state or the developing world. Capital is not nationalistic; it has no scruples about laying off workers in Europe if it can find better investments in China and India. What happened to Detroit, Michigan is a good example of what this phenomenon looks like in practice.

Capitalism in the developed world will continue to be dominated by rentiers and financiers. Capital will also attempt to take from the sphere of consumption what it cannot get from the sphere of production. In the US, the crisis in 2008 allowed banks to foreclose on properties and sell them to speculators, who have turned much of that housing into rental properties. The homeownership rate fell to its lowest level since the late 1980s, and even that rate is supported by high levels of ownership in people aged 65 and older. Rents are rising faster than wages and almost half of renter households paid more than 30 per cent of their income for rent in 2013. This exploitation reaches extreme heights for a quarter of renters, who pay more than half of their income for rent. Facing rising rents and declining wages or unemployment, more young Americans have been living in their parents' homes every year since 2002.[13] Quite literally, capital is attempting to get back in rent what it cannot get in profits.

Forecasting is difficult as the world delights in thrashing our expectations. It is still useful to try to establish a baseline scenario that we can test our predictions against and use to strategize about the future. Absent major shocks to capital like wars and revolutions, we should expect GDP growth in the developed world to decline slowly in the next few decades of the 21st century. This is consistent with observed trends. Countries with faster demographic growth, unsurprisingly, will grow faster than countries with stagnant or declining populations. Overall, the developed economies—the US, Europe, Japan, Canada, Australia and New Zealand—will probably grow at a combined average rate of 1–2 per cent per year over the next two decades, albeit with significant yearly fluctuations. Compounding annual growth of just 1 per cent is pretty significant over the long run. An economy growing at a rate of 1 per cent per year will double in value every seventy years or just a little over two generations. That is still a rate of growth that dwarfs any period of time prior to the Industrial Revolution, but it is not enough to sustain the fiction that a rising tide really does lift all boats. Growth figures will almost certainly be inflated for multiyear stretches by asset bubbles. Growth in Japan and the EU as a whole will probably be more anemic than that of the US. We will examine the implications of these trends for the working class in further detail in the next chapter.

The Developing World

The so-called developing world, including most of Asia, the Middle East and North Africa, sub-Saharan Africa, Eastern Europe, and Latin America and the Caribbean, contains more than four fifths of the world's population. It is made up of countries with rapidly developing economies like Brazil, India, Turkey and China, and countries as poor as Haiti. The very idea that there is such a thing as a "developing world" is something of a Western conceit and is as much a product of colonialism as the stymied development of the countries that comprise the vast majority of humanity. Nevertheless, as far as capital is concerned, the developing world is going to be where most of the action is for the duration of the 21st century.

From the 16th to the mid-20th century, European states established colonial empires that dominated most of today's developing world. These colonies were sources of raw materials, cheap labor and markets for European goods. Colonized peoples were conscripted to fight Europe's wars, as when the UK used Indian troops to cement their occupation of Afghanistan. Some settler colonies, like the US, broke free of European control and established their own empires. After a period of military modernization in the late 1800s, Japan also established its independence and built an empire. Most of Asia, Africa and the Middle East only slipped free of formal Western control after a heroic series of anti-colonial struggles after the Second World War. Even after these brief successes, most decolonized nations still remained in the grasp of the West's outsized military and economic might. They were still dependent on international capital, and they were vulnerable to coups and invasions if they provoked the ire of the US and the capitalist bloc.

This relationship is going to change in the 21st century. States in the emerging economies—China, India, Brazil, Russia, South Africa, Turkey and so on—are developing independent bases of capital and the capacity to assert their will in international politics. This transition will not be smooth or easy. Emerging economies have to compete with international capital based in the West that already dominates many of the world's established markets. Two firms—Boeing and Airbus—control 100 per cent of the global market share for large commercial aircraft. Two firms—Intel and AMD—dominate almost 100 per cent of the market for PC microprocessors.[14]

These are extreme examples, but the general trend of rising capital requirements to compete in many industries makes it difficult for developing economies to build local industries. They also have to confront a global system dominated by the military might of the US and NATO, and economic institutions like the IMF and the World Bank. However, this military might is not invulnerable, as demonstrated by the disastrous invasions of Iraq and Afghanistan. The US still has the world's strongest military by a long shot, but it is overextended. It is going to be increasingly difficult for the US to dominate the entire world when its strength is declining relative to every emerging economy over the long run. This is the ultimate source of the US's aggressive behavior from Ukraine to the South China Sea—a creeping anxiety that it will no longer be able to rule the entire world and will instead have to deal with regional powers who may be able to outflank it in their own backyards. There are few historical examples of such a power transition that have not ended with war and bloodshed.

The global power transition is the product of changing global patterns of capital accumulation. When capital started to run up against its limits in the developed economies, it broke down international barriers, and created a world market for commodities and labor. This process not only benefited Western capital by giving it an outlet for investment, but it also provided emerging economies with the means to develop as independent economic powers. China, for instance, cleverly used its large labor force as leverage to force advanced international firms to partner with its own firms, gaining expertise in manufacturing and a domestic base of industrial capital.[15] However, the relationship between Western capital and developing nations is still extremely asymmetric.

From 1980 to 2008, the foreign direct investment of firms from the advanced capitalist economies grew from $503 billion to $13,623 billion. By the end of this period, the "foreign" employment and sales of these companies exceeded their "domestic" numbers. Firms from developing countries also increased their foreign investments, but these totaled less than a fifth of the advanced countries' investments. The Netherlands, a country of only 16 million people, has more investments abroad than Brazil, Russia, India and China combined.[16]

This massive inflow of capital supported profits in the Western world and started one of the most rapid periods of capital accumulation in history in the developing world. From 1982 to 1987, the emerging economies accounted for only around 30 per cent of the world's economic growth. By 2012, three quarters of global growth came from the developing world.[17] There is no reason to expect that this trend is going to reverse; after all, we're talking about four fifths of humanity. Still, the catch-up effect is slowing down. Decades of globalization at maddening speeds and manufacturing-driven growth could only last for so long.

Emerging market growth peaked at almost 9 per cent per year before the crisis, before settling in at around 5 to 6 per cent in the aftermath of the first phase of the global recession.[18] This rate will slow, too, as the emerging markets crisis develops. Crises and slowdowns in the developed world are not going to be a boon for Western capital. Money fleeing emerging markets will somehow have to locate trillions of dollars of profitable investments in the advanced economies, which is a dubious proposition absent a world war. This surplus capital would have to be satisfied in part with investing in government bonds that will probably yield negative real interest rates, as inflation will often outpace the interest on state debt. Global capital will thus rely on the continued existence of frontiers for investment in the developing world.

Capital accumulation in the emerging economies, which include a massive variety of societies with different political histories, economic bases and cultures, is going to be very uneven. In recent decades, the fastest rates of growth occurred in East Asia and the former Soviet Union. China is still well positioned for GDP growth in the coming decades, though not at a rate of 10 per cent per year. Manufacturing employment in China peaked in absolute terms in 1996 and it has been drifting gradually downward ever since as Chinese firms automate more of their production.[19] This is good for Chinese capital. It is going to be increasingly difficult to use cheap labor to compete with machinery in the coming decades, particularly in manufacturing. Despite inevitable difficulties, China will probably continue its transition toward an economy more heavily focused on the service industries, finance and middle-class consumption. While there are real differences between countries like China and India, we can expect roughly similar transitions in the strongest emerging markets: Brazil, India, South Africa, Turkey, Indonesia, Malaysia and others.

As growth inevitably slows in these countries, capital will turn to the last earthly frontiers of accumulation. Globally, around 1 billion people support themselves as smallholder farmers. Subsistence agriculture is often only barely integrated into chains of commodity production. This population, which is heavily concentrated in sub-Saharan Africa and South Asia, represents the limit point of future growth through the absorption of land and labor into the capitalist economy. In 2000, the service sector surpassed agriculture as the largest source of employment on the planet.[20] As we have seen in the past, the percentage of the world's population employed in agriculture will continue to decline in relative terms and will eventually decline in absolute terms.

Those regions where subsistence agriculture is common will likely follow the established script: debt-encumbered farmers will be forced to sell their land to large landowners and corporations, become incorporated into the capitalist workforce and watch as local subsistence goods are replaced with commodities from all over the world. This process will be responsible for a substantial portion of global economic growth as the 21st century continues and may become a primary source of profits for global capital. Even this growth has its limits, as we will see later, because bringing these regions up to Western "standards of living" — really, standards of waste — would impose unbearable ecological costs on the planet.

The changing nature of production will create additional hurdles for developing nations in the coming decades. As computers and machinery outcompete labor in traditional industries, the potential uses of cheap labor may become increasingly limited. This is already starting to happen in manufacturing, but agriculture could become another candidate if landowners in the developing world consolidate land holdings and find ways to adapt machinery to local conditions.

If language barriers are overcome, it is possible that developing nations will face competition from automated foreign service industries ranging from accounting to customer service lines. It will probably be more difficult for other nations to repeat the Chinese model of development in future decades, not least because the world market is increasingly saturated with goods from both the advanced capitalist countries and the strongest emerging markets. At present, this lights-out vision has to be tempered by the real world, which is propelled by dangerous, labor-intensive *maquilas*, sweatshops, strip mines and prison labor as much as it is by robotized factories.

The role of distributed production in emerging markets will be more ambiguous. Demand for computers, 3D printers and whatever else emerges in the coming decades will be mostly fulfilled by refineries and factories in the developing world. Even self-replicating 3D printers will need microchips built from rare earth minerals. These means of production will be used in a variety of ways. Distributed production can be mobilized as counter-power, allowing local communities to develop resistance economies by reducing their dependency on the owners of industrial capital. This use, however, relies on energy and a communications infrastructure capable of supporting these machines, which many of the world's poorest regions lack. Furthermore, Nick Dyer-Witherford points out that technologies like cell phones are used to mobilize precarious labor in developing nations.

From El Salvador to India, finding poorly paid, intermittent work now requires a cell phone. Financial institutions are using cell phones to extend micro-credit, or small loans with often usurious interest rates, to populations who have traditionally escaped the financial system.[21] In this way, technologies that facilitate distributed production can simultaneously make us more vulnerable to precarious labor and help to saddle us with debt. Just as was the case with industrial production, new productive technologies cannot develop to their full potential within the fetters of the old system.

Disregarding the inevitability of disruptions, wars and other shocks to capital, we can gradually expect growth in the developing world to trend downward over time. I expect GDP growth in the emerging markets to average around 5 per cent annually after they emerge from the crisis that they are currently entering at the time of this writing. Depending on how the convergence of technological change, demographic shifts and geopolitical maneuvering impacts the developing nations, which will not be uniform, we should expect growth to decline to anywhere between 3 and 4 per cent annually within a couple of decades. After this point, global economic growth will probably slow markedly, given that much of the catch-up effect in East Asia, Eastern Europe, the Middle East and North Africa, and Latin America will be exhausted. This would leave sub-Saharan Africa and South Asia to account for the majority of economic growth and population growth by 2050.

Does Capitalism Have a Future?

The limits that capitalism faces in the 21st century are not just technological; they are geographic, as well. Capital does not go quietly into the night when accumulation becomes difficult. It searches the world for new areas where it can continue accumulating value, by pulling more labor, resources and markets into its system. Infinite growth is not possible on a finite planet. As capital accumulates in China, Brazil and India, it will ultimately be forced to go searching for value elsewhere in frontiers like sub-Saharan Africa. The last time that capital faced a general crisis of overaccumulation, the Great Depression, these frontiers were actually quite vast. Most of the world was almost completely underdeveloped from a capitalist perspective. This is no longer the case today. Global economic growth is already slowing and capital's frontiers are starting to close in. As capital expels labor from the production process in the advanced economies, it continues to exhaust the geographical limits of its expansion.

Capitalism's prospects for growth are still significant and it may be able to afford decades of growth globally even while it deals with chronic instability in the developed world. But this process cannot go on forever. The adjustment mechanism for the problem forecast by US agriculture, the collapse of commodity production, is simple: the constant addition of new industries and new markets. This mechanism is already starting to run out of steam. In the coming decades of the 21st century, we will watch as capital overaccumulation transforms from a local into a global problem. By its very nature, this transition is not going to be smooth. It will be punctuated by crises, bubbles, wars, uprisings, revolutions and ecological pressures. It is even possible that a global war on the scale of World War II might set the clock of capital accumulation back a few years. Overall, such a disaster could only provide a temporary reprieve. If this hypothesis is correct, then capitalism is not destined to go on endlessly accumulating value until the sun burns out. Capitalism will collapse of its own internal contradictions within the 21st century, within the lifetime of children born today.

Endnotes

1   Harvey, D. (2014) *Seventeen Contradictions and the End of Capitalism*. (London: Profile Books) p. 232.

2   Maughan, T. "The dystopian lake filled by the world's tech lust," *BBC*. April 2nd, 2015. Available at: http://www. bbc.com/future/story/20150402-the-worst-place-on-earth. [accessed 7 June 2017]

3   Lord, L. "How Many People Were Here Before Columbus?" *US News and World Report*. August 18th, 1997. Available at: http://www.bxscience.edu/ourpages/ auto/2009/4/5/34767803/Pre-Columbian%20population.pdf. [accessed 7 June 2017]

4   Piketty, T. *Capital in the Twenty-First Century*, trans. A. Goldhammer. p. 74, 78–80.

5   This variance depends on how birth and death rates are affected by medical trends, like battling HIV/AIDS, and evolving social norms about family size. Global population could be anywhere between 9.6 billion and 12.3 billion by 2100. However, few of these studies account for the likely stresses that climate change will place on food and water supplies. Talbot, D. "U.N. Predicts New Global Population Boom," *MIT Technology Review*. September 18th, 2014. Available at: http://www.technologyreview.com/ news/530866/un-predicts-new-global-population-boom/. [accessed 7 June 2017]

6   Piketty, T. *Capital in the Twenty-First Century*, trans. A. Goldhammer. p. 93.

7   Ibid. pp. 100–1.

8   See: Roberts, M. "Thomas Piketty and the search for r," *Historical Materialism*, Vol. 23, No. 1. (2015) pp. 86–105. Available at: http://bit.ly/1k2DepI. [accessed 7 June 2017]; Rognlie, M. "A note on Piketty and diminishing returns to capital." June 15th, 2014. Available at: http://www.mit.edu/~mrognlie/piketty_diminishing_returns.pdf. [accessed 7 June 2017]

9   Thompson, D. "The Death of Music Sales," *The Atlantic*. January 25th, 2015. Available at: http://www.theatlantic.com/business/archive/2015/01/buying-music-is-so-over/384790/. [accessed 7 June 2017]; Christman, E. "What's Behind the Digital Download's Decline and Can Streaming Save the Day?" *BillboardBiz*. January 10th, 2014. Available at: http://www.billboard.com/biz/articles/news/record-labels/5869521/whats-behind-the-digital-downloads-decline-and-can-streaming. [accessed 7 June 2017]

10 Tabuchi, H. "When Consumers Cut Back: An Object Lesson From Japan," *The New York Times*. February 21st, 2009. Available at: http://www.nytimes.com/2009/02/22/business/worldbusiness/22japan.html?fta=y. [accessed 7 June 2017]; "Waging a new war," *The Economist*. March 9th, 2013. Available at: http://www.economist.com/news/finance-and-economics/21573133-shinzo-abe-wakes-up-political-risk-higher-prices-without-higher. [accessed 7 June 2017]

11 Gordon, R. (August 2012) "Is U.S. Economic Growth Over? Faltering Innovation Confronts the Six Headwinds," *NBER Working Paper Series*, No. 18315. Available at: http://www.nber.org/papers/w18315.pdf. [accessed 7 June 2017]

12 See: Raphael, A. "TaskRabbit Redux," *The New Yorker*. July 22nd, 2014. Available at: http://www.newyorker.com/business/currency/taskrabbit-redux. [accessed 7 June 2017]

13 Joint Center for Housing Studies of Harvard University. (2015) *The State of the Nation's Housing 2015*. Available at: http://www.jchs.harvard.edu/sites/jchs.harvard.edu/files/

jchs-sonhr-2015-full.pdf. [accessed 7 June 2017]; Matthews, S. "Here's Evidence That Millenials Are Still Living With Their Parents," *Bloomberg Business*. September 18th, 2015. Available at: http://www.bloomberg.com/news/articles/2015-09-18/here-s-evidence-that-millennials-are-still-living-with-their-parents. [accessed 7 June 2017]

14 Nolan, P. and Zhang, J. (July/August 2010) "Global Competition After the Financial Crisis," *New Left Review*, No. 64. p. 99. Available at: http://content.csbs.utah.edu/~mli/Economies%205430-6430/Nolan-Global%20Competition%20after%20Financial%20Crisis.pdf. [accessed 7 June 2017]

15 See: Arrighi, G. (2007) *Adam Smith in Beijing: Lineages of the Twenty-First Century*. (London: Verso) pp. 351–78. Available at: http://digamo.free.fr/adambeijing.pdf. [accessed 7 June 2017]

16 Nolan, P. and Zhang, J. "Global Competition After the Financial Crisis," *New Left Review*. p. 101.

17 O'Brien, M. "Emerging Power: Developing Nations Now Claim the Majority of World GDP," *The Atlantic*. June 4th, 2013. Available at: http://www.theatlantic.com/business/archive/2013/06/emerging-power-developing-nations-now-claim-the-majority-of-world-gdp/276543/. [accessed 7 June 2017]

18 "When giants slow down," *The Economist*. July 27th, 2013. Available at: http://www.economist.com/news/briefing/21582257-most-dramatic-and-disruptive-period-emerging-market-growth-world-has-ever-seen. [accessed 7 June 2017]

19 McAfee, A. (September 2012) "Technological Unemployment: Not Just for the U.S.," *Race Against the Machine: Jobs. Economy. Wages.* Available at: http://digitalcommunity.mit.edu/community/featured_content/race-against-the-machine/blog/2012/09. [accessed 7 June 2017]

20 United Nations Environment Programme. (2013) *Smallholders, food security, and the environment.* Available at: http://www.unep.org/pdf/SmallholderReport_WEB.pdf. [accessed 7 June 2017]; Food and Agriculture Organization of the United Nations. "Labour." Available at: http://www.fao.org/docrep/015/i2490e/i2490e01b.pdf. [accessed 7 June 2017]

21 Dyer-Witheford, N. *Cyber-Proletariat.* pp. 102–23.

Chapter 9

The Future of Labor

Machines are the new proletariat. The working class is being given its walking papers.

Jacques Attali, adviser to Socialist President of France
François Mitterrand

The rise and fall of cybernetic capitalism will be experienced as a profound transformation in the nature of labor. In the developed world, this transformation is already underway. Capitalism is a system founded upon abstract, homogenous labor represented in the form of money. Where capitalism historically expanded by incorporating more labor into the production process, it now develops by expelling labor in fits and reincorporating it in increasingly precarious forms. In the past, when an industry expanded by investing more capital in production and expelling labor, it inevitably reached a crisis of profitability. Capital resolved these crises by establishing monopolies and subsidy systems to extract surplus value from more profitable industries, and by integrating labor-intensive production into supply chains, like Apple does. As global capitalism reduces its total reliance on labor, it also undercuts its own means of survival.

Radical automation and distributed production erode necessary labor by their very nature. Technologies that capitalism itself produced are laying the foundations for a society without labor. This is currently seen as a disaster of almost unprecedented proportions. The majority of people directly rely on wage labor or that of friends and family to clothe, house and feed themselves. Our entire economic system depends on this system of exploitation. Even state programs that redistribute wealth (really, re-redistribute) need taxes on profits and income, and many pension systems are funded by investments in the stock market. The erosion of wage labor is even being experienced as the slow death of organized labor, throwing the entire Left into disarray and confusion. After all, the revolution was supposed to be led by the most organized segments of the working class: the industrial proletariat. Today, the industrial working class is a shell of its former self in the most advanced economies, even as it rises and organizes itself in the developing world. We are moving into the 21st century bereft of our old guideposts. It is essential that we get a grasp on this process.

A Brave New World

If we zoom out and look at the world as one coherent system, we get a very different picture of the world than we might if we just focus on Europe, Japan and the US. Agriculture was still the world's largest occupation up until the dawn of the 21st century. Industry still accounts for somewhere around 20 per cent of world employment, much of which is in labor-intensive sectors like the Bangladeshi garment industry. The majority of the global working class is non-white and female. Decades of globalization pulled manufacturing based on cheap labor into the developing world, while debt and international competition pushed farmers into towns and cities. But even as capitalism doubled the global labor supply, it began to develop ways to reduce its reliance on labor in general.

We have seen the first stages of the process over the last couple of decades in the US. From 2000 onward, the total demand for labor hours in the US economy has been in decline. Crises amplified the trend, but did not alter its fundamental direction. The US is something of a perfect storm among the major economies as far as radical automation is concerned. US industries make use of advanced automation, Americans work longer hours than comparable nations and union strength has seriously declined from its post-war peak. Nevertheless, the US is a good case study precisely because of its extremity. It exemplifies almost all of the trends that can be attributed to radical automation in the developed economies, where countries like Germany and Japan might only exhibit a few.

We have to look at a few different trends if we want to understand what is happening to labor in the US. First, let's get some basic official definitions out of the way. A person is considered *employed* if they worked for at least one hour in a formal paying job in the previous week. Someone is considered *unemployed* if they do not have a job and are looking for work. If you do not have a job and are not actively looking for work, you are considered to have dropped out of the labor force. The *labor force* consists of everyone who is both employed and unemployed. The *labor force participation rate* is the percentage of people in a given group who are either employed or looking for work. The *employment to population ratio* is the percentage of people in a given group who are employed. Each of these indicators can tell us something about the state of labor, and the structural conditions that shape the nature of work, wages and worker struggles.

The US labor force participation rate for people aged 16 years and older peaked at 67.3 per cent in 2000. It increased almost 9 per cent from the mid-1960s to 2000, as women entered the workforce in greater and greater numbers (the male labor force participation rate has fallen continuously since 1950). From 2000 to 2015, the labor force participation rate fell almost 5 per cent. This means that nearly 5 per cent of the adult population dropped out of the workforce. It is possible that a portion of this decline could be accounted for by an aging population and growing numbers of students, as economists often suggested before 2008.

If we look at statistics for prime-age workers—those between 25 and 54 years old—we find that this cannot possibly be true. Cutting out the young and old should minimize the effect of retirees and students, but the prime-aged labor force participation rate fell from almost 85 per cent in the late 1990s to around 80.5 per cent in 2015. Prime-aged workers dropped out of the labor force at roughly the same rate as the whole population. The picture gets even clearer if we add the unemployed to those who dropped out of the labor force. The prime-age employment-to-population ratio peaked in 2000. Employment dropped dramatically during the recessions in 2001 and 2008, and *job growth never returned employment to the rate it reached before each recession.*[1]

U.S. Employment to Population Ratio (1971-2015)

Women enter workforce

Decline

— All (age 25-54)   - - - - Men (age 25-54)

This drop accounts for around 4.6 million working-aged people who are no longer employed. The idea that shifting trends in employment are simply caused by normal fluctuations is difficult to believe, as these trends took place across multiple boom-bust cycles. While the Great Recession accelerated job losses, the long-term decline in labor force participation was already underway before the crash. An interview conducted by Brynjolfsson and McAfee suggests a reason why modern recessions destroy more jobs than recoveries create:

> A few years ago, we had a very candid discussion with one CEO, and he explained that he knew for over a decade that advances in information technology had rendered many routine information-processing jobs superfluous. At the same time, when profits and revenues are on the rise, it can be hard to eliminate jobs. When the recession came, business as usual obviously was not sustainable, which made it easier to implement a round of painful streamlining and layoffs. As the recession ended and profits and demand returned, the jobs doing routine work were not restored. Like so many other companies in recent years, his organization found it could use technology to scale up without these workers.[2]

Economists have been at a loss to explain the declining use of labor in the past 15 years. Many simply admit that they do not understand what is happening, while others argue that the trends can be reduced to an aging population or the cyclical impact of the Great Recession. More recently, some mainstream economists have started to wonder if automation might be responsible for consecutive jobless recoveries.[3] What we are really seeing is the beginning of a structural change in the capitalist economy. Radical automation is finally converging with a decline in the growth of outlets for capital's expansion.

The costs of the falling demand for labor are not evenly distributed throughout the labor force. Instead, the burden of underemployment and poverty is foisted on vulnerable social groups: the disabled, the young, and marginalized racial and ethnic groups. Where changing working conditions appear like a trickle for the workforce as a whole, these groups have experienced the inequities of the post-2000 world as a flood. From 2000 to 2014, the unemployment rate for disabled adults in the US rose from 8.7 per cent to 15.8 per cent. According to the

American Community Survey, the labor force participation rate for disabled persons aged 25–64 fell uninterruptedly from 50.3 per cent in 2000 to 39.2 per cent in 2013, a drop of 11.1 per cent. During this same period the poverty rate for disabled adults spiked from 19.9 per cent to 31.9 per cent. This rate includes payments from programs like Social Security, which means that the adults in question were still impoverished after receiving welfare.[4]

As any young person can tell you, the state of the youth job market is extremely poor. In 2013, 45 per cent of the unemployed in the US were between 18 and 34 years old. Unemployment is disproportionately high among black and Hispanic youth, and those without college degrees. Even college-educated young people found it extraordinarily difficult to find work consistent with their education and many have been forced to work in low-paying, part-time service jobs, all whilst being saddled with large amounts of student debt.[5] Enraged and frustrated declassé middle- to upper-class youth formed the core of the Occupy movement, just as unemployed college-educated youth played a significant role in the 2011 uprisings in the Arab world.[6]

From the 1980s onward, long-term unemployment became progressively more common after each crisis. It took over 2 years for jobs to recover their absolute losses after the 1981 recession, two and a half years after the 1990 recession, almost 4 years after the 2000 recession and over 6 years after the crisis of 2008. Again, after 2000, employment as a percentage of working-aged people never recovered to its pre-crisis levels. After the 2000 recession, the share of unemployed workers who were out of work for over 6 months peaked at over 20 per cent. During the Great Recession, this number shot up to 45.5 per cent by 2011—the highest number seen since the end of World War II.[7]

Even the work created in partial compensation for lost jobs is precarious and poorly compensated. During the Great Recession, high-wage industries accounted for 41 per cent of lost jobs, while medium-wage and low-wage industries accounted for 37 per cent and 22 per cent respectively. The recovery basically reversed this pattern. In 2014, low-wage jobs made up 44 per cent of the jobs created in the aftermath of the crisis.[8] The proportion of workers in "non-standard" jobs like part-time work, temporary work, contract work and day labor jumped up 5 per cent to 40.4 per cent from 2006 to 2010. Many of these jobs tend to have little to no benefits, more dangerous work conditions and little job security.[9] The pressure to accept low-paying, precarious work is a result of persistently high unemployment and the erosion of union power, both of which can be traced directly to automation.

At the other end of the phenomenon of radical automation is the rapid growth of what David Graeber calls "bullshit jobs." The popularity of this idea is proof of its simple truth. A bullshit job is essentially pointless—it is employment that requires little, if any, meaningful work. The contemporary office is full of such jobs; indeed, there are entire careers based upon extracting 8 hours' pay for less than an hour of work. To quote Graeber's poetic formulation, "It's as if someone were out there making up pointless jobs just for the sake of keeping us all working."[10]

The bullshit job is a preservation of the image of labor even as its function wanes. It is one of the most bizarre manifestations of labor's growing irrelevance. In the bullshit job, work becomes totally absurd. Office workers must pretend to be hard at work when their supervisors walk by, even though they have absolutely nothing to do. Corporate lawyers and administrators create mountains of useless paperwork while remaining fully aware that society would run perfectly well if they all suddenly vanished. There is something truly tragic about this idea. Unemployment at least presents itself as a serious crisis, but the endless expansion of bullshit jobs is the dream of capitalism's apologists. One could probably win the Nobel Prize in Economics by finding a way to endlessly multiply 40-hour paper-pushing jobs for the unemployed.

The conditions we find in different countries vary widely, but almost all demonstrate some aspect of a creeping decline in the demand for labor. The International Labor Organization (ILO) estimated that around 201 million people were unemployed in 2014, around 31 million more than before the Great Recession. Official global unemployment stands at around 6 per cent, though it is as high as 9.9 per cent in Europe, 11 per cent in the Middle East and 12.5 per cent in North Africa. Youth unemployment is almost three times higher than the rate for adults. Global labor force participation fell around 0.7 per cent from 2007 to the present, even though older women pushed European rates higher by entering the labor market in droves to support their families. Indeed, the ILO predicts that even with steady growth in low-paying service-sector jobs, global employment rates are probably slowly going to deteriorate throughout the rest of the decade.[11] Even in Germany, which is widely hailed for its "successful" recovery and high employment rates, the crisis exacerbated existing trends of rising precarious employment. A survey by the German metalworkers' union IG Metall shows that only 5 per cent of new hires gained permanent contracts. The other 95 per cent were on fixed-term contracts or were temps.[12]

The point of the preceding pages is not to bury you under an avalanche of statistics, but to demonstrate that we are living through the beginnings of a real change in the way that capitalism works. Capital is reducing its dependence on labor. We should not expect this trend to reverse itself. Automation and distributed production are only going to become progressively more sophisticated. Traditional models of employment are based on incorrect assumptions that will be revised over the next couple of decades. The question is not whether the demand for labor is going to fall, but where and how quickly.

There is no simple way to predict the speed of these trends. Declining growth and perceived stagnation can act as a break on the introduction of automation. Capitalists are less likely to introduce productivity-boosting technologies if they do not foresee much growth in their markets. However, a falling rate of profit can spur competition between capitalists for a greater share of existing markets. We saw how changes in the US auto industry were spurred by an influx of Japanese competitors.

A decline in working hours can also be distributed in different ways. It may be cheaper for firms to employ fewer employees on a full-time basis and hire more part-time employees, or the opposite may be the case. The structure of wage and benefit regulations, the strength of unions, the amount of competition for work and other factors will all influence how firms in different contexts decide to employ labor. Regardless of the factors influencing these decisions, firms will almost always choose the cheapest possible way to employ as much labor as can profitably be used in their particular enterprise. Of course, declining labor hours could simply be distributed evenly by reducing the length of the workday without a reduction in pay, but there is no reason why capitalists would voluntarily agree to do this. Unemployment forces wages down and capitalists want to get the maximum amount of labor hours out of workers. Politely ask the people who own your company for a 4-hour workday and you will probably get laughed at, fired or both.

The declining demand for labor will be felt as an intensification of decades long trends: rising structural unemployment, the increasing precariousness of work, stagnant or declining wages and skyrocketing inequality. Unemployment does not have to be universal before the vast majority of workers feel its effects. Unemployment creates pressure on all workers to accept lower wages and poor working conditions. If you can easily be replaced, your bargaining power as a worker declines.

Education is not a solution to this problem. First, the idea that there is a "race between technology and education" is patently absurd. No amount of education can teach you how to build cars better than a robotic arm and no amount of education will teach you how to calculate faster than a computer. Secondly, if the demand for labor is falling generally, then pushing more people through higher education just increases the competition for available jobs that require a university degree. Indeed, this is already happening. As it becomes more and more difficult to get a job without a degree, people are going to do what they can to get an education. Even if we do not expect teaching or art to be meaningfully automated in the near future, competition for these posts will increase as unemployed workers search for ways to make a living. If they cannot, the unemployed will fall back upon what they always have: hustling in the informal economy to survive.

The decline of labor may heighten uneven development around the world. China, India and Brazil accumulated a significant amount of capital in the past few decades compared to countries like Haiti and Ethiopia. Their industries have spawned their own peripheral zones in poorer nations, where rock-bottom wages and labor-intensive production fuel the stronger manufacturing industries. The emerging economies developed their industries by manufacturing goods for export. As their industries become more productive, they may saturate the world market for manufactured goods. The door to export-oriented development would be partially shut to the poorer nations, who could find themselves stuck as a permanent periphery to the world's economic core. Many of the least developed countries would have to industrialize by producing commodities for their own markets, which are both underdeveloped and already heavily penetrated by imported goods. Suffice it to say that this would be quite difficult, particularly with barriers to trade being as low as they currently are. As automation becomes more efficient, even the potential uses for cheap labor will decline; though they will still exist as long as capitalism survives. The least-developed nations may have to find an alternative path to development, ideally one which jettisons the skewed values and injustices of capitalism.

The Labor Struggle

In 2014, 40,000 Chinese workers went on strike at Yue Yuen, the world's largest shoe manufacturer, demanding higher pay and pension contributions. Four years earlier, striking workers at Honda's Chinese auto-part suppliers shut down all of Honda's plants in China, winning large raises. Over the past half-decade Chinese workers engaged in well over a thousand wildcat strikes and labor actions, with little to no support from China's state-controlled union.[13] In 2012, South African miners initiated a wildcat strike over poor wages and brutal working conditions, despite opposition from the government and the National Union of Mineworkers leadership. Police opened fire on the strikers, killing 34 and wounding 78 in what would come to be known as the Marikana massacre. Still, the miners refused to back down and won a 22 per cent raise.

By contrast, consider the US. In 2014, workers at a Volkswagen plant in Chattanooga, Tennessee voted against representation by the United Auto Workers (UAW). Volkswagen actually invited the UAW to organize in its plant, as many German companies use a management system that co-opts labor unions. US companies typically fight union organizing like the plague and the UAW's loss in Chattanooga shocked some observers. Others suggested a host of explanations: Tennessee was a conservative state, politicians and the media came out hard against the union, and the UAW's historical record was full of cronyism and poor compromises with management.[14]

Such examples show how dramatically the fortunes of organized labor have changed since the middle of the 20th century. On the one hand, in the developed world, union strength has almost universally decayed, often in a spectacular fashion. On the other hand, developing nations are seeing a new wave of worker militancy. These divergent outcomes clearly trace the general trend of capitalist development. In the advanced capitalist economies, diminished demand for industrial labor weakened organized labor's main weapon in negotiations with capital. As industrial employment rose in the developing nations, newly concentrated workers began organizing to demand dignified working conditions just as their Western counterparts had a century before.

This story may be just a little too simple in order to understand what happened to organized labor in the West. The history of the labor movement varies greatly between countries. The Scandinavian countries—Denmark, Sweden, Norway, Finland and Iceland—still have large, powerful trade unions, while US unions have basically collapsed. Different strategies of resistance can modify the impact of grand dynamics like globalization and deindustrialization. Inequality rose in Scandinavian countries over the past few decades, though not nearly as much as in countries like the US, the UK and Germany. Even though German unions used corporatist strategies—pursuing grand bargains between labor, capital and the state—similar to those of Scandinavia, German unions weakened in recent years while Scandinavian unions did not.

This is not the place for an exhaustive history of the labor movement. Instead, I want to offer a short discussion of the prospects for today's workers. In the developed world, unions in many countries were devastated by capitalism's wave of adaptations in the late 20th century. US unions were particularly ill-prepared and are a perfect example of how poor strategy can make a bad structural trend much worse. By the end of the Second World War, unions in the US were incorporated into the legal and political structure of the country. The largest US unions purged radical elements in the name of decommunization, and most accepted pragmatic bargains with capital in exchange for higher wages and pensions. Militant rank-and-file workers often criticized the union leadership for its stultifying bureaucracy, cronyism and undemocratic practices. For their part, union leaders earned those critiques. Union leaders often intervened on the side of management to suppress wildcat strikes, stymieing grassroots challenges to capital. With the exception of the Industrial Workers of the World, unions organized themselves on an industry-by-industry, shop-by-shop basis, fragmenting their influence. Many unions did not even attempt to organize "unskilled" workers and contracts often showed a complete disregard for the unemployed.

These weak strategic decisions made the US labor movement extremely vulnerable to automation and globalization. Unions could be attacked piecemeal, since the union leadership had no real tradition of industrial solidarity. Faced with the alternatives of fighting for workers' broad interests and locking in existing benefits for older union members, most unions chose the latter. Two-tiered systems saved the wages and pensions for old, soon-to-retire members, and condemned new workers to cuts. Most importantly, because they had entirely abandoned an anticapitalist vision, union leaders felt they had no choice but to accept wage freezes and pension cuts to support corporate profits. By accepting the existence of capitalism as the limit of the possible, organized labor condemned itself to a slow death in much of the developed world.

The conditions for unions are not going to get much better in the 21st century, at least as far as the production process is concerned. Automation will continue to be a potent weapon in the hands of capitalists. We have already seen how corporations like McDonald's threaten to automate work when workers stand up for themselves. It is also now much easier to simply move production lines to get around labor unrest. If workers' struggles in the developed world remain piecemeal efforts bound by a fundamental adherence to capitalist logic and legality, they are doomed to repeat the failures of the last century.

The labor struggle in the developing world will continue to intensify in the coming years. By bringing large numbers of workers together under factory roofs and in industrial cities, capital is recreating the explosive dynamic that gave birth to the Western labor movement. Unfortunately, the labor movement in countries like China and South Africa will have to deal with many of the problems that unions in the advanced capitalist economies currently struggle with.

Unlike European workers in the 19th century, Chinese workers will have to compete with cheap, easily accessible labor in other developing nations. Chinese industries are already taking advantage of labor in places like Ethiopia, Tanzania and Senegal, where factory labor costs are less than 10 per cent of their level in China.[15] Wedged between cheaper labor and a wave of machines, workers in the developing world will have to struggle with a form of capitalism that is more adaptive and powerful than its 19th-century predecessor.

I do not mean to be overly pessimistic. I only want to highlight the structural challenges that workers in capitalist societies will face in the 21st century. Workers are not powerless in the face of globalization and automation, as many capitalist authors would certainly like to suggest. They simply have to adopt strategies that adequately reflect reality.

There have been some encouraging signs of dynamism in the developed world's labor movement. The Fight for 15 campaign for a $15 an hour minimum wage is not revolutionary, but it is a step toward organizing low-wage, part-time workers, who were traditionally ignored by unions. More radical initiatives include occupying and operating closed factories to fulfill social needs. In Greece, workers occupied and began running the Vio. Me factory as a cooperative after its old owners abandoned it in 2011. The cooperative is run as a non-profit, and it helps to supply Greece's solidarity economy and local clinics.[16] These are early steps and we can hope that they blossom into something more. However, labor struggle will only ultimately succeed in the 21st century if it is part of a larger social movement that can bring down the capitalist system.

Before the Fall

The death of labor seems like capitalism's ultimate triumph. After all, capital has been locked in centuries of perilous struggle with the working class. The more that capital substituted machines for workers, the more it weakened their ability to resist its demands. By pushing labor farther away from the production process, capital undercut its ability to bring production to a halt. Labor's interventions now often have to use alternative methods: blockades, occupations and sabotage. Along with globalization, automation has become capital's preferred weapon against the worker. Why strike for higher wages when you might be replaced by a machine? Why risk your job when unemployment is already so high?

Armed with the computer and the machine, contemporary capitalism intensifies its worst aspects. What could be more alienating than being reduced to simply monitoring a group of machines and programs, waiting to fix some minor glitch? What could be more humiliating than losing your job to a computer through no fault of your own and being forced to beg for work in a petty service job with no hope of advancement? In the classical battle between labor and capital, capital at least *needed* the worker, however much it hated to admit it. Now, entire groups of people are becoming superfluous to capital's expansion. Hatred, at least, is better than indifference. One hates those with power, but one treats the superfluous with contempt.

In many industries, the worker really has become a mere accessory to the production process. How many workers are needed to grow US corn or churn out Fanuc's industrial robots? In other industries, labor persists as exploitatively as ever.

Congolese miners slave away in open-pit mines, US prisoners churn out goods for cents on the dollar, and Bangladeshi garment workers toil away in dangerous and unsanitary conditions. These seeming extremes are two faces of the same process. The gleaming white halls of an Apple or Google need the brutal foundations of cheap labor and extractive industry to exist. There are no iPhones without rare earth minerals. *There is no capitalism without labor.*

This is the central contradiction of capitalism. Capitalist development requires the accumulation of an ever-increasing mass of value. Capitalists pursue this, often only semi-consciously, by expanding labor's productive power with organization, technology and machinery. Eventually, capital approaches the limits of this incredible expansion: the workerless farm, the lights-out factory and the computerized office. But capitalism is not a system for accumulating wealth or lightening the burden of work. It is a system for accumulating value. You cannot accumulate value, which is crystallized labor time, without living labor. There is no such thing as fully automated capitalism. As capitalism approaches this point, commodity production will inevitably collapse. The law of value will be abolished, as a society with negligible labor cannot have an economy based on labor values. Cybernetic capitalism will make production for profit impossible. The most advanced system for exploiting human labor in history digs its own grave.

Heraclitus once said that the way up and the way down are one and the same. We would do well to remember this wisdom. We already know what 21st-century capitalism's ascension looks like. Industrial giants consolidate their power and industrial capital accumulates in fewer hands. Automation throws masses of workers into unemployment and precarious jobs, while corporate elites and financiers make more money than ever. The tiny minority who own capital enrich themselves obscenely, while the vast majority struggle to get by and find stability on constantly shifting foundations. State power is wielded almost universally to prop up capitalist interests and suppress the resistance of working people. In a crisis, even the pretense of democracy gets wiped away. Unelected technocrats take power, slashing basic social commitments to restore capitalist profits. Convinced of the fundamental corruption of the present system, people look for alternatives. Some shift to the Left and some become radicals. Others turn to the fascists, exchanging their freedom for the bleating of the herd.

At the same time, capitalism gnaws away at its own foundations. While industrial capital centralizes, distributed production places a widening range of productive technologies in the hands of individuals. Some of these technologies facilitate capitalism's growth, but others foretell something different. Instead of producing things for exchange and profit, people cooperate with one another and produce things directly for their own use. They eschew private property and copyright, sharing goods freely.

In this new world, scarcity is artificial. Armed with their own machines, the people square off against industrial capital and they often win. There is a cost to this victory. The rise of a mode of production based on freely shared work and use cannot simply coexist with wage labor and exchange value. While it remains trapped within a capitalist society, distributed production cannot flourish to its full extent. Instead, it acts as a steadily growing vision of a new world within the shell of the old: a world without scarcity and a world without labor.

The apex of industrial capitalism and the rise of distributed production are evolutionarily twinned. The one concentrates power in fewer hands and the other disperses it. These seem to be inherently contradictory, but they proceed toward the same fundamental outcome. Both are creating the foundations for a society without labor and a system beyond capitalism. Radical automation and distributed production will create very real pain and dislocation, but this has nothing to do with the inherent qualities of these technologies. This suffering is only the result of these technologies being developed within an irrational social system.

The death of labor is a good thing. It makes it possible for us to envision a world where economic problems and meaningful scarcity are banished from our day-to-day concerns. We could live in a world without poverty, and a world with plenty of goods to go around and plenty of free time to pursue our passions. We just cannot get to that world with capitalism. If a mode of production is a social relationship mediated by technology, then no amount of technological progress can fix a fundamentally broken social system. Today's technologies reveal the path to the future, but they cannot bring us there alone. Left to its own devices, capitalism will bring us more crises, poverty and war. The choice we face, as Rosa Luxemburg once wrote, is simple: *socialism or barbarism*.

Endnotes

1   U.S. Bureau of Labor Statistics. "Civilian labor force participation rate." Series ID LNS11000000. Available at: http://data.bls.gov/cgi-bin/surveymost?bls. [accessed 7 June 2017]; U.S. Bureau of Labor Statistics. "Labor force participation rate: men," retrieved from FRED, Federal Reserve Bank of St. Louis. October 17th, 2015. Available at: https://research.stlouisfed.org/fred2/series/LNS11300001; U.S. Bureau of Labor Statistics. "Civilian labor force participation rate: 25 to 54 years," retrieved from FRED, Federal Reserve Bank of St. Louis. October 17th, 2015. Available at: https://research.stlouisfed.org/fred2/series/LNU01300060; U.S. Bureau of Labor Statistics. "Employment to population ratio, 25–54 years." Series ID LNS12300060; U.S. Bureau of Labor Statistics. "Employment-population

ratio: men," retrieved from FRED, Federal Reserve Bank of St. Louis. October 17th, 2015. Available at: https://research. stlouisfed.org/fred2/series/LNS12300001.

2   Brynjolfsson, E. and McAfee, A. *The Second Machine Age: Work, Progress, and Prosperity in a Time of Brilliant Technologies.* p. 140.

3   For a confused economist, see: Hall, R. "Secular Stagnation in the US," *Vox.* April 22nd, 2015. Available at: http://www. voxeu.org/article/secular-stagnation-us. [accessed 7 June 2017] For economists arguing that declining labor force participation is cyclical, see: Erceg, C. and Levin, A. "Labor Force Participation and Monetary Policy in the Wake of the Great Recession." April 9th, 2013. Available at: http:// www.bostonfed.org/employment2013/papers/erceg_levin_ session1.pdf. [accessed 7 June 2017]

4   Bruenig, M. "Unemployment for Disabled Adults Up 80%," *Demos.* July 7th, 2015. Available at: http://www.demos.org/ blog/7/7/15/unemployment-disabled-adults-80. [accessed 7 June 2017]; VonSchrader, S. and Lee, C.G. "Disability Statistics from the Current Population Survey (CPS)," *Cornell University Employment and Disability Institute (EDI),* retrieved October 18, 2015. Available at: https://www. disabilitystatistics.org/reports/cps.cfm?statistic=poverty.

5   Ruetschlin, C. and Draut, T. "Stuck: Young America's Persistent Jobs Crisis," *Demos.* April 4th, 2013. Available at: http://www.demos.org/publication/stuck-young-americas-persistent-jobs-crisis. [accessed 7 June 2017]

6   The word *declassé* refers to people who were once members of a higher social class—for example, the wealthy—but who have lost their status owing to some misfortune.

7   Benanav, A. "Precarity Rising," *Viewpoint Magazine.* June 15th, 2015. Available at: https://viewpointmag.com/2015/06/15/ precarity-rising/. [accessed 7 June 2017]; Mishel, L., Bivens, J., Gould, E., and Shierholz, H. (November 2012) "Jobs," in

The State of Working America, 12th Edition. p. 352. Available at: http://www.stateofworkingamerica.org/subjects/jobs/? reader. [accessed 7 June 2017]

8   High-wage jobs are defined as having hourly wages between $20.03 and $32.62, adjusted for 2013 dollars. Medium-wage jobs are defined as having hourly wages between $13.73 and $20.00. Low-wage jobs are defined as having hourly wages between $9.48 and $13.33. Evangelist, M. (April 2014)"The Low-Wage Recovery: Industry Employment and Wages Four Years into the Recovery," *National Employment Law Project.* Available at: http://www.nelp.org/content/uploads/2015/03/ Low-Wage-Recovery-Industry-Employment-Wages-2014-Report.pdf. [accessed 7 June 2017]

9   U.S. Government Accountability Office. "Contingent Workforce: Size, Characteristics, Earnings, and Benefits." April 20th, 2015. Available at: http://www.gao.gov/ assets/670/669899.pdf. [accessed 7 June 2017]

10 Graeber, D. "On the Phenomenon of Bullshit Jobs," *Strike!* August 17th, 2013. Available at: http://strikemag.org/ bullshitjobs/. [accessed 7 June 2017]

11 International Labor Organization. (2015) *World Employment and Social Outlook: Trends 2015.* Available at: http://www.ilo. org/wcmsp5/groups/public/---dgreports/---dcomm/---publ/ documents/publication/wcms_337069.pdf. [accessed 7 June 2017]; Porter, E. "Why Europe's Job Picture Looks Different," *The New York Times.* February 7th, 2014. Available at: http:// economix.blogs.nytimes.com/2014/02/07/whyeuropes-job-picture-looks-different/. [accessed 7 June 2017]

12 Dörre, K. "Germany after the Crisis: Employment Miracle or Discriminating Precarity?" *Friedrich-Schiller-Universität Jena.* March 5th, 2011. Available at: https://www.tcd.ie/policy-institute/assets/pdf/Dorre_Speech_March11.pdf. [accessed 7 June 2017]

13 Barnes, T. and Lin, K. "China's growing labour movement

offers hope for workers globally," *The Conversation*. April 16th, 2015. Available at: http://theconversation.com/chinas-growing-labour-movement-offers-hope-for-workers-globally-39921. [accessed 7 June 2017]; Chen, M. "China's Militant Workers Embrace Collective Action," *In These Times*. February 25th, 2014. Available at: http://inthesetimes.com/working/entry/16344/chinas_militant_workers. [accessed 7 June 2017]

14 DePillis, L. "The strange case of the anti-union union at Volkswagen's plant in Tennessee," *The Washington Post*. November 19th, 2014. Available at: http://www.washingtonpost.com/news/storyline/wp/2014/11/19/the-strange-case-of-the-anti-union-union-at-volkswagens-plant-in-tennessee/. [accessed 7 June 2017]; Yeselson, R. "After Chattanooga," *Jacobin*. February 17th, 2014. Available at: https://www.jacobinmag.com/2014/02/after-chattanooga/. [accessed 7 June 2017]

15 Hamlin, K., Gridneff, I., and Davison, W. "Ethiopia Becomes China's China in Global Search for Cheap Labor," *Bloomberg Business*. July 22nd 2014. Available at: http://www.bloomberg.com/news/articles/2014-07-22/ethiopia-becomes-china-s-china-in-search-for-cheap-labor. [accessed 7 June 2017] Found in Nick Dyer-Witherford. *Cyber-Proletariat*. p. 170.

16 Karyotis, T. "Vio.Me: workers' control in the Greek crisis," *ROAR Magazine*. May 1st, 2014. Available at: http://roarmag.org/2014/05/viome-workers-control-greek-crisis/. [accessed 7 June 2017]

Chapter 10

The Ecological Cliff

...the application of technology to apparent problems of resource depletion or pollution or food shortage has no impact on the essential problem, which is exponential growth in a finite and complex system.

The Limits to Growth[1]

Startling as the preceding predictions might be, they might offer a ray of hope to the despondent radical. Capitalism, it seems, is doomed to collapse of its own internal contradictions, regardless of what the working class does in the meantime. Were it only so simple! We could just wait for capitalism to reach its inevitable limits and collapse, hoping that a new society would arise from its ashes. Such a strategy is more likely to give us ashes than a new world. The problem is that capitalism is not an abstract system constructed in the minds of economists. It exists in the actual world—abstract value is embodied in physical things like land, metal and oil. Capitalism cannot just expand forever in the abstract, it has to actually grow. Expanding value means expanding the physical resources that a society consumes. If a capitalist society wants GDP growth, it needs to consume more land, trees, metals, oil and so on, into infinity. When capitalism cannot cannibalize any more of the Earth, growth stops.

Capitalism is reaching natural limitations on its continued growth, both in the sphere of production, which is limited by the contradictions of the system, and in the sphere of ecology. *Even if the entire thesis of the previous pages were incorrect, and capitalist development is not an inherently contradictory process, capitalism would still face an insurmountable external contradiction.* It is no longer possible to believe in a future of limitless economic growth and certainly not a future of steady expansion at the rate of 3 per cent compounded annually. This is a problem because capitalism is incapable of dealing rationally or humanely with what is logically obvious to any thinking person: *one cannot squeeze infinite resources out of a finite world.*

An ecologically sustainable society is one which can continue its current patterns of consumption and production for a long period of time without serious disruptions. There are simple standards by which one can judge whether a society is ecologically sustainable. A sustainable society must replace nonrenewable resources with renewable resources faster than the nonrenewable resources are consumed. It must also consume renewable resources at a rate that does not exceed the speed at which they can be replenished. Overall, a society cannot exceed the carrying capacity of its environment for long without eventually heading toward collapse.

These are obvious and simple ideas, but they have serious implications. If metals, oil and land are limited nonrenewable resources, then a society that consumes them in infinitely rising quantities must eventually run out of them at some point. If the Earth can only absorb a certain amount of pollution from industrial production and that pollution rises without end, then it will not be able to cope with pollution in future years. If the biosphere can only contain so many greenhouse gases, and capital keeps spewing more and more of them into the atmosphere, then there will inevitably be catastrophic ecological consequences.

Technological changes can mitigate some of these problems. We can find substitutes for certain kinds of metals, new sources of energy or learn how to produce more food on less land. But technology cannot erase the simple fact that limitless growth is impossible in a finite system. Yet, capitalism needs limitless growth to survive. Accumulating profit—a surplus—requires producing and consuming more commodities every year. For capitalism to become a sustainable system, it would have to stop growing. Nothing in the history of capitalism suggests any of this is possible without causing the system to collapse, even though this basic condition has to be met for the sake of humanity's continued survival on this planet. Capitalist society is fundamentally unsustainable, regardless of whether labor theory accurately describes how the system works.

Capital thrives on unpaid costs. A company that dumps toxic waste into a river does not have to treat that waste as an expense, even though it imposes a cost on society as a whole. Someone will have to clean the waste up eventually and people in the area will probably get sick from the pollution. When we buy a car or a chicken, we do not typically pay for the emissions it took to produce the car or for the cost of cleaning up pollution from chicken waste. When a rig pumps oil out of the Earth's crust or a farm uses up the fertility of the soil, the owners do not have to pay the Earth for what they took. At most, they have to pay rent to a government or some other landowner. Capital does not take these costs into account. For example, plastics started to replace leather in products like shoes after World War II because plastics needed less labor to produce.

> To produce the same value of output, the plastics industry uses only about a quarter of the amount of labor used by leather manufacture, but it uses ten times as much capital and thirty times as much energy. The substitution of plastics for leather in the production of these items has therefore meant less demand for labor, more demand for capital and energy, and greater environmental pollution.[2]

Many industries would not be profitable if they actually had to pay for all of the damage they do to humanity and the planet. The state can regulate these "externalities," but given the fact that the rich and powerful generally dominate parliamentary politics, these regulations are almost always insufficient. Even though current limits on carbon emissions are totally incapable of avoiding catastrophic global warming in the 21st century, most governments are unwilling to restrict their industries to the extent that actually addressing the problem requires. If a particular government is not totally owned by the rich, it still depends on profits to fund its operations. There are comparatively few states that are willing to ban profitable industries and drive workers into unemployment, even if those industries are extraordinarily destructive.

The looming ecological cliff confronts 21st-century capitalism with an insurmountable problem. Either capitalism must die or it will wreck the ecosystem upon which humanity depends. Every year that capitalism survives represents another year of ecological damage that will be increasingly difficult to repair. Climate change will destabilize ecosystems, create rising sea levels and amplify natural disasters. Pollution and overfishing will devastate the world's oceans. Valuable resources will become more difficult to extract and human activity may ultimately overshoot the planet's capacity to sustain production. The human cost of these tremendous failures would be extreme. It will become more difficult to grow food in many places, fresh water will become scarcer and many of the world's most populous regions will become difficult to live in. Today's conflicts may seem quaint in a world of dwindling resources and massive refugee populations. To understand the depth of these challenges, we have to briefly look at where current trends are headed. Like the previous investigations, they reveal a system running headlong toward its limits.

Capital and Climate Change

Let's picture our future for a moment. By the end of the 21st century, much of the Arctic tundra and the ice caps will melt.

Deserts like the Sahara may expand in some areas, wiping out farmland in neighboring regions. The band of evergreen forests ranging from Canada to Siberia will recede, along with the temperate forests of Southern France, Northern Italy and much of Eastern Europe. The ecological makeup of areas like Alaska, Scotland and Norway will change completely as native plants and animals are squeezed out. All told, 40 per cent of the world's biomes—major communities of plants and animals—will shift within the century, causing a massive disruption of all species[3]

Numerous species will not be able to adapt to such a rapid change. Between 67 and 84 per cent of genetic biodiversity—the range of genetic variation in living beings—could be wiped out by 2080. As local climates and patterns of rainfall change, many crops will no longer grow where they have traditionally been planted. Climate change will strain farming communities, and it will force local cuisines to change when once plentiful plants and animals are no longer around. As sea levels rise, islands nations like the Maldives, Nauru and the Marshall Islands may be wiped out completely. Coastal areas, where most of the world's population lives, will gradually lose land to erosion and rising tides. Absent a giant system of dikes, much of New York City will be underwater. Poorer areas may not be so lucky.[4]

These predictions are based on the climate change forecasts of the Intergovernmental Panel on Climate Change (IPCC). Because the IPCC's reports require the consensus of scientists from all over the world, some climate scientists suggest that its forecasts are actually quite conservative. In fact, over the past decade the IPCC's "worst-case scenario" predictions of carbon emissions, temperature increases and melting ice caps have all been exceeded by reality.[5] The IPCC suggests that limiting global warming to around 2 degrees Celsius within the 21st century could stave off potentially catastrophic effects. The preceding paragraph was based on this 2-degree scenario. Terrible as the preceding paragraph may be, we are not on course for a 2-degree increase in the world's temperature. If current trends continue, the average temperature of the Earth will increase between 3.5 and 5 degrees Celsius by 2100.[6]

I do not want to go into too much detail on how devastating these levels of warming would be. I find it too depressing to dwell on for very long. Climate change is already proceeding faster than at any previous point in Earth's history, but warming over 3 degrees within the century would probably push human civilization to the brink of collapse. An increase of 4 degrees of warming would trigger massive crop failures, droughts, calamitous natural disasters, the collapse of most ice sheets and the thawing of the permafrost. As the permafrost melted it would release at least half a trillion tons of carbon into the atmosphere, causing runaway warming. The consequences for humanity would be dire and unavoidable: mass migrations away from the equator, rationing of basic goods like food and water, and waves of famine.[7]

Climate change is a normal part of the Earth's natural systems. All the things that appear timeless and stable to us — continents, climates, plants and animals—constantly change over millenia. Today's climate change is not like natural change. Energy from coal and oil powered the Industrial Revolution. Burning these power sources released carbon dioxide (CO_2) into the atmosphere. (Methane, another major greenhouse gas, is also released by fossil fuel extraction and livestock production.) Humanity raised the amount of CO_2 in the planet's atmosphere by 40 per cent from 1750 to 2015, increasing the amount of the sun's energy that would be trapped in the atmosphere instead of radiating into space.[8] This trapped energy turns into heat, causing climate change.

The same process that allowed capitalism to begin its runaway accumulation of value put humanity on a collision course with the planet's ecological limits. Capitalists got rich in part by dumping the waste from production into the atmosphere. Climate change accelerated from a glacial pace to the fastest rates in planetary history. The last time the Earth was 2 degrees colder on average, we were in the middle of an Ice Age. A mile-thick glacial sheet stretched all the way to New York from the North Pole. It took around 18,000 years to get from then to today's world. Today, we are on course for an equivalent level of warming in as little as a few decades.

Rapid climate change is particularly dangerous, because ecological systems do not gradually adapt to changing climate conditions. There are a series of tipping points that can cause rapid and drastic changes in biomes and weather patterns. When one part of an ecosystem declines or collapses, it often creates feedback mechanisms that disrupt other parts of that system. For example, warming of 1 to 2 degrees Celsius may cause a significant transformation in the Altiplano of the Bolivian Andes. As Lake Titicaca dries up owing to global warming, rainfall will diminish and the local climate will actually cool down. This could trigger a feedback mechanism that would turn the lake into a salt marsh. Ultimately, the Altiplano might turn from a viable agricultural region into a dry climate hostile to plant life. The Bolivian farmers who depend on the region's natural climate would be ruined.[9]

In order to keep warming below the 2-degree Celsius limit, we need to reduce carbon emissions. This does not mean we need to reduce the growth of emissions. We need to engineer an *absolute* decline in total global emissions and we need to do it very quickly. When economic activity creates carbon emissions, and it does, *any* economic growth means that carbon emissions will rise if all else holds equal. It takes resources and energy to produce virtually any commodity. Even "immaterial" services like counseling require computers and phones, which rely on electric lighting, power plants and mining.

Carbon emissions are closely correlated with economic growth—emissions fall during recessions and rise during recoveries. Unsurprisingly, the countries whose carbon emissions are growing fastest are those with rapid economic growth driven by industrialization. China is now the largest emitter of CO_2. Pinning the blame for climate change on the developing countries, however, is complete hypocrisy. Developed countries accumulated capital by producing colossal levels of emissions and Western capital fueled the rise of industrialization in the developing world. Western corporations and consumers who rely on Chinese goods are as responsible for "Chinese" emissions as the firms that create them.[10]

It is becoming very common for economists to reconcile economic growth and ecological stability by suggesting that capitalist economies pursue "green growth." In this fanciful model, growth and profits can actually be supported by transitioning to an ecologically sustainable economic model. These escapists argue that societies can boost demand while reducing emissions by promoting renewable energy, a service-oriented economy and more efficient resource use. This idea is a dangerous and misleading fallacy. The global economy became 23 per cent more efficient in terms of carbon emissions per dollar of GDP between 1980 and 2008, but total emissions still expanded rapidly, because global economic and population growth offset these gains. If the developing countries catch up to European GDP per capita standards by 2050, carbon intensity would have to fall to less than 1 per cent of its current level to meet the IPCC's targets. To achieve these targets while maintaining economic growth, we would immediately and permanently need to decouple carbon emissions from growth.[11]

This is even harder than it sounds. Under capitalism, making the production of energy more efficient tends to make people use it more. This is called the "rebound effect." When cars use fuel more efficiently, people tend to drive more because it becomes cheaper. Economic growth in the service sector still creates a lot of emissions. As stated earlier, service industries require a large base of carbon-heavy capital to function and people who work in service industries still need to consume things that produce emissions. If an economy is going to grow, these people need to consume more each year. US teachers buy goods from China and drive Japanese cars. Developed nations still produce the most carbon emissions per person because of the sheer quantity of goods they consume. Using more renewable energy is not going to resolve this problem, either. It takes a lot of resources to produce solar panels, wind turbines and the electric grids to support them, and the majority of fossil fuels are used for transportation. Until cargo ships, trucks and airplanes no longer run on oil, renewable energy is not going to miraculously halt emissions. A transition to renewable energy can reduce carbon emissions per unit of GDP, but this can easily be offset if economic growth outstrips these gains.[12]

The problem, then, is not just that the global economy is inefficient or wasteful in the way that it produces commodities. The problem is that economic growth *in general* creates more carbon emissions, even while energy production becomes more efficient. Green growth is an attractive idea, because it suggests that contemporary society can become ecologically sustainable without any major social or economic changes. Per usual, technology is made into a fetish capable of solving any ill. Absent an unforeseeable miracle technology that rapidly makes the carbon impact of economic growth negligible, there is simply no way that present patterns of growth and consumption can continue if we intend to limit global warming. It is naive and self-serving to think otherwise. Because the elite cannot foresee or abide any other economic system than capitalism, they are incapable of admitting that capitalism and ecological sustainability are fundamentally incompatible.

Climate change and capital will interact in both contradictory and mutually reinforcing ways throughout the 21st century. The contradictions are obvious. Mitigating climate change requires severe limitations on emissions, which imposes costs on every company that previously received a free ride while it dumped greenhouse gases into the atmosphere. Raising the cost of capital by requiring emissions controls should lower profits. Industries and individual capitalists often try to fight these regulations, either by preventing them from being implemented or by trying to secure exemptions. Despite this, there is a growing effort to address climate change, even from otherwise tepid reformists and conservatives. There are very few people who want to watch helplessly as their way of life is destroyed by runaway global warming. Most states feel pressured to at least appear to do something, spawning an endless series of conferences and agreements on climate change.

When I first wrote this chapter, representatives from most of the world were engaged in the latest phase of negotiations for an international agreement on climate change. The Paris talks were split along typical lines: developed and developing nations both want the other group to bear most of the burden of reducing global emissions.[13] This just reflected the basic reality we saw above. Reducing emissions will necessarily bring down profits for most industries and slow economic growth if all else holds equal. (On the other hand, the industries that sell emissions-control technologies and goods like solar panels will benefit.) There is almost no chance that the agreement reached in Paris will be able to keep global warming below the 2-degree limit. For that to happen, total carbon emissions have to level out immediately and start falling by 2020. The longer we wait to make these adjustments, the more difficult and costly it will be to mitigate climate change later on.

The first international climate negotiation, the Kyoto Protocol of 1992, helped to almost stabilize emissions in some regions (like Europe), but it was not nearly enough to reach the basic target. We already know that the 2015 pledges submitted in Paris will not meet the targets, either.[14] We should not expect any future agreements negotiated by governments that represent the interests of capital to perform any differently. For his part, US President Trump has already pulled out of the Paris Agreement. Most states will introduce certain restrictions, but they will be too gradual to have a meaningful impact. Tackling climate change requires a dramatic reorganization of society, as soon as possible, that brings humanity beyond the limits of capitalism.

Climate change may aid capital in some ways in the short run. Global warming will make natural disasters more severe. While the dynamics of weather patterns are complex, global warming tends to make wet areas wetter and dry areas drier. This increases the likelihood and damage of blizzards, floods, wildfires and droughts. As the temperature of the ocean increases, typhoons and hurricanes gather more energy. When sea levels rise, coastal areas become more vulnerable to flooding. Hurricane Sandy, which struck the Northeastern United States in 2012, caused $75 billion of destruction and 233 deaths. Hurricane Sandy was fueled by unusually high ocean temperatures, part of which were a direct result of man-made climate change. Additionally, rising sea levels owing to climate change made the storm surge much worse. Some scientists have suggested that New York's subways and tunnels would not have flooded without human-induced rising seas. Of course, the question of whether or not some particular extreme event is a result of global warming is the wrong one. There is only one atmosphere. By pumping more energy into this atmosphere and changing weather patterns, climate change impacts all of the weather on the planet.[15]

Perversely, disasters can actually be good for capitalism. A natural disaster destroys accumulated capital and creates new opportunities to make money. Disasters can also break up existing patterns of life and disrupt people's ability to resist assaults on their wellbeing. After Hurricane Katrina in 2005, New Orleans became a capitalist playground. Thanks to rampant speculation, real estate values and rents doubled, and even quadrupled in some neighborhoods. Public housing was turned over to private developers. The city's public schools and the University of New Orleans sustained a coordinated assault designed to deliver education over to neoliberal "reformers." New Orleans' public schools were completely privatized and all of the city's 4700 teachers were fired.[16] But even if environmental disasters aid capitalism by destroying accumulated wealth and paving the way for privatization, this will only contribute to system-wide instability. Rebuilding cities takes resources and energy, generating more emissions and pollution in the process.

Exhausting the Seas

Just as capitalist growth imperils the stability of our planet's climate, it also threatens to exhaust the world's oceans. Oceans make up most of the Earth's surface and most of the life on Earth lives in them. Humans have always had a productive relationship with the ocean. The seas are a source of sustenance and wealth. The oceans provide us with oxygen, fish, medicines, transportation and now even electrical power. Despite our incredible dependency on the Earth's oceans, capitalism is exploiting and polluting them to an unconscionable and unsustainable extent.

When CO_2 gets dumped into the atmosphere, it does not just impact the climate. As much as 30 per cent of it dissolves into the oceans. Algae absorbs some of this CO_2, using it to produce food and releasing oxygen as a byproduct. However, ocean life cannot absorb all of the CO_2 that humanity is producing. The excess CO_2 reacts with water to produce carbonic acid. As these reactions take place, the ocean becomes more acidic. This process is known as ocean acidification. Since the Industrial Revolution, the acidity of the ocean has increased around 30 per cent. Life is extremely sensitive to changes in the balance of acidity in water. Calcifiers—like corals, shellfish and small creatures known as pteropods—build their shells out of calcium in the ocean. Ocean acidification makes it harder for these animals to get calcium to build their shells, making them weak and vulnerable. Thus, even seemingly small changes in the balance of acidity in the oceans can make many the shells of many species dissolve, ultimately causing them to die.[17]

Ocean acidification is even worse than it initially sounds. Calcifiers are one of the most important foundations of the ocean's food chains, as many of the species caught in fisheries depend on them directly or indirectly for food, including commercially vital species like salmon, cod, herring and mackerel. Lobsters, crabs and other shellfish (all calcifiers) are also extraordinarily important to many cultures and the fishing industry. Coral reefs support the most diverse marine populations in the ocean, providing nurseries and food sources for huge numbers of species. They also protect shorelines from erosion and natural disasters.

Studies are starting to show that fish growth and reproduction will probably be directly harmed by an increasingly acidic and CO_2-heavy ocean.[18] We are already seeing the impacts of acidification on ocean life. Since 2005, oyster farms on the US Pacific Coast have been having difficulty raising oysters, which is a direct result of acidification. Coral reef growth is also slowing down as acidification, pollution and warming waters take their toll. If ocean acidification continues to worsen, as it inevitably will if CO_2 emissions keep rising, the damage to ocean life will be severe.[19]

Oceans support the livelihoods of 10–12 per cent of the world's working population by providing jobs in fishing and related industries.[20] Fish and shellfish are the main source of protein for around a billion people worldwide and they are one of the healthiest sources of protein even for those who do not rely on them completely.[21] This resource is under threat. Fish populations are being depleted by chronic overfishing and environmental pressures. Around 85 per cent of the world's fish stocks are are overexploited, depleted, fully exploited or recovering from disastrous exploitation. Overexploitation means that fish numbers will decline, as reproduction cannot keep up with fishing.

States often worsen this trend by heavily subsidizing massive fishing fleets that would otherwise not be able to pursue declining numbers of fish. Instead of encouraging conservation, countries like Spain are ensuring the ultimate destruction of their own fishing industries. Thanks to these short-sighted policies, swathes of the Mediterranean and the North Sea are virtual deserts almost entirely devoid of fish.[22]

Pressures on fish populations are only going to get much worse if present trends continue. Many fish stocks could collapse by the middle of the 21st century.[23] Ocean acidification will compound overfishing by decreasing vital food sources. As the concentration of CO_2 in the oceans and fresh water increases, algae will multiply. Algae feed on CO_2, which can help to balance carbon emissions. However, too much algae can create toxic algae blooms or "red tides." Elevated numbers of algae can also create dead zones, where fish and other species cannot survive. As CO_2 levels increase and run-off nutrients from farms rise, algae grow in excessive levels in areas like the entry to the Mississippi Delta. The algae initially produce oxygen, but when they die and decompose in large numbers oxygen gets sucked out of the water by other microorganisms. These low-oxygen zones kill fish, which need oxygen to breathe. Ocean dead zones are already getting worse and this will only continue as climate change progresses.[24]

Climate change also causes the oceans to warm up as they absorb heat from the atmosphere. Aquatic life is as sensitive to temperature as it is to acidity and the survival of some critical species, like Antarctic krill, may be threatened by rising temperatures. Warming seas hurt coral reefs by forcing them to expel symbiotic algae, transforming them into dead, bleached white husks.[25] Global warming of just 2 degrees Celsius is likely to destroy almost all of the world's coral reefs. Rising sea temperatures also produce more extreme weather like hurricanes and blizzards.

An equally serious threat to humanity is rising sea levels caused by warming seas. First, warming seas speed up the pace at which the ice sheets in the Arctic and Antarctic melt. Secondly, water expands as it gets hotter, so that the oceans increase in volume when they warm. Most of the world's population lives less than 100 miles from the coast and increasing numbers of people live in coastal cities. If carbon emissions continue as usual, sea levels could rise 1 to 2 meters (and possibly even more) by 2100. This would subject around 177 million people to regular flooding, seriously threatening the viability of life in many coastal areas. Most of these people are in Asia. More than a quarter of the population of Vietnam would be threatened by regular flooding, along with over 50 million Chinese residents.[26] Some areas will copy the model of the Netherlands and build dikes to protect high-value areas like major cities. However, it is hard to believe that it will be possible to protect the entirety of the world's coast from rising seas. To escape constant flooding, coastal populations will flood inland.

Our Finite World

In 1972, a group of scientists produced a report called *The Limits to Growth*. In the report, they suggested that the natural limits of arable land and resources would be outstripped by economic growth in the 21st century if contemporary trends continued. Many capitalists hold up this work as an example of environmental catastrophism or misguided panic based on faulty assumptions.[27] These arguments are typically based on deliberate misreadings of the report, which misconstrue it as stating that the world system would collapse by the end of the 20th century. If these individuals actually took time to read *Limits*, they might have noticed that its predictions have been largely confirmed.

As Graham Turner wrote in 2014, the simulation used in the paper has been remarkably accurate up until the present day. From 1970 to 2010, reality largely corresponded to the model that *Limits* authors described as "business as usual" or a society that made no major modifications to pursue sustainability. Global population, industrial output per capita, food production, pollution and estimates of remaining nonrenewable resources all broadly tracked this scenario.[28] This does not necessarily mean that the future will proceed exactly as the model suggests, but it does demonstrate important concerns that need to be addressed if human society is to become ecologically sustainable.

The basic contradiction identified by *The Limits to Growth* is the one I highlighted at the beginning of this chapter. Infinite growth in physical consumption is not possible on a finite planet.[29] If population grows without end, more resources will have to be used to support the standard of living that people expect. If per capita growth continues, then more nonrenewable resources will have to be consumed. Even if 100 per cent of goods are recycled, which would be both unrealistic and extremely energy intensive, endless growth must inevitably outstrip the reserves of resources on this planet. If pollution—as discussed previously—continues to rise, then this will inevitably trigger negative feedback mechanisms that force economic growth and resource consumption to fall.

Fishing industries cannot exist if there are no fish and spending money on adaptation to climate change diverts it from being invested elsewhere in the economy. *Limits* helpfully shows how negative and positive feedback loops can impact global development. For example, if an increasing population fuels further industrial production, then resource consumption can rise very quickly. On the other hand, if industrial production requires so many nonrenewable resources that it becomes increasingly expensive to extract those resources, then investment will be diverted from production to resource extraction.

We often hear about "peak oil" and various other peaks of a wide variety of critical resources. What this seems to suggest is that the Earth will literally run out of oil or copper or gold in the near future. While this is certainly true over the very long run, it is actually quite misleading. The issue in economics is not whether something can be extracted hypothetically, but at what cost. Vast quantities of many of the world's most important nonrenewable resources—aluminum, copper, rare earth minerals and oil—are scattered throughout the Earth's crust in tiny concentrations. If productive copper mines were to be exhausted, theoretically it would be possible to get copper from these other sources. Something similar has been happening in recent years with the emergence of fracking as a way of producing oil. Chinese rare earth mineral refineries are another example—rare earth minerals are really not that rare, it is simply the case that most countries are unwilling to invest the money and accept the environmental damages required to extract them.

As the global economy continues to grow, as it must if capitalism is to survive, then more nonrenewable resources are going to be consumed every year. When this rising consumption starts to exhaust cheaper sources of resources, companies will start to produce them in more expensive ways. In and of itself, this expense includes higher requirements of energy, nonrenewable resources and capital. When it takes more investment to extract the same resource, the price of that resource rises. For example, fracking is currently uneconomic when the price of oil is lower than $70 a barrel. Absent technological innovation, an economy that depends heavily on fracking is not going to be able to get oil cheaper than $70 a barrel. Higher resource costs suppress the profits of all capitalists except the rentiers who own oil fields and mines. This price can also be measured in environmental terms. If it takes more energy to extract resources, then carbon emissions and other forms of pollution will rise. As the capitalist economy adapts to keep these resources flowing, it also undermines its future by fueling global warming.

Capitalist price signals are totally counterproductive from a social standpoint, as they are incapable of accounting for long-term environmental costs. For instance, when oil prices rise owing to scarcity, this makes it profitable for oil companies to extract oil by drilling in the Arctic and fracking. Rising oil prices should tell people to use less oil, but it also prompts oil companies to pull more of it from the earth, including reserves that simply cannot be burned if we want to limit global warming. When reserves are plentiful and energy is cheap, people and companies use more of it. China, for instance, has many years of cheap coal readily available in the ground. Why should Chinese capitalists stop burning coal when cheap energy is such a critical component of economic growth? By the time coal prices rose to levels that would encourage a switch to other energy sources, the Earth would already be condemned to catastrophic global warming. There is simply no way one can expect capitalist pricing to tell people to stop using resources even if the long-term environmental costs of that use exceed its benefits.

There are real ecological limits to growth in the 21st century. This is no place for a simplistic prediction of resource exhaustion or population growth outpacing the food supply. Instead, we should acknowledge a simple truth: continued economic growth will place rising strains on the Earth's ability to sustain our way of life. We can shift these strains around by investing more energy in extracting nonrenewable resources, but we will create more emissions in the process. We can cut emissions radically to forestall future catastrophe, but this will impose a cost on today's capitalists. This is a circle that cannot be squared. Unless economic growth can be completely decoupled from resource consumption and pollution—and this remains to be demonstrated—continuous compounding growth will only push us further toward the brink of disaster. The alternative to this truth is the willful blindness of today's plutocrats. Gesturing at vague yet-to-materialize technologies has no impact on the real and already-present costs of ecological damage.[30] We have to be honest about the challenge facing humanity, which may rank higher than any other problem in human history. In order to sustain private profit, capitalism is sending us headlong toward ecological disaster.

Capitalism is Barbarism

When Rosa Luxemburg suggested that her society faced a choice between socialism and barbarism, she was right. The two world wars wreaked unimaginable devastation on the world, killing millions of people and laying waste to fields, factories and cities. The monstrous crimes of the fascist governments shook the world's confidence in humanity's relative capacity for good and evil. Yet, capitalism was saved. This destruction paved the way for decades of rapid growth and full employment. Capitalism emerged from barbarity stronger than ever.

Today, such a solution seems more unlikely, though the peril of fascism is re-emerging. The slow disintegration of capitalist societies is creating a new wave of reactionary politics. This reactionary impulse is equally the property of self-identified fascists and polite liberals who struggle to keep out refugees while fueling imperialist wars abroad. But contemporary capitalism faces greater challenges today than those it faced during the Great Depression. Labor is being expelled from production, capital accumulation is proceeding toward global rather than local limits and the world is headed off an ecological cliff from which there can be no return. For Luxemburg, barbarism meant mass murder. For us, it means mass murder and the devastation of our world. Barbarism isn't a unique form of society. It is capitalism reaching its heights of power and capitalism heading toward collapse. In many ways, it is all too ordinary. What could be more normal today than the rapacious destruction of a natural world we once considered sacred, or callous disregard for human life outside the narrow confines of the nation state?

Our relationship with nature and our relationships with each other are inextricably linked. As Murray Bookchin wrote, "if we are faced with the prospect of outright ecological catastrophe, toward which so many knowledgeable people and institutions claim we are headed today, it is because the historic domination of human by human has been extended outward from society into the natural world."[31] Capitalism is founded on a dual oppression—the ruthless exploitation of the working class and the Earth. It is based on a warped system of values that can only conceive of human beings and nature as instruments for making money.

This idolization of domination has poisoned our culture. Nothing characterizes the pathology of the elite more than a profound resentment of everything that resists their mastery. A ruling class that treats other human beings as objects for degradation cannot help but degrade the natural world. This ideology of domination and resentment permeates our society. Racism, patriarchy, homophobia and antisemitism—the pillars of fascist and nationalist thought—are delusional expressions of a desire to found one's fragile dignity on the domination of the Other. Nature suffers equally from this pathology. We have been deluded into believing that humanity can "master nature," ruling over it like a petulant little toddler.

One cannot master nature any more than one can shackle the sun or abolish gravity. Humanity does not stand above and apart from nature—it is part of it. We depend on the ecosystem to furnish all of our basic needs, including food, clean water, breathable air and every natural resource. At least 30 per cent of crops and 90 per cent of wild plants need natural pollinators like bees to survive, and yet our use of pesticides has caused an unprecedented collapse of the bee population.[32] Air pollution in the industrial regions of China has reached staggering proportions, leading to all kinds of terrible health problems. Communities in the coal-producing regions of West Virginia, where coal ash and other chemicals leach into the soil and water, have cancer rates double that of nearby areas.[33] Damage done to nature is always damage done to ourselves.

Humanity as we know it cannot survive an ecosystemic collapse, but capitalism is still driving us headlong into unmitigated disaster. We have to realize that we are part of a coherent whole—the global ecosystem—which we must cooperate with and learn from if we are to survive and thrive. By contrast, life on this planet does not require humanity for its continued survival. Even in the event of total nuclear war, which would wipe out humanity completely, seeds and other traces of life would live on and recolonize the planet. Nature is indifferent to our ultimate fate and we should not delude ourselves into thinking that it will prevent our self-destruction.

That I even have to couch the argument in these terms demonstrates the corrosive effect that capitalism has on our values. Instead of arguing that clean air and beautiful natural spaces are a good in themselves, environmentalists are being forced to frame nature as a force of production. There are a proliferation of papers that attempt to measure the dollar value of the services that nature provides to capital, putting a price tag on something that simply cannot be valued. The alternative to capitalism's waste and destruction cannot be based on the law of value. It must be founded on an affirmation of life. To triumph over barbarism, we need to go beyond just slashing emissions and pollution to save ourselves. We need to transform our relationship with the world and transform ourselves in the process. We must revalue our values.

The question facing us is not just whether we want to save jobs for fishermen, avoid the devastation of coastal communities or protect farming from a changing climate. It is a question of what kind of world we want to live in. Do we want to live in a world where our favorite crops have to be replaced by select genetically modified organisms designed to withstand higher temperatures? Do we want to live in a world where salmon, lobster and killer whales are replaced by jellyfish and algae blooms? Do we want to live in a world where our favorite wild places and ecosystems are irreversibly damaged by a changing climate? Again, the question is simple: Will we impoverish the world and ourselves or will we rise to the challenge of this century? We cannot have any illusions that addressing this problem is possible within the capitalist framework. It isn't. By its very nature, capitalism must run roughshod over the planet's natural limits. When we dwell on these questions for long, we come to an inevitable conclusion: another world is not just possible, another world is necessary.

Endnotes

1   Meadows, D., Meadows, D., Randers, J., Behrens III, W. (1972) *The Limits to Growth.* (New York: Universe Books) p. 145. Available at:http://www.donellameadows.org/wp-content/userfiles/Limits-to-Growth-digital-scan-version. pdf. [accessed 7 June 2017]

2   Bellamy Foster, J. (1999) "The four laws of ecology and the four anti-ecological laws of capitalism," from *The Vulnerable Planet.* Available at: http://climateandcapitalism. com/2012/04/02/four-laws/. [accessed 7 June 2017]

3   Bergengren, J., Waliser, D., and Yung, Y. (August 2011) "Ecological sensitivity: a biospheric view of climate change," *Climate Change*, Vol. 103, No. 3. pp. 433–57. Available at: http://link.springer.com/content/ pdf/10.1007%2Fs10584-011-0065-1.pdf. [accessed 7 June

2017]

4   Bálint, M., Domisch, S., Engelhardt, C.H.M., Haase, P., Lehrian, S., Sauer, J., Theissinger, K., Pauls, S.U., and Nowak, C. (July 2011) "Cryptic biodiversity loss linked to global climate change," *Nature Climate Change*, Vol. 1. pp. 313–17. Available at: ftp://norbif.uio.no/pub/outgoing/runeho/KR/Vali&al11NatureCkimCh1-313.pdf. [accessed 7 June 2017]

5   Scherer, G. "How the IPCC Underestimated Climate Change," *Scientific American*. December 6th, 2012. Available at: http://www.scientificamerican.com/article/how-the-ipcc-underestimated-climate-change/. [accessed 7 June 2017]

6   Peters, G., Andrew, R., Boden, T., Canadell, J., Ciais, P., Le Quéré, C., Marland, G., Raupach, M., and Wilson, C. (January 2013) "The challenge to keep global warming below 2 °C," *Nature Climate Change*, Vol. 3. pp. 4–6. Available at: http://bit.ly/1OMoEQ1. [accessed 7 June 2017]

7   Thanks to Charles Rodda for introducing me to the *Climate Reanalyzer* while I sat in on a discussion at the University of Maine. The Reanalyzer is a remarkable tool that allows one to project the likely impact of climate change on biomes and natural systems, and I highly recommend it. Climate Change Institute at the University of Maine. *Climate Reanalyzer*, Available at: http://cci-reanalyzer.org/ECM/. [accessed 7 June 2017]; Pidcock, R. "What happens if we overshoot the two degree limit for limiting global warming?," *Carbon Brief*. December 10th, 2014. Available at: http://www.carbonbrief.org/what-happens-if-we-overshoot-the-two-degree-target-for-limiting-global-warming/. [accessed 7 June 2017]; Plumer, B. "We're on pace for 4°C of global warming. Here's why that terrifies the World Bank," *The Washington Post*. November 19th, 2012. Available at: http://www.washingtonpost.com/news/wonkblog/wp/2012/11/19/were-on-pace-for-4c-of-global-warming-heres-why-the-world-bank-is-terrified/. [accessed 7 June 2017]

8   Again, my thanks to Charles Rodda for offering the Andean climate as an example of non-linear climate change. Blasing, T.J. (February 2014) "Recent Greenhouse Gas Concentrations," *Carbon Dioxide Information Analysis Center.* Available at: http://cdiac.ornl.gov/pns/current_ghg.html. [accessed 7 June 2017]

9   Bush, M.B., Hanselman, J.A., and Gosling, W.D. (December 2010) "Nonlinear climate change and Andean feedbacks: an imminent turning point?" *Global Change Biology,* Vol. 16, No. 12.

10   Goldenberg, S. "CO_2 emissions are being 'outsourced' by rich countries to rising economies," *The Guardian.* January 19th, 2014. Available at: http://www.theguardian.com/environment/2014/jan/19/co2-emissions-outsourced-rich-nations-rising-economies. [accessed 7 June 2017]

11   Hoffman, U. (July 2015) "Can Green Growth Really Work and What Are The True (Socio-) Economics of Climate Change?" *United Nations Conference on Trade and Development Discussion Papers,* No. 222. Available at: http://unctad.org/en/PublicationsLibrary/osgdp2015d4_en.pdf. [accessed 7 June 2017]

12   Ibid.

13   Clark, P. "Climate talks fail to break deadlock," *Financial Times.* October 23rd, 2015. Available at: http://www.ft.com/intl/cms/s/0/c31543fe-79a2-11e5-933d-efcdc3c11c89.html. [accessed 7 June 2017]

14   Plumer, B. "The math on staying below 2°C of global warming looks increasingly brutal," *Vox.* October 19th, 2015. Available at: http://www.vox.com/2015/10/19/9567863/climate-change-ambitious-cuts. [accessed 7 June 2017]; Plumer, B. "Two degrees: How the world failed on climate change," *Vox.* April 22nd, 2014. Available at: http://www.vox.com/2014/4/22/5551004/two-degrees. [accessed 7 June 2017]

15   Trenberth, K., Fasullo, J., and Shepherd, T. (August 2015)

"Attribution of climate extreme events," *Nature Climate Change*, Vol. 5. pp. 725–729. Available at: http://bit.ly/1OYj6Aq. [accessed 7 June 2017]; Abraham, J. "New study links Hurricane Sandy to climate change and other extreme weather events," *The Guardian*. June 22nd, 2015. Available at: http://www.theguardian.com/environment/climate-consensus-97-per-cent/2015/jun/22/new-study-links-global-warming-to-hurricane-sandy-and-other-extreme-weather-events. [accessed 7 June 2017]

16 Adams, T.J. "How the Ruling Class Remade New Orleans," *Jacobin*. August 29th, 2015. Available at: https://www.jacobinmag.com/2015/08/hurricane-katrina-ten-year-anniversary-charter-schools/. [accessed 7 June 2017]; Walters, J. "A Guide to Hurricane Katrina and Its Aftermath," *Jacobin*. August 28th, 2015. Available at: https://www.jacobinmag.com/2015/08/hurricane-katrina-bush-gulf-new-orleans-climate-change-racism-fema/. [accessed 7 June 2017]

17 Harrould-Kolieb, E., Huelsenbeck, M., and Selz, V. (November 2010) "Ocean Acidification: The Untold Stories." *Oceana*. Available at: http://oceana.org/sites/default/files/reports/Ocean_Acidification_The_Untold_Stories.pdf. [accessed 7 June 2017]

18 Johnson, S. "Fish unable to rapidly adapt to ocean acidification," *Ars Technica*. October 10th, 2014. Available at: http://arstechnica.com/science/2014/10/fish-unable-to-rapidly-adapt-to-ocean-acidification/. [accessed 7 June 2017]

19 Harrould-Kolieb, E., Huelsenbeck, M., and Selz, V. "Ocean Acidification: The Untold Stories."

20 Food and Agriculture Organization of the United Nations. (2012) *The State of World Fisheries and Aquaculture*. p. 10. Available at: http://www.fao.org/docrep/016/i2727e/i2727e.pdf. [accessed 7 June 2017]

21 World Health Organization. "Availability and consumption of fish," in *Global and regional food consumption patterns and*

trends, accessed October 24th, 2015. Available at: http://www. who.int/nutrition/topics/3_foodconsumption/en/index5. html.

22   Vince, G. "How the world's oceans could be running out of fish," *BBC*. September 12th, 2012. Available at: http://www. bbc.com/future/story/20120920-are-we-running-out-of-fish. [accessed 7 June 2017]; Harvey, F. "Tuna and mackerel populations suffer catastrophic 74% decline, research shows," *The Guardian*. September 15th, 2015. Available at: http://www.theguardian.com/environment/2015/sep/15/ tuna-and-mackerel-populations-suffer-catastrophic-74-decline-research-shows. [accessed 7 June 2017]

23   Plumer, B. "Just how badly are we overfishing the oceans?" *The Washington Post*. October 29th, 2013. Available at: http:// www.washingtonpost.com/news/wonkblog/wp/2013/10/29/ just-how-badly-are-we-overfishing-the-ocean/. [accessed 7 June 2017]

24   Zielinski, S. "Ocean Dead Zones Are Getting Worse Globally Due to Climate Change," *Smithsonian Magazine*. November 10th, 2014. Available at: http://www.smithsonianmag. com/science-nature/ocean-dead-zones-are-getting-worse-globally-due-climate-change-180953282/?no-ist. [accessed 7 June 2017]

25   Innis, M. "Warming Oceans May Threaten Krill, a Cornerstone of the Antarctic Ecosystem," *The New York Times*. October 19th, 2015. Available at: http://www.nytimes. com/2015/10/20/science/australia-antarctica-krill-climate-change-ocean.html. [accessed 7 June 2017]; Markey, S. "Global Warming Has Devastating Effects on Coral Reefs, Study Shows," *National Geographic News*. May 16th, 2006. Available at: http://news.nationalgeographic.com/ news/2006/05/warming-coral.html. [accessed 7 June 2017]

26   Jones, N. "Rising Waters: How Fast and How Far Will Sea Levels Rise?" *Yale Environment 360*. October 21st, 2013.

Available at: http://e360.yale.edu/feature/rising_waters_
how_fast_and_how_far_will_sea_levels_rise/2702/.
[accessed 7 June 2017]; Neumann, B., Vafeidis, A.,
Zimmerman, J., and Nicholls, R. (March 2015) "Future
Coastal Population Growth and Exposure to Sea-Level Rise
and Coastal Flooding – A Global Assessment," *PLoS One*,
Vol. 10, No. 3. Available at: http://www.ncbi.nlm.nih.gov/
pmc/articles/PMC4367969/. [accessed 7 June 2017]; Aisch,
G., Leonhardt, D., and Quealy, K. "Flooding Risk From
Climate Change, Country by Country," *The New York Times*.
September 23rd, 2014. Available at: http://www.nytimes.
com/2014/09/24/upshot/flooding-risk-from-climate-change-
country-by-country.html. [accessed 7 June 2017]

27 For example, see the following useful idiot: Lomborg, B.
"The Limits of Panic," *Slate*. June 26th, 2013. Available at:
http://www.slate.com/articles/business/project_syndic
ate/2013/06/climate_panic_ecological_collapse_is_not_
upon_us_and_we_haven_t_run_out.html. [accessed 7 June
2017]

28 Turner, G. "Is Global Collapse Imminent?" *MSSI
Research Paper No. 4.* (August 2014) Available at: http://
sustainable.unimelb.edu.au/sites/default/files/docs/MSSI-
ResearchPaper-4_Turner_2014.pdf. [accessed 7 June 2017]

29 Harnessing the vast resources available in outer space would
meaningfully eliminate this contradiction, but this is not a
reasonable response to resource constraints at the moment.
For space to replenish Earth's diminished resources, it
would have to become economically feasible to extract and
transport billions of tons of metals and other resources from
sources within the solar system to our planet. Even if space
travel becomes more common, it will likely be a long time
before this is possible.

30 Compare the techno-optimism of today's capitalist
apologists to the discussion of technology in the first section

of this book. The analysis of the first section was deliberately limited to technologies that already exist and work. Extant technologies still often take decades to become widely used. Similar questions can be applied to any "miracle technology" that will supposedly save us from ecological limits: Where are these technologies? How do they work? How much do they cost? Can we reasonably expect them to be implemented in time to avert serious damage?

31 Bookchin, M. (2015) "The Ecological Crisis and the Need to Remake Society," in *The Next Revolution*. (New York: Verso) p. 31.

32 Sass, J. (March 2011) "Why We Need Bees: Nature's Tiny Workers Put Food on Our Tables," *Natural Resource Defense Council*. Available at: https://www.nrdc.org/wildlife/animals/files/bees.pdf. [accessed 7 June 2017]

33 Ward Jr., K. "Study finds increased cancer rates near Coal River mine sites," *Charleston Gazette-Mail*. July 27th, 2011. Available at: http://www.wvgazettemail.com/News/201107271037. [accessed 7 June 2017]

Part III

The Coming Revolution

Each generation must out of relative obscurity discover its mission, fulfill it, or betray it.

Frantz Fanon, *The Wretched of the Earth*

Chapter 11

What is to be Done?

Capitalism in the 21st century faces three major contradictions, each of which might be significant enough on its own to cause its collapse. Capitalism accumulates wealth by exploiting labor, but it is making labor increasingly obsolete. Capitalism requires monopolistic control of the means of production by one class, but it is creating a new production paradigm that will permanently erode monopoly production. Finally, capitalism requires infinite growth, but we live on a finite planet. We are witnessing the simultaneous development and intensification of each of these contradictions. I do not believe that they can be resolved within the capitalist framework. Therefore, the collapse of capitalism within the 21st century is very likely.

Overcoming these tremendous challenges will require a revolutionary reconstruction of society. In order to move beyond the contradictions of capitalism, we must create an economic system based on the fulfillment of genuine needs and liberation from toil, rather than private profit and the accumulation of value. We must adapt to radical automation and the rise of distributed production without producing mass unemployment or unconscionable inequality. We must evolve beyond crass materialism and create a way of life that exists in balance with our planet's ecosystem. Finally, we have to dismantle the systems of oppression that buttress the status quo, and replace them with social systems that guarantee actual freedom and equality to every person on Earth.

It is time for the radical Left to reorient its vision. We have to conduct an honest assessment of today's world and build a strategy based on this assessment. We are not living in proto-industrial Czarist Russia, industrializing Britain, or Europe during the collapse of the post-war order. We are living during the last great period of global capitalist expansion. Most of the world has been integrated into the world market and the industrial working class is dwindling in the world's wealthiest countries. We can already see the beginning of the end of living labor as a source of value and with it the end of the law of value itself. The political and technological foundations of these facts make today's capitalism more powerful than that of any previous generation. However, the uniqueness of our era also provides tremendous opportunities. Put simply, we have already reached a level of economic and technological development that will allow us to eliminate material want, burdensome labor, and social and political inequality. These possibilities are immanent in the very machines that today threaten to throw us into unemployment and destitution.

As stated earlier, the question that faces us is how we can reconstruct our society in a way that eliminates the contradictions of capitalism. I do not have the final answers to this question. I have no tablets to bring down from the mountaintop. But it is long past time to start debating and reworking our strategies. One might expect that the turmoil and unrest of the previous years would have created a renaissance in radical thought. On the contrary, much of the Left remains devoid of a coherent strategy for radical change, and has fallen back time and again on nostalgic appeals to 20th-century reforms. This problem is particularly acute in Europe and the US. After years of crisis it should be clear that a return to the conditions of the past is neither possible nor desirable.

In this sense, I hope that the following proposals provide a small starting point for today's radical movement. I propose five basic ideas that should be embraced by any modern revolutionary movement:

1. Labor hours should be progressively reduced to eliminate

unemployment and increase free time, until we reach the point where necessary labor has been abolished.

2. The means of production should be socialized, so that working people own and control their own workplaces and direct production across the entire economy democratically. A comprehensive social system should be established to provide social security, education, healthcare and the means to live a dignified life to all.

3. Debts should be abolished. The vast majority of mortgage, consumer, student and sovereign debts should be forgiven as part of a global jubilee, which will be feasible only with the socialization of the financial system.

4. The state—including the bureaucracy, military, police and the prison system—should be dismantled and replaced with a direct, radical democracy responsible for political decision-making and the administration of public affairs.

5. Society should establish a comprehensive system for managing production and consumption that ensures that humanity lives in balance with the planet's ecological limits. Carbon emissions and pollution should level off and then be reduced, nonrenewable resources should be replaced by renewable resources wherever possible, and relatively unspoiled ecosystems should be protected from encroachment and destruction.

Reduce Labor Hours

Labor is dying. As a system of distribution and a way of life, wage labor is being steadily eroded by today's technological developments. Capitalist society is so dependent on the social construct of labor that panic is the normal response to this trend. Virtually every day we see frantic new schemes for creating jobs: offering wages for housework or Facebook posts, paying citizens to perform community service and so on. Watching these attempts to save labor is like watching a child on the beach trying to save his sandcastle by stopping the tide. It is time to stop clinging to the past and start adapting to reality. We can adapt to this process with a simple but powerful tool: reducing the amount of time that workers are required to work without a reduction in pay.

For example, a country with a standard 40-hour workweek could reduce its workweek to 30 hours. Every worker would work 10 fewer hours while taking home the same pay. Firms would have to make up for this deficit of work hours by making their current workers more efficient—by rationalizing production or introducing labor-saving machinery—or by hiring more workers. This is a win-win scenario for working-class people. At the very least, workers have to work less, giving them more free time to spend with their friends and family, and to pursue their own interests. Any increased demand for more laborers will reduce unemployment, reduce poverty and raise the bargaining power of workers by reducing the pool of possible replacements.

The reduction of labor hours should be the cornerstone of any radical strategy for reorganizing the socioeconomic structure of society. First, reducing labor hours is the only sustainable way to compensate for a long-term decline in the demand for labor. As we have seen in previous chapters, a decline in the demand for labor is presently experienced as a disaster for working-class communities. Steady jobs evaporate, often only to be replaced by precarious, part-time and poorly paid work. Some people are forced to work long hours of overtime to make due, while others cannot find any paying work at all. Traditionally, this problem is addressed by either constantly increasing the amount of goods a society produces or through the state employing workers unproductively.[1] The first will inevitably fail. We live on a finite planet, which cannot tolerate the limitless expansion of production. Secondly, history suggests that the demand for goods is likely not infinitely elastic—there is actually a point at which markets become saturated. Finally, unproductive state employment creates a rising tide of debt that must eventually be redeemed by value-producing labor if the state is to avoid default.

A shortage of opportunities to employ labor profitably is the very thing that unproductive employment is intended to compensate for, which suggests that over the long run debts will inflate to unsustainable levels. Instead of pursuing these fruitless paths, we can eliminate unemployment and underemployment by equitably distributing the available work.[2]

Secondly, reducing labor hours turns surplus value appropriated by capitalists back into free time for working people, reducing the rate of exploitation. Any reduction in the workday lessens the surplus time that workers give to the capitalist for free. For example, say it takes a worker 4 hours out of an 8-hour workday to produce the commodities whose value equals what is necessary to support their family. Reducing the length of the workday to 6 hours still allows the worker to support themselves, but it slashes the surplus time in half. Instead of working 2 extra hours for the capitalist's benefit, the worker now has 2 extra hours every workday to use as they sees fit. Of course, capitalists will vigorously object to any attempt to reduce the length of the workday, since unpaid labor time is the source of profits. This is not a bad thing. The struggle to reduce labor hours clearly reveals the direct contradiction between the interests of capitalists and working people, and any success pushes capitalism further toward dissolution.

Thirdly, reducing labor hours invests rising levels of productivity in increased free time, not in producing an endlessly rising tide of commodities. As we now know, limitless economic growth will lead to catastrophic climate change, making our world much more hostile to human life. When productivity rises, we can choose either to produce more goods in the same amount of time or to produce the same amount of goods in less time. Those of us who live in the developed world are not suffering from a lack of goods—if anything, complete abundance is only prevented by the distributive injustices and artificial scarcity created by the capitalist system. It is time to stop investing in an endless stream of useless commodities that can never satisfy our fundamental desires to create, explore and connect with one another. Instead, we should use our technological advances to free ourselves from the burden of work, giving us precious time to pursue what we want.

Finally, the reduction of labor hours is a progressive process that ultimately leads to the creation of a society in which the compulsion to labor has been permanently eliminated. Reducing labor time is not a one-time fix for a temporary problem. It is a political technique that can be used to replace an economic system based on the law of value—capitalism—with an economic system based on freedom and the fulfillment of human needs—communism. By continuously reducing labor hours, production for profit can be abolished by eliminating surplus value. As productivity continues to rise and as non-market alternatives to market production continue to develop, labor time—or waged work—can ultimately be reduced to zero. A society without labor will finally shatter the law of value. Work, rather than being compelled by the need to earn a wage, would be purely voluntary, and goods would simply be distributed and used on the basis of need. This is not a utopian fantasy. Given contemporary technological developments and social trends, it is both feasible and necessary. I will outline how this can be accomplished in further detail later.

Every economist and social theorist who seriously examines the problem of automation agrees that labor time must be reduced. This includes unapologetic capitalists like Keynes and Rifkin. Every reduction of labor hours is a further step toward the abolition of labor and the abolition of meaningful scarcity itself. Thus, everyone who seriously considers the effects of automation agrees that the movement toward the eventual abolition of capitalism is both necessary and inevitable, even including some capitalists. The question, then, is how this movement can be advanced given the political, social and technical conditions of our time.

A successful program to reduce labor hours must abide by certain rules. Any cuts in labor hours must be hard cuts. When France reduced its work week to 35 hours, employers reportedly responded by speeding up production and expanding overtime. Today, French workers average 39.5 hours of labor a week thanks to the numerous loopholes allowed by the law.[3] Workers in many countries already work a substantial number of overtime hours, because it is often cheaper for employers than hiring new workers. If the burden of labor is to be fairly distributed in our society, overtime pay must be substantially more expensive than regular work hours, at least three to four times higher. Otherwise, firms will find it more lucrative in most instances to avoid hiring new workers by forcing existing employees to work overtime or work at unhealthy speeds. Even with these regulations any reform of capitalism, including reducing labor hours, will run into difficulties so long as its implementation remains in the hands of capitalists.

The size of a proposed reduction in labor time should reflect the economic conditions in a given society: its level of technological and economic development, the magnitude and persistence of unemployment and underemployment, and its existing labor laws. A country like the Netherlands, which has the lowest average workweek of any industrialized nation at 29 hours, can and should immediately implement a 20-hour workweek. A country like the US, which averages over 40 hours per week, should immediately slash it to 30 hours. Developing nations like Burundi, which may average up to 50 hours per week, should consider sizable reductions—cutting anywhere from 10 to 15 hours based on local conditions. If these reductions in the length of the workweek do not fully eliminate unemployment after a short period, and it is entirely possible that they would not, then the society in question should continue cutting labor hours until the unemployed are absorbed.[4]

The political struggle to shorten the workday will be acute and dire. Every hour returned to working people is an hour of profit taken back from the capitalist class. A capitalist society cannot accommodate the progressive reduction of labor hours over the long run, because this process will bring down the rate of profit. Capitalism is already suffering from a global shortage of opportunities for profitable investment. We can thus expect the capitalists to fight any attempt to reduce labor hours like a death sentence. Only a socialist society will be able to live up to the promise embodied in modern technology, liberating us from toil while ensuring prosperity for all.

As an aside, I briefly want to discuss another proposal for addressing structural unemployment. Many leftists are starting to advocate for a universal basic income or a certain amount of money that every citizen would receive regardless of their status. A basic income is a potential method of addressing poverty that lacks the paternalism of many welfare schemes. However, it is not a useful response to unemployment. In essence, a basic income scheme taxes the product created by those workers who are employed and provides a portion of it to the unemployed. While some workers work overtime, others receive a minimal sum not to work at all. It is patently unjust to ask a certain portion of the population to labor for longer than necessary, when a simple solution can equitably share both labor hours and free time. Even as a welfare program, a basic income stacks up poorly against targeted payments to those who cannot work, like children, the elderly and the disabled. Given a certain amount of money to distribute, basic income payments will always be smaller to non-workers than targeted programs, because much of the money will be distributed to wage earners.

Politically, a universal basic income is a minimal, not a maximum, demand. This very idea is built into its name: it is a "basic" income or an absolute minimum threshold of money given to those who are no longer needed in the production of value. Milton Friedman famously advocated for a basic income (a "negative income tax," in his terms), arguing that it was entirely compatible with capitalism. I am inclined to agree with him. Unlike a reduction of labor hours, a basic income scheme redistributes surplus value without pointing the way toward the abolition of capitalism's social relations. To paraphrase André Gorz, there is an important difference between "reformist reforms" and "radical reforms." A true radical reform lays the foundations for reconstructing society, even while remaining attainable within the confines of the present system. Reducing labor hours is a radical reform, a basic income scheme is not.

Socialize the Means of Production

Capitalism is a fundamentally contradictory social system. While it is founded on the pursuit of private profit and the limitless accumulation of value, capitalism must ultimately produce so much real wealth that production for profit becomes impossible. If capitalism is destined to collapse, then it must be replaced by an alternative socioeconomic system. Such a system should value life over private profit, free time over labor time and the fulfillment of genuine needs over the enrichment of the few. The only system that can fulfill these demands is socialism.[5]

First, we have to clarify what two highly misunderstood words actually mean. *Socialism* is a socioeconomic system where the means of production are owned by, controlled by and operated for the benefit of the working class. *Communism* is a state of society in which wage labor and the production of value have been abolished. Each person contributes what they can according to their abilities and each person receives goods according to their needs. In a modern communist society, burdensome work would be reduced to an absolute minimum and free time would be maximized, so that every person would have the opportunity to pursue their passions and desires. Both socialism and communism are first and foremost *social* systems rather than technical ones. It is possible to establish either kind of society at any level of technological development. Indeed, many early human societies were essentially communist prior to the development of patriarchy, agriculture and accumulated wealth.

In order to create a socialist society we have to fundamentally alter the basic rules about the ownership and control of wealth. The first step is transferring the ownership of the means of production from shareholders to workers. The ownership and control of all large enterprises—say, those with 50 employees or more—should immediately be transferred to their workers. Firms should be democratically run by their workers, who will establish their own system of rules and regulations, and select officers if necessary. Rather than working for a capitalist's profit, working-class people will control the conditions of their work and directly receive the product of their labor. Workers' control should also be immediately established in all public- and state-controlled entities, such as hospitals and administrative departments.

This step will immediately resolve many of capitalism's contradictions. Worker-owned cooperatives would not need to make a profit. They would be able to pay worker salaries and cover their other costs by simply breaking even. With no shareholders to answer to, a decline in the rate of profit would not create catastrophic disruptions in the system of investment. A socialized investment system, which I will describe in more detail later, would be able to smooth out the peaks and troughs of capitalism's boom-bust cycle. Just as importantly, democratizing the economy would help to eliminate the petty tyranny of many workplaces, which are presently run like miniature feudal states. Workers would be responsible to each other instead of bosses and shareholders, and could take pride in the fact that they owned their workplace. Rather than being treated as instruments for the production of profit, workers would take control of their lives within the workplace and assert their dignity.

As is the case with any economy, basic rules would have to be set to ensure a fair playing field and dignified working conditions for all. The minimum wage would be set at a level significantly above the poverty line, enough to provide all of the essential comforts of life to any family with a working member. Dangerous and unhealthy working conditions would be eliminated as much as possible. Workers would be protected from arbitrary dismissals by coworkers, discrimination and abuse. A socialist society should guarantee paid maternity and paternity leave, disability and injury pay, paid vacation and other forms of compensation for necessary absences from work.

So long as they are capable of operating by the same rules as the cooperatives, the owners of small enterprises should not be coerced into transferring ownership of their businesses. It will already be difficult enough for these enterprises to compete with larger cooperatives and seizing the property of smallholders would unnecessarily alienate a class that makes up a significant portion of the population. Instead, a socialist society could offer incentives for small property owners to transform their businesses into cooperatives—such as compensation and/or 1 to 2 years of paid vacation—without having to resort to forms of coercion that encourage reactionary responses. If smaller businesses find themselves unable to compete in a socialist environment, they can be consolidated into larger cooperatives with the assistance of the socialized financial system.[6]

The capitalist financial system is based on mortgaging, selling and trading claims to private property. Shares of private firms make up much of this activity. With the socialization of the means of production, the stock market would cease to exist. The financial system would need to be socialized and transferred to communal ownership, both to avoid chaos in the markets and to transition to a new system of investment. As part of this transition, many previously existing debts and speculative financial instruments would simply be wiped off the ledgers, as their value would no longer be relevant. I will go into more detail about this process later in this chapter.

A socialist financial system would eliminate most forms of today's risky and quasi-fraudulent financial activity. Existing financial institutions would be consolidated into a single institution with two main branches, which we may provisionally call the "People's Bank." The first branch would simply serve the role of a traditional commercial bank, offering a safe place to store one's earnings and borrow credit (at a non-usurious interest rate of less than 1 per cent). The second branch would act as a clearinghouse for transactions between the cooperatives and the public. When cooperatives sell goods to one another, the Bank will facilitate the transfer of money between the two. If a cooperative requests investment to finance expansion, the Bank will provide this credit from the surpluses of other cooperatives. During the Spanish Revolution from 1936 to 1937, the worker cooperatives established by the CNT used this method to facilitate production in a socialist economy. They quickly learned that they needed both a system of accounts to clear transactions between cooperatives and a means of investment to finance their operations.[7]

A socialist financial system would not be held hostage by the need to accumulate private profits. Instead of chasing value, the Bank would be responsible for maintaining economic stability by providing investment during potential downturns and restricting investment to sectors that were expanding beyond reason. A socialist society could make the political decision to direct investment to important sectors regardless of their profitability. For example, a society with poor public health would want to subsidize the construction of new clinics and hospitals. Every contemporary society would need to heavily subsidize investment in clean and renewable energy sources in order to face the challenge posed by climate change. While perhaps competing against one another to create better products, the cooperatives would in fact be part of a network designed to offer mutual support and prevent economic disruptions.[8]

Finally, a socialist society would establish a comprehensive social system to provide basic social rights to all and care for all those who are unable to work. Healthcare, education and a pension are social rights that should be provided to all. A socialist society must additionally create systems to distribute goods through channels other than labor income. In the US, two out of three impoverished persons are unable to earn a wage income simply because they belong to an unemployable class. A significant majority of the impoverished population is made up of the disabled, the elderly and children.[9] Capitalism is not capable of alleviating these forms of poverty, because it does not provide income to people who do not or cannot be used to produce value. By contrast, a socialist system would provide generous disability payments, pensions and child credits for families earning less than a relatively high threshold. This social system would be funded directly by taxes on the cooperatives.

By themselves, these steps would be enough to create a socialist society where the means of production were owned and controlled by the working class. They would end poverty and, combined with the reduction of labor hours, eliminate unemployment. However, these accomplishments would only represent the beginning of the revolutionary transformation of society. Just like capitalism, socialism is a temporary stage of development. The form of socialism outlined previously is still based on labor, with the workers instead of capitalists reaping its fruits. It still requires forms of money, coercive taxation and meaningful scarcity to function. I believe all of these are necessary evils within a wrenching transition from one kind of society to another; although we should be more than happy to do away with them as soon as possible.

As I stated earlier, a communist society would not compel its members to work for a wage. It would provide goods to its people for free, allowing them to fulfill their needs without having to worry about artificially produced scarcity. Production would be carried on entirely through voluntary work and would be defined by a cooperative spirit. Throughout history, much of the Left has pictured the final transition from socialism to communism as an uncertain and perhaps unachievable process. There is a wide gulf between working-class control of the means of production and the abolition of labor. However, I believe that we can consciously pursue this transition given the political will to do so. We can gradually substitute non-market forms of production for market ones and we can steadily replace the elements of wage labor preserved in cooperatives with voluntary forms of work. We can harness the power of distributed production and radical automation to significantly reduce the amount of human effort required to produce the things we need. Finally, we can manage this process and adapt to its dislocations with a powerful tool: the reduction of labor time.

Communization—creating a communist society—requires us to reduce labor hours to zero. However, communism does not require full automation. It simply requires us to produce goods directly for their value as useful objects and to distribute those goods equitably to those who need them. This seemingly far-off goal is already immanent in the technologies that are revolutionizing contemporary production. A powerful trend in distributed production is the tendency for users to share their work freely with one another simply because it is the best possible way to distribute things like texts and software.

These technologies show that another world is possible, but these possibilities are trapped within the confines of a capitalist society. After all, the producers of free software somehow have to get money to eat, and pay rent and taxes. A socialist society would strive to remove these fetters and unleash the technological potential of distributed production.

First and foremost, we must encourage any form of production based on the voluntary participation of the producers and the free provision of goods. We are already witnessing the first phase of this process with the emergence of solidarity-based economies in places like Detroit, Jackson, Mississippi and Greece. For now, free clinics and farms are programs intended to help people survive the wreckage of capitalism's failures. There is no need to try to do away with these programs and experiments. Instead, we can subsidize these forms of production, treating them as a commons that benefits society as a whole. Where necessary, these producers could be provided with a socially guaranteed income. Agriculture is a prime candidate for treatment as a commons along this model. Farmers and farmworkers could be guaranteed a dignified income and working conditions—including autonomous workers' control of production—but production for profit would be abolished. Instead, food would be provided for free to consumers. Necessary capital for investments would be provided by society as a whole through the People's Bank. Through this mutually beneficial bargain, farmers and the rest of society could forge a new paradigm based upon cooperation and mutual support.

Secondly, we should push radical automation to its limits. As the century continues, it will become possible to substitute machines and software for labor in an increasingly wide number of fields. When the productivity of a particular industry increases past a certain point, it will no longer be feasible simply to leave its management to the care of a now largely superfluous workforce. For example, driver-less vehicles will gradually render the vast majority of the labor in the transportation industry obsolete. Should taxi drivers suffer because their work can now be performed more efficiently by machines? Absolutely not. But should we also expect nurses to work 6-hour days while taxi drivers barely need to work at all? Again, certainly not.

When a particular field passes a certain threshold of efficiency, its firms should have their ownership and management transferred to the relevant communal body, and become part of the commons. New York's political assembly, for instance, would assume the management of New York's automated transportation services. The revenues of these commonly held firms could then be used to pay for social services, or to gradually eliminate taxes, or their products could be provided for free. The net effect of the reduced demand for labor would be compensated by a further reduction of working hours through increased holidays and paid leave, shorter workdays and shorter weeks. The individuals previously employed in these firms would be generously compensated, socially supported, and be given the opportunity to pursue further education and training that would help them integrate into the remaining workforce.

Managing these transitions will be difficult, but it will be a far superior process to the merciless dislocations that are the norm in contemporary capitalism. The strategy proposed in this section would allow us to equitably distribute the benefits of automation and gradually increase the free time of all members of society. Again, we should think of this strategy as a progressive process. Over time, more and more basic goods and services will be provided for free. At the same time, necessary labor time will be continuously reduced—freeing us all from the burden of labor. Some people will devote part of their free time to voluntary projects, sewing the seeds for a further reduction of the remaining ghosts of wage labor. Ultimately, labor time will be reduced to zero. The means of production will be commonly held, work will be purely voluntary, and goods and services will be provided for free to all who need them. Doubtlessly, some questions about the distribution of certain particularly scarce goods may remain and we will have to find equitable solutions to those questions. However, meaningful scarcity will cease to exist. Humanity will solve its economic problem.

Abolish Debts

Debt is a mortgage on the future that cannibalizes the present. Capitalism survives by extracting rising promises of future payment from the state and from individuals, because it cannot accumulate enough value in its own time. Everything is bought and sold on credit—everything from an education to a grain of rice is purchased with the promise of future time. When this payment inevitably cannot be made, capital seeks to recover its losses by any possible means. Take Greece, for example: an entire country has been put up for sale to the highest bidder to "repay" a debt that every financier agrees can never be repaid. Creditors demand cuts to wages, pensions and basic social services, all to squeeze every last penny out of a destitute people. The Greek youth who shouted "We are an image from your future!" was more right than any of us could have known. The collapse of the last massive debt bubble in 2008 did not lead to a re-evaluation of the role of debt in society. Instead, even more debt has been accumulated, far exceeding the rate of economic growth. At the time of this writing, global debts have surpassed their pre-crash levels. We know where this road leads and we also know why it is happening. Capitalism must postpone its final reckoning by bleeding the many and it will continue to try to do so for as long as it possibly can.

To begin, we have to do away with the idea that debt has anything to do with morality or ethics. There is nothing ethical about extorting years of someone's labor just so that they can gain access to an education, healthcare or housing. These goods are only scarce because capitalism bars access to them to those who do not have enough money to afford them. The idea that people "must pay their debts" is a silly, unexamined prejudice.[10] Debt is a system of coercion, designed to transfer the future production of value from those who have little to those who already have too much. The ethical response to the problem of debt is not paying them. It is struggling to abolish the very concept of debt, thereby freeing us from the shadow it casts over our future.

The simple response to the problem of debt is wiping the slate clean. As David Graeber has written, many ancient societies periodically forgave all debts in order to avoid a decline into a state of near-permanent debt slavery. The Biblical Jubilee, for example, required the forgiveness of all debts and the freeing of slaves every 50 years.[11] We should embrace this tradition and go further. We should not just aim to wipe the slate clean. We should do away with systems of debt altogether. Instead, we can choose to promote relationships based on free giving and mutual respect. We should help one another and provide each other with what we need, not because we want to extract some future reward for doing so, but simply because human beings should treat one another with decency. Doing away with debt requires both an economic and an ethical transformation. We will have to learn to stop thinking in terms of the guilt-laden hierarchies of creditor and debtor, and we will have to embrace the idea that all people are equal in terms of both dignity and power.

A socialist society should immediately move to abolish all possible debts, including consumer debt, student debt, mortgage debt and sovereign debt. The capitalist financial system is based entirely on the system of debts and credits, and as such it could not survive a Jubilee. Almost all bank assets would be wiped out and the existing monetary system would collapse. New money enters the financial system as debt through government bond sales. Wiping out sovereign debts would choke off the money supply, and render many institutions and firms insolvent.

Socializing the financial system would be absolutely necessary in order to avoid catastrophic economic dislocation.[12] Consumer bank deposits would have to be guaranteed and transferred to the People's Bank. Old currencies would have to be exchanged for a new currency whose value would be guaranteed by the products of the cooperatives and the commons. The leftover debts of worker-owned firms to obsolete financial institutions would have to be carefully examined, consolidated and possibly canceled.

A Jubilee would effectuate a massive transfer of wealth from creditors to debtors. In and of itself, this process would not be as simple or equitable as it might initially seem. Many of the largest debtors are super-rich individuals or institutions who have taken out massive lines of credit to finance speculation in real estate or financial markets. Many of the largest creditors are pension funds, whose assets are usually invested in stocks, bonds and other equities. A Jubilee would have to be a carefully supervised process, with considerations of justice placed first. Wiping out mortgage debts should not deliver four or five properties over to landlords who purchased those properties with massive credit lines. Erasing debts should not bankrupt pensioners and retirees. These may seem like obvious principles, but ensuring that we actually follow them will require the careful consideration of each individual case.

A socialist society will thus have to balance potential dislocations and prevent transfers of wealth that only worsen inequality. Private pension funds, for instance, would be replaced by guaranteed public pensions for all. Individuals or firms who have multiple mortgages would have their obligations examined. If someone owns more properties than they can possibly use, these properties can be transferred to common ownership and used to house the homeless, found new cooperatives and so on. These kinds of decisions are inherently political and will have to be dealt with situationally.

A Jubilee should include state debts. At present, states borrow money for purposes ranging from funding wars to paying for social services. From a capitalist's perspective, state deficit spending can absorb surplus capital through borrowing and dispose of it unproductively, relieving some of the pressure caused by capital accumulation. A socialist society that has done away with the pressures of production for profit will not require this mechanism to support capitalist profits or employment.[13] More importantly, a Jubilee for public debt will remove the enormous pressure that is currently being placed on the peoples of both the developed and developing world on behalf of creditors. Ethically speaking, the vast majority of this debt is odious—it was contracted on the backs of people who have never had a real say in the creation of state economic policy. The people at large should not be made to suffer for the mistakes of dictators, technocrats and "representatives" whose main objective has always been the enrichment of their own class.

Canceling outstanding debts will be immensely liberating. We will no longer have to submit to years of labor in jobs that we hate in order to pay off enormous sums borrowed for education, medical treatment or housing. We will no longer have to live in fear of banks and debt collectors. We will no longer be subjected to the thousands of little mechanisms designed to remind us constantly of our debts and the obligation to be a docile, reliable borrower. Our future should not be overshadowed by the shackles of the past.

Dismantle the State

The state is a coercive apparatus that exists clearly distinct from and above the people. It is made up of government officials, the bureaucracy, the army and the police. The state's purpose is to reproduce the domination of the preeminent social classes. In the contemporary world, states protect the dominance of capitalism, nationalism and patriarchy. States guarantee the existence of the system of private property. After all, a deed is just a piece of paper without police to enforce it. Symbiotically, states live off surplus value appropriated through taxes. The state thus forms one relatively autonomous pole of a capitalist society and is absolutely essential to its preservation.[14]

Modern states function by appropriating power from the people of a given society and acting as an idealized representative of the competing interests within that society. Ideologies like nationalism encourage people to identify themselves and their interests with the state, even when that state transparently serves the rich and powerful. If it is functioning effectively, a state can create "social peace" between conflicting classes by appearing to mediate their interests through legal channels. For example, a parliamentary system allows parties representing different political opinions to confront each other safely in the halls of government without threatening the basic foundations of society. This system discourages the direct participation of citizens in politics by rendering it almost impossible for them to have any immediate say in the affairs of their own government. Instead, they elect "representatives," who can choose to do whatever they wish the day after their election. These representatives typically have remarkable autonomy from their constituents and can only be held accountable, if at all, once every 2 to 6 years.

Outside of the electoral system, a much larger unelected bureaucracy actually handles the day-to-day affairs of government. An incredible range of departments handle issues ranging from environmental regulations to the prison system. While it is theoretically accountable to elected representatives, the bureaucracy often takes on a life of its own, as bureaucrats try to enlarge their authority and cement their spheres of influence. Thus, the actual task of governance is in the hands of a massive, unwieldy organization that mediates the power of political representatives, who themselves mediate the power of ordinary citizens. The entire system is designed to place power far, far away from the people who are affected by it.

What most people refer to as "Western democracy" is not democracy, at all. The word "democracy" comes Ancient Greek, meaning "people's power." Representative government is not designed to give people power over their own destinies; it is designed to alienate as much power as possible from them while retaining a minimum level of consent. At present, states across the world are losing this basic level of consent and legitimacy. Faced with extraordinary economic and social dislocation, people are confronted with the simple fact that states do not represent their interests and actively perpetuate their oppression.

People are responding to this realization in a number of different, contradictory ways. Many have thrown their support behind a variety of insurgent populist parties on the Left and Right, who have promised to get a hold of state power and wield it for the benefit of their constituents. Some have called for vaguely outlined reforms to "democratize" the state, make governance more "transparent" and enable citizens to have greater input into the political process. Others, like the Kurds in Rojava and the Zapatistas in Chiapas, have experimented with new political forms in an attempt to build a new society beyond the state.

States were born when class societies arose and they will die when class society dies. The first states were created to protect the power of warrior aristocrats; today's states protect the power of capitalists. Ministries and police forces exist because ordinary people cannot be trusted to reproduce class relations without an external power imposing them from above. Thus, a society that does away with classes will also have to do away with the state—it will have to place power and responsibility directly in the hands of the people.

Many leftists seem to believe that capturing state power is the only path to social transformation. This idea is definitionally incorrect. The state—parliaments, ministries, armies and police—was designed to serve the interests of the elite. It was not designed to give the people the means to govern themselves and care for themselves. Modern states function best when they are fulfilling their intended purpose and when they resist attempts to use them for other purposes. They depend on existing class relations. After all, state revenues are drawn from surplus value, meaning that the health of the state goes hand in hand with the health of capitalism.

State power is a chimera for any would-be revolutionaries. Popular movements view the state as an extremely powerful force, because it confronts them with its legions of riot police, its prisons and its armies. Then, when a radical political party takes office, it is suddenly bewildered when it finds itself incapable of making any of the changes it promised its constituents. No matter who governs, the state is still prey to the demands of the global capitalist market. The bureaucracy resists encroachments on its power and changes to existing practices. If social reforms cause capitalist profits to fall, then the state's revenues will decline, as well. If the bureaucracy refuses to implement the agenda of the elected party, then the party is powerless to create change.

Greece's Syriza is a perfect example of this problem. Placed in power in the midst of a crisis and hemmed in by forces that it was powerless to control, Syriza surrendered to Greece's creditors and reneged on almost every single plank of its election platform. Within a few months of winning the 2015 elections, Syriza implemented the exact same austerity measures that it had denounced before it was in power. In mere months, a "party of the radical Left" began proposing drastic cuts to pensions in order to shore up capitalist profits.

In order to dismantle capitalist society, we have to dismantle the state, as well. We have to place political power directly in the hands of the people, with as little mediation as possible. We will have to replace a global system of dictatorships, technocracies and parliaments with radical democracy. The local forms of this democracy will vary, but all should reflect the basic principle that people should have direct control over and responsibility for their own destinies. At the same time, these democracies—which would necessarily be local and immediate—must create an interdependent network that spans the globe and eliminates the maladies of the state system, including war and international borders. In the next chapter, I will outline how this new kind of political organization may function and how we can build the revolutionary power to transform our society.

Build an Ecologically Sustainable Society

Our struggle is not just for the working class or for human beings. Ours is a struggle for life itself, which links the fate of working people to the fate of every living being on Earth. It is no mere coincidence that the form this struggle takes is that of labor against capital or that of living, breathing work against dead, soulless money. Capitalism cannot respect the Earth's ecological limits, because it must grow endlessly or die. It has spent the better part of two centuries destroying much of our natural heritage, eliminating sacred spaces, and wiping out plant and animal species that had lived on this planet for thousands of years. Capitalism is finally reaching the point that its continued expansion poses a potentially existential threat to our civilization and yet it continues pushing the planet past the point of no return. There is no alternative to this fate under the present system—if we allow production for profit to continue, catastrophic climate change is inevitable.

A socialist society must re-establish the essential balance between human civilization and the planetary ecosystem. We need to seriously alter our patterns of production and consumption, and we need to radically restructure our values. The basic principles of sustainability are simple. A sustainable society must replace nonrenewable resources with renewable resources faster than the nonrenewable resources are consumed. It must also consume renewable resources at a rate that does not exceed the speed at which they can be replenished. This means that we have to use all resources on our planet—including energy, land, fresh water and nonrenewables like metals—at a rate that at most equals the rate at which they can be regenerated. We will have to do this all while attempting to fulfill our vision of eradicating poverty and ensuring a dignified standard of living for every human being.

The politicians and businessmen who promise a pain-free transition to a sustainable society are liars. There is a huge gulf between contemporary capitalism and a future society capable of fulfilling the principles outlined in the previous paragraph. The choices we face will be very difficult, and we will have to struggle and make sacrifices if we want to leave a world worth living in to our grandchildren. We will have to learn how to stop pursuing certain activities if they are incompatible with our basic ecological principles. Most crucially, we must abandon the culture of waste and thoughtlessness that currently permeates our society. For example, it is presently common to package everyday consumption items like food in plastic that will never degrade and will never be recycled. Each and every one of these packages represents a wasted resource that may permanently languish in a landfill. The entirety of the present-day production system is based on this sort of waste.

Socialization does not just mean we reap the rewards of production. It also means that we have to take responsibility for our decisions and learn to forgo short-term benefits that have unacceptable long-term costs. Building popular power must pave the way for a political movement for ecological sustainability. Through their democratic bodies, the people will have to create guidelines for sustainable production, limit unsustainable consumption, and invest in technologies that eliminate waste and pollution. Ecological concerns affect everyone on the planet and these decisions must be made collectively.

We should aim to halt rising carbon emissions within 10 years and start bringing them down immediately afterward. This can be achieved, with much difficulty, by imposing hard emissions limits on the cooperatives and by subsidizing investment in technologies that reduce and capture emissions. This is a baseline proposal that must be adopted if we want to avoid catastrophic climate change within the 21st century. Each additional year that carbon emissions continue rising will require us to shorten this time frame, and make even more extreme and painful adjustments. If the capitalist system survives for 2 decades and continues along projected patterns of growth, then it will be all but impossible to avoid catastrophic climate change.

In this case, we will still need to implement a rapid plan to halt emissions. However, we will also need to divert a substantial portion of our productive capacity into adaptation to climate change's inevitable consequences.[15] Instead of spending this capacity on improvements in living standards, we will need to build miles of dikes around populated coastlines, protect fresh water supplies, create modified crop varieties that can survive in the new environmental conditions, and transport millions of people away from the equator and into more temperate regions. Again, this is why it is so critical that we overthrow capitalism as soon as possible. We also need to bring an end to the many other forms of pollution that are harming local communities and devastating the Earth's remaining natural spaces. Just as is the case with carbon emissions, we should introduce hard limitations on air pollutants like sulfur dioxide, water pollutants like agricultural runoff and soil pollutants like harmful pesticides. We should subsidize large investments in filtration technologies and redesign industrial facilities so that they minimize or eliminate these harmful outputs.

In order to achieve these goals, we will need to transform the way that we generate and use energy. Presently, the vast majority of the world's energy comes from burning fossil fuels like oil, coal and natural gas. These energy sources were revolutionary in the 19th and early 20th centuries — today, they shackle our potential to develop as a society. If we continue to burn fossil fuels to power our civilization, catastrophic climate change is inevitable. We need to shift to a new paradigm of energy generation. This requires massive investments in renewable energy sources including solar, wind, tidal and geothermal power. However, many forms of renewable energy have a "density problem" — they tend to generate power over a relatively large area and their output needs to be compacted by other energy sources. Even if we were able to transition to 100 per cent renewable energy use by 2050, per some current proposals, this might still be insufficient to reach our goal of reducing carbon emissions over the next few decades.[16] Many people are understandably wary of nuclear power. Nevertheless, it may be our only medium-term solution to generate enough power for our society without creating irreversible damage from carbon emissions.

We also need to restructure the way that we power and use transportation. Some of this restructuring will entail phasing out gas-powered cars for electric ones powered by renewable energy sources. However, automobiles are the most inefficient form of transportation in terms of both fuel and energy use.[17] We need to remake our transportation systems and redesign the urban environment. Every city and town should have a robust public transportation system made up of some combination of buses, trams, subways and trains. Since access to transportation is a basic necessity of life, these services should be provided free of charge to the public. Cities and towns also need to be designed to make walking and biking feasible and attractive options for getting around. This means abandoning industrial-era urban design principles — including the ridiculous obsession with large, single-use districts — in favor of mixed-use neighborhoods that keep residences, leisure activities, work and shopping areas within a walkable area. Streets and highways should not just be seen as utilitarian devices for shuttling people back and forth from work. They should be beautiful, clean, and designed to give ample space for pedestrians and bikers.

Human population growth will need to slow, and eventually stabilize, if we intend to achieve any of our aforementioned goals. We should not try to force the issue with quasi-fascist policies like birth limits. Instead, a program for sustainable development must include free access to birth control and family planning options, health education and a vigorous struggle for the rights of women to determine their own destinies. Historically speaking, birth rates have declined in most societies as living standards rose. Thus, the best way to ensure that human population growth reaches sustainable levels is not by imposing draconian limitations, but by eliminating poverty and giving women the tools to secure control of their own bodies.

Finally, we have to radically reorient our values. Capitalist society is obsessed with endless growth, churning out a never-ending tide of shoddy, soon-to-be-obsolete commodities. Economic growth, as measured by GDP, is unnecessary for continued social and technological progress. As living standards require less and less labor to attain, we can increasingly spend our time on our research and technological development. Instead of using these new technologies to waste even more time working, we can liberate ourselves from the burden of work. Labor hours can decrease steadily in exact proportion to increasing productivity. Managed in this fashion, our society will be able to ensure that each of its members can enjoy more leisure and products of a higher quality without increasing resource consumption to unsustainable levels.

If we want to live in such a society, we have to value ourselves and our loved ones more than our material possessions. We have to center our lives on our shared experiences and interpersonal connections, rather than the next new smart phone. We must realize that development is prosperity and the time to enjoy it. Economic freedom is not the ability to choose between 20 different cereals produced by the same corporate conglomerate. It is freedom from want, and the freedom to dedicate our lives to whatever we desire. We can only free ourselves, and save our planet from ruin, by abolishing this system based on endless labor and endless growth.

Endnotes

1   Remember, "unproductive" is not a judgment of worth in this sense, but a statement about whether the activity in question produces value. Both public sector teachers and soldiers are unproductive workers from the standpoint of capital, because they are not employed in the production of surplus value, even though capitalism requires their existence.

2   Orthodox economists may reply that this claim is based on the "lump of labor fallacy" or on the supposed belief that only a certain amount of labor is available in a given economy, which must be divided amongst the available workers. They argue that it is conceivable that a reduction in labor hours could actually lead to reduced employment, given the administrative costs associated with hiring more workers and the possibility that firms could simply speed up work. As far as I am aware, the only attempted mathematical demonstrations of this so-called fallacy rely on the idea that compensation per hour is fixed, so that workers work less and earn less. Keynesian models would thus suggest a possible demand shortfall, leading to reduced employment. We can assuage our worried economists by holding compensation steady while reducing labor hours. As an aside, the historical periods in which labor hours were

reduced in the face of rising productivity without causing increased unemployment give the lie to this transparently self-interested doctrine.

3   Alderman, L. "In France, New Review of 35-Hour Workweek," *The New York Times*. November 26th, 2014. Available at: http://www.nytimes.com/2014/11/27/business/international/france-has-second-thoughts-on-its-35-hour-workweek.html. [accessed 7 June 2017]

4   One reason to suspect that more than 10 hours can be cut from a 40-hour week is the fact that there are diminishing marginal returns for each additional hour that a worker labors. Every additional hour worked creates less value than the last, as workers tire and lose focus over time. Thus, the hours of labor being cut are always the least productive hours that the worker labors.

5   Marx argued that the collapse of capitalism would necessarily usher in a socialist society. While I think that socialism is a likely possible result of capitalism's development, I do not believe it is the only one. It is entirely possible to imagine a barbarous, authoritarian society that is no longer premised on the law of value. For example, one could establish a fascist society based on a hierarchical rationing of goods (use values), where the ghost of labor is maintained through performance without producing value.

6   In this case, property is used to mean productive property—like a business—and not real estate.

7   For those who advocate for the immediate abolition of money and any form of finance, the Spanish Revolution is a particularly interesting case study. Many anarchist-dominated towns abolished money immediately during the revolution, only later to reinstitute forms of money to create systems of accounts. Money was only no longer used for goods, like bread, that were no longer meaningfully scarce. A communist society would be able to abolish money for

most goods, but it would still require a system to distribute scarce items equitably. See: Dolgoff, S. (1974) *The Anarchist Collectives: Workers' self-management in the Spanish Revolution, 1936-1939.* (New York: Free Life Editions) Available at: https://libcom.org/files/25020337-The-Anarchist-Collective-Sam-Dolgoff_0.pdf. [accessed 7 June 2017]

8   It should be noted that the socialist system outlined above requires neither central planning nor price-setting. Cooperatives are free to price goods as they want and consumers are free to purchase what they wish. This allows the one benefit of the current pricing system—transferring signals about what people are willing to buy to producers—to be maintained and would require no major shift in behavior for ordinary people.

9   Bruenig, M. "If You Really Want Low Poverty, Market Income Is Not Going to Get You There," *Matt Bruenig Politics.* May 25th, 2015. Available at: http://mattbruenig.com/2015/05/25/if-you-want-really-low-poverty-market-income-is-not-going-to-get-you-there/. [accessed 7 June 2017]

10   Nietzsche put forth a compelling case for the mutually reinforcing nature of a religious morality based on spiritual debt (Christianity) and the everyday regime of economic debts.

11   Graeber, D. *Debt: The First 5,000 Years.* Chapter 4, Note 20. p. 403.

12   The abolition of debts logically follows from a socialized financial system. After all, it makes little sense to continue extorting the people for large sums of money that they simply owe to themselves.

13   A socialist society will not need public deficit spending to support private investment, because all investment will be public and no longer subject to the constraints that face private investors, such as the need to make a profit.

14   The idea of relative autonomy argues that the state and state

officials can have interests that differ from other segments of the ruling class. While the capitalist ruling class generally shares an interest in the preservation of capitalism as a broad system, the fine details of how the system operates—namely, how groups within the ruling classes distribute power and benefits—can vary widely. For example, state officials can reign in the activities of a particular group of property owners (manufacturers, rentiers, etc.) in order to stabilize the system or increase their own relative power. These disputes appear as ideological material conflicts between political parties, bureaucrats, nongovernmental organizations and firms. A current example of such a dispute in the US centers on the prison system. One group—among them private prison owners—wants to maintain existing US laws that promote mass incarceration. Others, seeking to assuage popular anger about the injustices of the carceral system and divert taxes elsewhere, argue that sentencing laws should be made more lenient. Neither of these disputant groups argues that prisons should be abolished, nor that the systems of capitalism and white supremacy are responsible for mass incarceration and popular outrage.

15 Even if capitalism is toppled relatively soon, we will still need to make substantial investments in climate change adaptation. The scale of these investments will only increase with every year that capitalism survives.

16 Shwartz, S. "Stanford scientist unveils 50-state plan to transform U.S. to renewable energy," *Stanford News*. February 26th, 2014. Available at: http://news.stanford.edu/news/2014/february/fifty-states-renewables-022414.html. [accessed 7 June 2017]; "100% Renewable Energy," *Stanford University*. Available at: https://100.org/wp-addons/maps. [accessed 7 June 2017]

17 "Planes, trains and automobiles: Traveling by car uses most energy," *University of Michigan Transportation Research*

Institute. January 10th, 2014. Available at: http://www.umtri. umich.edu/what-were-doing/news/planes-trains-and-automobiles-traveling-car-uses-most-energy. [accessed 7 June 2017]

Chapter 12

The Revolutionary Struggle

We may continue to speak of a crisis of capital, but what
really confronts us is a crisis of the left.

Jerome Roos[1]

It is not enough to suggest a series of techniques that might
be used to move our society beyond capitalism. Capitalism
is not a technical problem. It is a social system defended
by governments and their security forces, political parties
and reactionary movements, and a range of ideologies and
entrenched prejudices. Capitalism must be overthrown by the
concerted effort of the oppressed. But how can we overturn such
an entrenched system, which spans the entire globe and governs
every facet of our lives? In the past years we have waged a series
of desperate struggles against our immanent destitution, against
authoritarianism and against imperialism. Yet, we seem just as
far from abolishing capitalism as we were before the crisis. This
problem demands a response. We need a revolutionary strategy.

We need to wage a struggle to build our capacity to
resist capitalism and the state, and lay a foundation for the
revolutionary reconstruction of society. *Politics* is a struggle
to shape and determine the power relations in a society. It
is a dynamic contest between competing social forces and
individuals. This definition of politics is different from the
common usage of the word, which places the well-worn arena
of representative politics, institutions and voting on a bizarre
pedestal. Transgressing gender norms, occupying a factory and
obstructing evictions are all political acts. These struggles are
often inherently *more* political than the actions of a parliament or
congress, because they push the boundaries of what is possible

in a given society. In this broad sense, we have to wage a political struggle to build our capacity to overturn the power relations in contemporary society.

The guiding strategy of any struggle must reflect the actual conditions of that society and the struggle's ultimate aims. In this book, I laid out an economic analysis of present-day capitalism and the trends that will shape it in the coming decades. Capitalism is entering its final phase of expansion. It is expelling labor from the production process and giving birth to a new production paradigm. Economic instability will continue to rise, along with structural unemployment, poverty, and the attendant waves of racial and religious prejudice. Climate change will exacerbate these trends. Absent a world war to reset the clock of capital accumulation, there is no foreseeable path back to the economic conditions and political arrangements of the post-war period. Capitalism is headed for collapse.

The capitalist system *must* be overthrown as soon as possible and replaced with a superior system capable of guaranteeing a dignified life, freedom and equality to humanity. We must create a socialist society, where the economy is controlled by the people and run for their benefit. We must liberate ourselves from work and we must eliminate poverty. We must create a society that eliminates economic crises and lives in harmony with our planet's ecological systems. We must tear down the state and its oppressive institutions, and replace them with arrangements that give us control over our own lives. In essence, we have one critical goal that ties all of our separate objectives together: we must take power from the few and put it back in the hands of the people.

If we want to achieve this, we need to build popular power from the ground up. We can do this by building a form of political organization that has been the foundation of many modern revolutions, including those in France, Russia and Spain. This organization is the commune, based on the assembled power of the people and their communities. Today, this radical form of political organization has re-arisen in the struggles of the Zapatista movement in Mexico and the Kurdish movement in Rojava and eastern Turkey. We can learn from these strategies and adapt them to our own local conditions. To understand why we should adopt this particular strategy, we need to understand the historical successes and failures of the radical Left.

Our History

The struggle against capitalism is as old as capitalism itself. Throughout history, a massive number of movements, organizations and political parties have advocated varying strategies either to reform or overthrow capitalist society. Many of these movements achieved varying degrees of success, forcing key concessions, and even seizing power from state authorities and the capitalist class. However, the latter half of the 20th century witnessed the almost universal failure and collapse of the most influential tendencies of radical political struggle. In the West, parliamentary socialists and other reformist leftists were unable to defend their post-war victories, leading to a prolonged assault on social democracy and the welfare state. "Actually existing socialism" in states like the Soviet Union and China collapsed of its internal contradictions and capitalism swiftly established itself in both countries. It is not enough to reject the historical experience of 20th-century socialism outright. If we are to have any hope of success in our own century, we must study and learn from the mistakes of those who came before us.[2]

As the Industrial Revolution sent shockwaves throughout Western society in the 19th century, the first socialist and labor movements sprung into existence. New organizations struggled for better wages and working conditions, political rights for the working class and even for revolutionary change. Throughout the early 19th century, this kind of agitation was illegal in most countries, and radicals faced constant repression and harassment. By the end of the century, working-class men gained the right to vote in major nations like the German Empire. (There were few places in Europe where women were given the right to vote until the 20th century.) States eased restrictions on the activities of mass political parties, reigniting a fierce debate between leftists who advocated gradual reform and those who fought for an immediate revolution.

As the primary workers' party in one of Europe's most populous and developed nations, Germany's Social Democratic Party (SPD) was the most powerful voice in the global socialist movement until the outbreak of the First World War. In 1890, the German state revoked the Anti-Socialist Laws, allowing the party to work and campaign openly. This posed a problem for the party: its activities were now legal and its demands for democratic inclusion were no longer a threat to the capitalist state.[3] In response, the SPD articulated a new strategy. Since any party could now openly campaign for control of the state through parliamentary politics, and since workers made up the vast majority of the population, the SPD proposed a legal route to socialism. In 1891 the SPD put forth the Erfurt Program, demanding ten key reforms that it hoped to win through the ballot box. Despite this gradualist orientation, the SPD still advocated for the abolition of capitalism and class society. It simply hoped to achieve its revolutionary objectives through legal means.

By throwing itself into parliamentary politics, the SPD won important reforms like social security and taxation of the rich, but it undermined its capacity to fight for radical change. By becoming a mature political party, the SPD naturally developed an institutional structure and bureaucracy that separated its leaders from its base. As they transformed themselves into established politicians, the SPD's leaders increasingly identified their interests with those of the German state and attempted to tamp down on more militant workers. SPD politicians distanced themselves from and even helped to suppress wildcat strikes and uprisings.[4] Ultimately, the gap between achieving the SPD's ultimate aim—instituting socialism—and the challenges of participating in the management of a capitalist state proved unbridgeable.

The crucial test of German social democracy arrived in the lead-up to the First World War. Socialists had long held, as Marx wrote, that workers have no country. Class exploitation cuts across national boundaries and socialists argued that nationalism and militarism were tools that the ruling classes used to manipulate workers into slaughtering each other on the battlefield. In 1864, socialist, communist and anarchist groups founded the First International, which aimed to unite the global working class. In the coming decades, Europe's major powers pursued massive military build-ups driven by their colonial and imperial rivalries. In the early 20th century, it became clear that Europe was heading for a general war. In 1912, the Second International unanimously resolved to oppose the coming conflict, arguing that it was the duty of the socialist parties "to intervene in favor of its speedy termination and with all their powers to utilize the economic and political crisis created by the war to arouse the people and thereby to hasten the downfall of capitalist class rule."[5] But in 1914, working-class unity shattered.

The crisis between Austria, Serbia and Russia threw the contradictions in the SPD's program into sharp relief. The SPD should have been bound by its internationalist principles to oppose a war between capitalist powers, in which the working class would suffer immensely. However, opposing the war would have placed the SPD in an immediate and desperate conflict with the German state, which it had been struggling to gain control of for over 4 decades. The SPD could continue on the path of political respectability and support the war effort, or it could embark on a dangerous new road. When Germany declared war on Russia in August of 1914, the SPD voted in favor of the war budget. On the floor of parliament, its chairman declared: "In the hour of danger we shall not desert our Fatherland." The SPD's betrayal of the Second International's resolution shocked its counterparts and within weeks, social democrats across Europe lined up behind the war efforts of their respective governments.[6]

The First World War killed millions of workers, who were almost universally failed by their representatives in Europe's parliaments. This tragic experience did little to correct the shortcomings of Europe's social democrats. After its defeat in the war, the German government was on the verge of collapse. In 1919, militant workers aligned with the German Communist Party rose up throughout Germany. The SPD allied itself with proto-fascist paramilitary groups known as the *freikorps* to crush the uprising. The *freikorps* killed over 1000 workers across Germany, and murdered revolutionary leaders Rosa Luxemburg and Karl Liebknecht. The SPD's subsequent stint in power was short. In a little over a decade, the Nazis came to power, abolishing the short-lived Weimar Republic and outlawing the SPD.

The story of the SPD is by no means an exception in the history of social democracy. Throughout Europe and the rest of the world, parliamentary socialists were unable to resolve the contradiction between their immediate reformist goals and methods, and the ultimate revolutionary aim of creating a socialist society. This is not the place for a lengthy discussion of the histories of the UK's Labour Party, France's Socialist Party and so on, but most bear a striking resemblance to the SPD's trajectory. Particularly in the aftermath of the Second World War, social democratic parties won reforms that ushered in the modern welfare state and legal protections for organized labor. Some parties even enjoyed substantial terms in office. But despite these victories, social democratic parties abandoned their commitments to socialism in favor of "capitalism with a human face." After the crisis of the 1970s, social democracy's victories were not as durable as its proponents might have hoped. In response to the long neoliberal assault, Western social democrats moved even further to the Right, taking part in governments that slashed the welfare state and forced austerity on the working class. Parliamentary social democracy proposed an alternative way to manage capitalist society, but it ultimately proved incapable of challenging the capitalist system.

While parliamentary socialism attempted to win reform through the ballot box, revolutionary socialists proposed a direct challenge to the capitalist state. The most influential current in 20th-century revolutionary socialism was Marxism-Leninism, named for Vladimir Lenin's political interpretation of Marx's economic thought. In contrast with the reformists, Lenin and the Bolsheviks held that capitalism could only be overthrown through revolution. In *What Is To Be Done?*, Lenin outlined a strategy for revolutionary change in Czarist Russia. He argued that workers would only develop "trade union consciousness" and agitate for economic concessions of their own accord. Because of this limitation, Lenin believed that a vanguard party comprised of advanced workers and intellectuals drawn from the upper classes was necessary to lead the masses in developing a revolutionary consciousness. This party would be organized according to the principles of democratic centralism: party policies would be debated internally and party bodies would be elected, but finalized decisions and party discipline would be strictly enforced by the organizational hierarchy.[7] Given the political conditions in Czarist Russia, this focus on internal discipline was an understandable strategic choice. Revolutionaries in Russia faced intense repression from the Okhrana, the Czarist secret police. In order to combat this repression, Lenin conceived of a party that would be able to operate as a disciplined, clandestine political and military organization.

Throughout the 20th century, Marxist-Leninist and Maoist

organizations struggled for and won power in an impressive number of countries.[8] This revolution erupted not in the most developed countries, as Marx predicted, but in the developing world. The Bolsheviks seized power in the Russian Empire in 1917 and the Chinese Communist Party finally prevailed after a long civil war with the Nationalists by 1950. Marxist-Leninist parties and guerrilla groups were extraordinarily influential in the struggles against colonialism and imperialism in Asia, Africa and South America. After their victories in the Soviet Union, China, Vietnam, Cuba and elsewhere, these vanguard parties set themselves to the project of "building socialism" in countries with backward, underdeveloped economies. Despite their successful seizures of power, these parties encountered contradictions that would ultimately prove fatal to this project. By the end of the 20th century, the "socialism" of the Soviet Union and China had collapsed.

In February of 1917, workers and soldiers overthrew the Czar of the Russian Empire and established a provisional government. The Russian Army was badly losing the First World War, and famine and scarcity fueled popular outrage at the Czarist autocratic government. In the following months, the Provisional Government—made up of appointed representatives from liberal and moderate socialist parties—was unable to resolve the many crises that plagued Russian society. As the Provisional Government floundered, Russian workers increasingly placed their faith in the *soviets*: popular democratic bodies made up of workers, soldiers and peasants founded during the February Revolution. As one of the only political parties that refused to participate in the Provisional Government, the Bolsheviks were well positioned to benefit from popular unrest.

As Alexander Rabinowitch has shown, during this crucial period in 1917 the Bolshevik Party displayed a remarkable degree of internal democracy and flexibility.[9] The views of influential leaders like Lenin were frequently overridden by other Bolsheviks in the Central Committee. The Party gained significant popular support by tuning its demands to the those of the people: bread, land and peace. Perhaps most significantly, it pledged to transfer power directly to the people through the soviets. As Lenin wrote:

"Power to the Soviets" means radically reshaping the entire old state apparatus, that bureaucratic apparatus which hampers everything democratic. It means removing this apparatus and substituting for it a new, popular one, i.e., a truly democratic apparatus of Soviets, i.e., the organised and armed majority of the people—the workers, soldiers and peasants. It means allowing the majority of the people initiative and independence not only in the election of deputies, but also in state administration, in effecting reforms and various other changes.[10]

Owing to its uncompromising stance against the war and for soviet power, workers and peasants flocked to the Bolshevik standard. By August and September, Bolshevik delegates had the majority in the Petrograd and Moscow soviets, and Bolshevik support in other soviets was skyrocketing. In October, the Bolsheviks allied with other Left opposition forces like the Left Socialist Revolutionaries and the anarchists, leading an uprising against the Provisional Government. The October Revolution ushered in a Bolshevik-led government pledging to bring about the rule of the working class in Russia through the soviets.

This commitment did not withstand the test of time. The Bolsheviks faced a number of immediate crises: Russia was still badly losing the First World War, the Russian economy was in tatters, and food and other goods were becoming increasingly scarce. Even if they overcame these immediate challenges, Russia would still remain among the most economically backward countries in Europe, with a small industrial base and a population comprised largely of peasants.

In 1918, a brutal civil war broke out, pitting the Bolsheviks and their allies against the reactionary White Army and its foreign supporters. The Bolsheviks responded to these crises with dictatorial measures. They sidelined workers' committees in the factories and implemented one-man management; they instituted martial law in many instances, suppressing strikes and demonstrations, and conducting mass arrests; they repressed and ultimately banned other political groups, including opponents on the Left such as the anarchists and the Left SRs; and they cracked down on dissent and internal democracy within the Party itself.[11] Leon Trotsky perhaps best summed up the Party's attitude by arguing that it was "obliged to maintain its dictatorship, regardless of temporary wavering in the spontaneous moods of the masses, regardless of the temporary vacillations even in the working class."[12]

The Soviet Union faced a crucial turning point with the outbreak of the Kronstadt rebellion in 1921. In the preceding months, widespread food shortages and the government's autocratic policies prompted mass unrest, including no less than 118 peasant revolts in February of 1921. In March, soldiers and sailors at the Kronstadt naval base rose up, demanding immediate elections to the soviets, freedom of speech, and assembly for the anarchists and Left socialist parties, and the liberation of political prisoners.[13] The Kronstadt sailors had long been among the most radical groups in Russia, playing a key role in the October Revolution, and the uprising sent shockwaves through the Bolshevik Party. Nevertheless, years of unrest and civil war had primed the Bolsheviks to respond forcefully to dissent. The Party ordered loyal Red Army units to assault Kronstadt, crushing the rebellion. The Kronstadt revolt persuaded Lenin to loosen state control of the economy, but it did not succeed in reinvigorating soviet democracy. Throughout the rest of the 20th century, worker democracy in the soviets was firmly subordinated to the Party and the party-state cemented its control of the Soviet economy.[14]

When the Chinese Communist Power (CCP) finally took control of most of mainland China in 1949, it faced serious political and economic challenges. As the journal *Chuang* relates, "Compared to China in 1943, Russia in 1913 (itself a largely undeveloped agrarian country on the eve of its revolution) already manufactured three times as many tons of steel, twice as many tons of iron, had twice as many kilometers of railways and produced thirty times as much petroleum."[15] This lack of industrial development was even more dramatic than these figures indicate, given China's much larger population compared to Russia.

As it sought to develop and modernize a largely agrarian economy made up almost completely of peasants, the CCP had only a scattering of small coastal enterprises and the remains of Japanese-built wartime factories in Manchuria at its disposal. China was still reeling from the devastation of Japanese invasion and occupation during World War II, in addition to a subsequent 4 years of civil war. Keen to do its part, the US immediately orchestrated and imposed a 20-year economic blockade on the mainland.

In the coming decades, the CCP pursued a difficult and contradiction-riddled campaign of rapid industrialization. Despite internal party conflicts about the best strategy to pursue industrial development, the CCP remained steadfast in its pursuit of accumulation throughout the "state socialist" period. Just as it remained the motive force behind the planning and execution of China's economic development, the Party maintained a political dictatorship and asserted its authority, to determine the ultimate social aims of that development.

In the years following the civil war, the state extracted a growing grain surplus from the peasantry, which it used to develop its urban and coastal industries. Nevertheless, rural

China remained radically undeveloped, lacking modern roads, railways and electricity.[16] Chinese agriculture needed to be modernized if it was going to supply the surpluses required to fuel industrialization, but many of the preconditions for modernization in the countryside were sorely lacking. Instead of slowing the pace of development, the Chinese state attempted to push the countryside to fund its own modernization.

Throughout the late 1950s, Chinese peasants were organized into larger collective bodies — "cooperatives," then "collectives," then "communes" — which allowed the mobilization of a sizable rural labor force to build infrastructure works. At the same time, livestock, tools and land were collectivized. During the "Great Leap Forward" in 1957 and 1958, rural labor was diverted into non-agricultural production, including the infamous backyard iron and steel factories. "Communes" had significant incentives to lie about increases in agricultural production, which they did en masse, prompting the central state to extract even more grain and divert rural labor to the cities. Agricultural production could no longer keep pace with demand. By 1962, grain production had dropped to just 79 per cent of its 1957 level. Coupled with bad droughts and crop failures, these policies contributed to the Great Chinese Famine of 1959–61, in which tens of millions perished. The "commune" system began to fall apart as party cadres lost control of much of the rural population.[17]

In the cities, the state's pursuit of rapid development fueled new conflicts. Unlike workers in the favored heavy industries, workers in smaller enterprises in coastal cities like Shanghai and Guangzhou suffered as the CCP pushed production targets higher. When "jointly owned" public-private firms in the coastal cities were nationalized in 1956, many of the firms' private owners and their management personnel "were simply transferred to positions of authority within the new industrial structure." The concessions that these workers had won over the past decade were slowly stripped away.

As production targets rose, enterprises required workers to work overtime even while "higher-level organs refused to pay extra money for wages." As a result, wages fell and new welfare benefits failed to make up for the decline.[18] These insults were too much to bear for workers in underprivileged positions. Strikes began to break out in 1956, before exploding in 1957. While these strikes were ultimately suppressed, the Party made a number of concessions, including the formation of workers' congresses of elected representatives in many factories. The influence of these congresses was uneven—some played a part in democratizing factory management, whilst workers in some factories simply "refused to elect representatives to the congresses." Despite these concessions, any level of worker self-management in the factories remained subordinate to overarching production plans established by the central government.[19]

By 1957, shortages of consumer goods were common and planning targets had to be reduced, leading to layoffs in both urban and rural areas. China seemed to be approaching an "industrial bottleneck," similar to the crises experienced during any developing capitalist economy's cycles of growth. True to form, the CCP decided to accelerate the pace of development instead of slowing down, mirroring its rural policies. The Party planned a new push of heavy industrialization alongside a massive expansion of the state sector, adding almost 30 million workers in 1958 alone.[20] At the same time that the Party pushed for an increase in the pace of development, it devolved much of the authority for economic planning and production targets to local authorities. Enterprises were permitted to set their own targets and were even "encouraged to competitively speculate" on them. The number of enterprises under central control fell from 9300 in 1957 to 1200 in 1958. Somewhat counterintuitively, this decentralization actually further increased Party control over production, as enterprises were essentially handed over to local Party committees.[21]

As the Party encouraged local enterprises to push their capacity to the limits, industrial employment expanded dramatically, drawing both from the rural labor force and urban temporary workers. Workers were encouraged to work at a frenzied pace, 7 days a week, with even Party cadre and technicians taking part in physical labor. Urban enterprises created their own socialized housework, dining and handicraft production services in what was known as the *danwei* system. Under the *danwei* system, enterprises directly provided social welfare benefits to their own employees, freeing up additional labor for factory production. The direct reliance of these welfare services on the individual output of factories encouraged workers to push even harder, given the obvious link between their enterprise's performance and the welfare benefits they received. This massive shake-up of the industrial structure, alongside key concessions like the temporary expulsion of unpopular Party cadre and technicians to the countryside, helped to subdue worker unrest for a few years.[22]

Despite its apparent initial successes, the productive frenzy of the Great Leap Forward in the cities was fueled by a completely unsustainable increase in the extraction of grain from the Chinese countryside. The collapse of agricultural production also spelled the collapse of the Great Leap's mobilization in the cities. In 1961, emergency measures concentrated production in a small number of efficient factories and by 1963, authorities managed to reduce industrial employment by around 40 per cent.

Around 20 million workers were deported to the countryside. This mass deportation formalized an enduring system of registration (*hukuo*) that defined workers as "urban" or "rural," with rural workers largely excluded from the superior welfare benefits available to urban residents. After the Great Leap Forward, factory managers were encouraged to make use of rural workers as cheap, temporary labor, who could be deported to the countryside at any time. Migrants who had come to the cities in search of a better life lost their benefits, while tens of thousands of old workers were involuntarily retired and often stripped of their urban registration. Just as the famine sapped support for the Party in the countryside, mass deportations and reductions in benefits created a simmering base of anger among deported workers.[23]

Chinese society was straining under the new power inequalities created by the country's developmental path, alongside the serious trauma of the Great Leap Forward. These growing social contradictions created the conditions for the monumental upheaval of the "Great Proletarian Cultural Revolution."[24] In 1966, Mao and his allies in the Chinese Communist Party launched a series of critiques aimed at the Party bureaucracy, claiming that it had been infiltrated by reactionaries who wanted to roll back the revolution.[25] Inspired in part by Mao's proclamations, millions of students rose up against the Party establishment in their schools and in local governments. Party leaders attempted to restore order over the restive students by dispatching "work teams" to the schools. Mao criticized this move, encouraging the students to "take charge of their own movement."

Millions of students organized themselves into groups known as Red Guards, engaged in widespread and often violent criticism of authority figures, attacked historical symbols like the tomb of Confucius and even seized weapons from the army. In Shanghai, temporary workers formed an umbrella organization known as the "Rebel Headquarters of Red Workers," boasting a membership of over 400,000 insurgents.[26] This organization was only one of many large rebel organizations that sprung up throughout China. In Hunan, the revolutionary committee published a manifesto demanding the immediate establishment of communes to replace the Party bureaucracy with the self-government of the working class. It cautioned that the Party was already beginning to backpedal on its revolutionary rhetoric. The committee warned that "[i]f dictatorship... is regarded as the ultimate object of the first great cultural revolution, then China will inevitably go the way of Soviet Union and the people may again return to the fascist bloody rule of the capitalists."[27]

Fearful of losing control of the people, Mao and his allies decided to reverse course. The People's Liberation Army put down embryonic communes and in 1968, Mao initiated the "Down to the Countryside Movement," sending millions of young urban intellectuals to live in rural China. While it was argued that privileged students needed to learn from the realities of life for China's rural poor, the movement benefited the Party elite by dispersing troublesome Red Guards throughout the countryside. At the same time, the PLA and Party-aligned "revolutionary committees" suppressed insurgent peasants and workers with often brutal violence. The Party ultimately re-established control over the municipalities and Party leaders feuded amongst themselves. By the end of the 1970s, Mao (who died in 1976) and his successors were marginalized and reformist moderates led by Deng Xiaoping ascended to power. Within a few years, Deng began transforming China into a modern capitalist economy. The Party abandoned its socialist rhetoric to simply pursue development on capitalist terms.

From the period between the Chinese Communist Party's victory in the civil war until China's transition to capitalism, the Chinese state attempted to balance its socialist rhetoric with its desire to develop the country rapidly. But despite uneven flirtations with worker democracy at the enterprise level, and fierce critiques of "bureaucratism" and "degeneration" in the Soviet Union, the CCP never resolved contradictions between pursuing economic growth and the socialist promise. Instead, the CCP-led state suppressed unrest where possible and gave small concessions where necessary, all whilst maintaining a ceaseless and sometimes disastrous drive to develop the Chinese economy as quickly as humanly possible.

This development did ultimately allow the largest society

in the world to transition from an agrarian to an industrial economy, pulling millions out of rural poverty. (Similar things, of course, can be said of many capitalist societies.) But the pursuit of development at the expense of all else laid the foundations for China's transition to capitalism and foreclosed the possibility of building a genuine socialist society. Furthermore, the CCP's monopolization of political power smothered chances for an alternative vision of China's future to emerge from below, despite the hints of other possibilities that surfaced during periods of crisis.

The 20th century witnessed major revolutions in two of the world's most populous countries—the Russian Empire and China. Yet, by the end of the 20th century, "actually existing socialism" in both countries had collapsed. To be certain, the Soviet Union and the People's Republic of China faced astounding developmental challenges, having scarcely been transformed by the touch of modern industrial capitalism when revolutionary forces took power. These developmental shortcomings were one of the primary causes of the development of dictatorial states in both countries, as only a strong state was capable of extracting the surpluses needed to develop industrial power rapidly in the absence of a dominant capitalist class.[28] These states facilitated the emergence of a new hegemonic class in place of the traditional capitalists. Many of the ceaseless debates about "what could have been" in the Soviet Union and China are now frankly pointless. A revolution in a contemporary capitalist economy would face little, if any, of the developmental challenges that plagued 20th-century socialist movements.

Nevertheless, there is something to be learned from China and the Soviet Union. These societies did not collapse simply because they were "undemocratic," as liberal commentators might argue. They collapsed because their political structures were fundamentally incompatible with socialism, which requires the equalization of political and economic power. China's history is instructive in this regard. The Chinese Communist Party faced little difficulty transitioning to a contemporary capitalist economy, because it had already monopolized political power in Chinese society. By monopolizing political power and control over the means of production, the Party constituted itself as a new bourgeoisie in waiting. When the left wing of the Party had been marginalized, opportunists only had to convince fellow political leaders—not the Chinese people—that capitalistic development would be a preferable path, that "to get rich would be glorious." Today, China is a nationalistic, capitalist power still ruled a "communist" party.

There are are still some anti-revisionist Marxists who look to the Soviet Union and pre-Deng China as models for a future socialist society. A typical line of argument suggests that these societies were genuinely socialist and thus worthy of emulation, but that some unfortunate combination of circumstances ultimately conspired to cause their collapse. The problem is that this stance is inherently contradictory. The idea that a socialist society could collapse of its internal contradictions and revert to capitalism defies the basic logic of Marxism.

Marx held that capitalism was a historical stage of development that would be superseded by the higher stages of socialism and communism. If the Soviet Union and China were socialist societies, how is it possible that they reverted to a more primitive stage of society? Neither society's transition to capitalism was prompted by a foreign invasion. Is Marx's theory of historical development wrong or were the Soviet Union and China not genuine socialist societies? Marxist-Leninists cannot have it both ways.[29] Even if this theoretical challenge can be overcome, it remains to be demonstrated why modes of governance that were designed for backward, scarcely industrialized countries should be applied to countries with massive, highly automated industrial bases, where human labor is increasingly superfluous to production.

Both parliamentary socialism and Marxism-Leninism failed to find a solution to the problem of power in a socialist society. The parliamentary socialists believed that they could adapt a form of government designed for capitalist rule to the needs of the working class. The Leninists believed that a party dictatorship could lead the way to socialism by holding the reins until the people were truly ready for self-rule. But the power relations in a socialist society cannot mirror those of capitalist society. A socialist society cannot be governed by a party bureaucracy or a hierarchical military organization. In order to secure popular control of the means of production, the people must hold direct political power, as well. They must be responsible for their own fates and fully capable of determining society's future. Freedom and equality can only exist where power is firmly in the hands of the people. The task we face is posing this question anew: What forms of power can we use to build a society that makes freedom and equality real?

Long Live the Commune

To build a revolutionary movement for the 21st century, we need to learn from and address the failures of past radical movements. Parliamentary socialism failed to pose a revolutionary challenge to capitalism, because its means of building power required it to participate in and protect the capitalist state. It was fundamentally incapable of overcoming the contradiction between its immediate reformist aims and tactics, and its long-term revolutionary aspirations. Marxism-Leninism, on the other hand, successfully seized power in numerous countries and set itself to the task of "building socialism." However, the contradiction between its stated aim of governing for the people and its actual modes of governance led to the degeneration of the most significant revolutions of the 20th century. Neither political movement overcame these fundamental limitations and, just as crucially, neither was able to move beyond the mutual antagonisms inherent in the geopolitical relations between competing nation states.[30]

At the same time, we must examine the shortcomings of common present-day forms of struggle and find a way to overcome their limitations. Since 2008, mass protests, strikes and riots have swept across most of the world, but capitalism remains seemingly as entrenched as ever. Thousands and even millions of people have taken to the streets in heightened moments of crisis, but they remain unsure how to push their movements beyond the largely symbolic arena of protest. Even in countries like Greece, which are experiencing destitution of an almost incomprehensible scale, radicals are uncertain how to organize a revolutionary challenge and the momentum of the movements has stalled.

The Arab Spring provides perhaps the best example of the present dilemma. In 2011, millions of Egyptians rallied against the Mubarak dictatorship, forcing his resignation. But few, if any, of the Egyptian revolutionaries were prepared to take power, much less dismantle the machinery of the Egyptian state. In 2013, a military coup quickly toppled Egypt's first democratically elected head of state, Mohamed Morsi. Today, Egypt is still governed by Mubarak's military dictatorship—but Mubarak himself has been replaced by a clone named Sisi.

Finally, we need a strategy that is capable of both pushing for revolutionary change and delivering concrete victories before "The Revolution." We do not have the luxury of waiting for the collapse of national governments or global capitalism before we can provide ourselves with basic necessities like food, clean water, housing, healthcare, and protection from the police and fascist paramilitaries. People do not want far-off promises of a hypothetical world to come after years of trying, often brutal struggle. We want solutions to our problems now and we want to implement these solutions as thoroughly as possible given realistic limitations. In short, we do not want to wait for the Revolution; we want to build the Revolution *now*, city by city, neighborhood by neighborhood, street by street.

The commune is the answer to the revolutionary question. A commune is a community that is directly responsible for its own governance and fate. Its participants have a shared life and a shared destiny, but they retain their autonomy, their freedom to move from place to place and their freedom to participate in politics on a completely equal footing. Its basic principles, though shifting across times and places, remain the same: it poses the power of the people against tyranny and mediated power, internationalism and egalitarianism against the narrow mindset of the nation state, and economic equality against the exploitation of capitalism. The theory of this form of organization is simply called *communalism*.[31]

The commune is something of the past and something of the future all at once. It evokes old notions of community and a politics based on the face-to-face interactions of ordinary people, mirroring ways of life eroded by industrial capitalism. At the same time, it is a conscious project to radically restructure society along liberatory, egalitarian lines. Participation in a commune is not restricted on the basis of ethnicity, citizenship, gender, age or any other arbitrary category, but is open to all who want to contribute to the project of liberation. It can expand, contract or divide itself based on the demands of its participants. Most importantly, it allows its participants to decide upon the forms of decision-making and execution that most suit their particular needs.

As a defined community, a commune covers a certain geographical area, which can be as small as a city block or as large as a small rural town. The area should be large enough so that its participants have enough power to address their local needs, but small enough that face-to-face decision-making is possible. Anyone in the commune's area of responsibility must have the right to participate in the commune. The commune looks after the collective responsibilities of the area, whether those responsibilities are putting in a new well, cleaning a city street or sending aid to comrades fighting oppression halfway around the world. But a commune is not simply a geographic or territorial unit. The commune is a new kind of social relation based on the direct participation of its members in the process of making decisions and the execution of those decisions. As such, it places power directly in the hands of those whom that power affects.

In English, the word "commune" is often associated a series of utopian social experiments premised on separating a group of people from the outside world. This practice is the exact opposite of what a commune must be.[32] Our enemies are organized internationally; capitalism is a global system. We cannot doom ourselves to failure by organizing ourselves within the confines of particular nations or localities. A commune is part of the world and as a part of this world, its fate is tied with the rest of our planet's inhabitants. It depends on outsiders and others for support, new ideas and growth. Communes must federate themselves in an allied network for mutual support, or they risk being crushed by the state or resigning themselves to irrelevancy. This grouping must keep the final say in political decision making in the hands of the communes themselves.

By joining together in larger and larger networks, communes can marshal the resources of an increasingly large area without surrendering their freedoms to a higher authority. When issues arise concerning areas larger than local communes, as will always be the case, the federated communes can form councils at higher levels — city, regional, national, global — for coordination and joint decision-making. With the advent of the Internet, there is no reason why these councils cannot also employ direct voting of all participants on issues of collective concern.

The commune is the starting point of democratic politics.[33]

The Revolutionary Struggle

Parliamentary government is not democracy. Democracy is people's power. Any alienation of political power from the people is an evil, because it necessarily diminishes the autonomy, power and dignity of every individual in our society. A democracy is an agreement between equals who decide to live and govern themselves together. Representation *as such* is illegitimate. To abrogate the responsibility and power of self-government is to destroy the foundations of democratic life. This is nowhere more apparent than in contemporary "representative" systems, where the corruption of political officials and the growth of an unaccountable bureaucratic state far outweighs all means of popular redress. The more "representative" the system, the more any harmony of desire between the people and their representatives becomes an effect of chance, and the fewer opportunities there are to engage in meaningful politics. As communalists, we must fight to take power out of the hands of the politicians and capitalists, and place it directly in the hands of the people.

There are compelling reasons to adopt a communalist strategy. Building communes places the burdens of political power and responsibility on the people. By creating a new kind of society within the shell of the old, we prepare ourselves for the demands of living in a socialist society. If we are to live without the oppressive power of capitalism and the state, we must learn how to manage the economy, resolve disputes and pursue social development on our own. By gradually assuming wider and wider responsibilities, we will build confidence in our ability to take control of our destinies without the intervention of so-called experts and the powerful. By dissolving the boundaries between the "activists" and the "masses," the commune cements an ethic of shared struggle, values and sacrifice in the everyday life of the community.

Just as crucially, the commune is an organ of political struggle that mirrors the kind of future society we struggle for. Instead of smuggling the prejudices and hierarchies of the old world into the new, the commune founds its practice on equality both before and after the conquest of power. Building the commune thus allows us to lay the foundation of the new world before the collapse of capitalism and the cataclysmic struggle of "The Revolution."

Communalism allows us to build power by rooting our political practice in the everyday struggles of our communities. The commune can begin as a site of convergence, organization and agitation around our demands as oppressed peoples. A commune can come into being simply by addressing something as simple as providing food for those who are hungry, a place to stay for those who are homeless or education for those who seek it. If the commune and its participants address the genuine needs of the community, then it will attract sympathy, support and wider participation. This allows the commune to take on greater responsibilities and struggles, pushing it further toward full autonomy and self-government. A commune can thus grow from humble origins into a substantial source of power capable of providing for the people, and posing a direct challenge to the state and capital.

The rise of a revolutionary commune gives birth to a durable insurgent community. As such, communalism benefits from and amplifies many of the strategic advantages of insurgencies. The participants in a commune are camouflaged from authorities, since their activities are undertaken in the name of the community itself. Like guerilla armies, communalist insurgents can seek shelter within a sympathetic larger community, when state forces inevitably attempt repression. A commune does not need presidents, chairpersons or commissars, and thus deprives the state of key leaders to bribe, jail or assassinate. A commune that is well-rooted in a community is extraordinarily difficult to uproot and destroy. When an entire community effectively functions as an insurgency, the imprisonment or killing of a single activist or group of activists can only harden the resolve of the other community members. In a conflict with a well-rooted commune, the state must either choose to settle in for a prolonged struggle, grant key concessions to the participants or collapse.

As a form, the commune is extraordinarily flexible. Its only requirement is a body of participants willing to envision and realize a new way of life in the present. After this point, a commune can change the way it operates, the territory and responsibilities it covers, and its organizational form, to suit local conditions. A successful revolutionary strategy can only emerge by responding to the needs and desires of the people living in a particular place. Communes will operate differently in New York and Cairo. Nevertheless, as long as commune participants recognize their shared interests in the larger struggle for the future of our world, they must provide each other with ideas and mutual aid, despite the wide variance in the forms that struggle takes in particular countries and cities.

Since 2012, Kurds and their allies in Rojava, or northern Syria, have fought to build a society based on the principles of "democratic confederalism." Rojava is governed by a network of local communes and councils, where its people take direct responsibility for political decision-making. Popular militias defend these communes from the violence of reactionary groups like the Islamic State. Despite years of lengthy sieges, an international blockade and a civil war, the people of Rojava have managed to maintain their commitment to democratic social transformation. In cities like Kobane, which was devastated by a months-long siege by the forces of ISIS, communes that once defended the city are now responsible for planning and stewarding the rebuilding process. The communes, in which men, women, and different minority groups participate on an equal footing, discuss and address problems as diverse as ensuring a steady supply of electricity and advancing the rights of women.[34]

Across the Turkish border, the Kurdish movement is using the strategies of democratic confederalism in what may be even more difficult conditions. The Turkish state has long denied the revolutionary aspirations of much of its Kurdish minority and its vibrant leftist movements with stark and brutal violence. Unlike in Syria, the Turkish state is still strong and can exercise control over the majority of its territory. Nevertheless, the Kurds and their allies in Turkey have been building local councils and communes as a means of organizing resistance since the mid-2000s, longer than their comrades across the border in Rojava.

From small villages in eastern Turkey to large cities, these grassroots organizations have taken on a growing role as protectors of women's rights, organizers of egalitarian economic projects and sites of convergence for revolutionary organizing. Since the Turkish government began its latest crackdown on leftist opposition forces within its borders, many of the cities and towns where the communes have taken root have declared autonomy and attempted to defend themselves from the state's attacks. At the time of this writing, it is still uncertain how the battle between the revolutionaries in Turkey and the Turkish state will end, but it is certain that the communes have created a resilient base for stalwart resistance.[35]

These are not perfect systems—there is no such thing as a perfect system—but they are examples of how communalism can create vital, effective and liberatory social systems, even under extraordinarily desperate circumstances. Communalism can move us beyond the symbolic arena of protests and demonstrations, and build our power to directly shape political reality. The oppressed majority across the world is desperate for change. People are well aware that the present system is failing them, that it is unsustainable, and that the elite are corrupt, self-serving and incapable of addressing their genuine needs. Communalism offers something new: a chance to seize control of the forces that govern our lives directly and steer the world in a radical direction.

If we are to rally our brothers and sisters around the world to finally take power back into our own hands, we have to articulate a compelling vision that we can believe in and fight for. Part of this must come from simply winning small victories in the present, showing those who have been beaten and oppressed for years on end that resistance can succeed. It also means making the connection between smaller acts of revolutionary love, like tending a garden or teaching a child, and the larger struggle for freedom that connects us all. Finally, we have to be able to turn our gaze from our particular local battles to the grand principles that drive us to struggle and to dare to win: freedom, equality and the brotherhood of all peoples across Earth. A movement that can inspire people in these ways will spread across the globe like a wildfire across dry brushland.

If we succeed, a small scattering of local experiments and tentative first steps will steadily grow as communes spring up throughout the city blocks, banlieus and villages of the world. New alliances will form between once distant groups, heralding a new coalition of the poor, the dispossessed, the marginalized and the disillusioned. At first, longstanding local political arrangements will be shaken up irreparably. The elite will struggle to understand a movement that defies its expectations, that has no mouthpieces and that has no single authority with which it can negotiate. Groups for the defense of communal life will arise alongside food distribution programs, free healthcare services and reclaimed housing. The agents of oppression will withdraw from some areas and they will be forced out of others. The state will attempt to repress the movement and many will suffer as a result. But draconian arrests and militarization will only fuel the people's anger, leading to a rising cycle of protests, riots, clandestine strikes and outright revolts.

Ultimately, the power of the people will reach a critical mass in one country and its government will fall. The commune will tear down the state and turn its seized resources to the task of radically restructuring society. Other governments will fall and the communes will join together in a federation of free peoples. What began as a droplet will end as a flood: the remnants of capital's power will be crushed beneath the revolutionary wave, ushering in a new era beyond the poverty and oppression of capitalism. We will erect the home of humanity's next evolutionary leap, forged in struggle and tested by the fires of revolution: the Commune of communes.

Endnotes

1   Roos, J. "Towards a New Anti-Capitalist Politics," *ROAR Magazine*. December 9th, 2015. Available at: https://roarmag. org/magazine/anti-capitalist-politics-21st-century/. [accessed 7 June 2017]

2   Fellow travelers will likely object to my exclusion of the short-lived, anarchist-dominated Spanish Revolution from 1936 to 1939. While Spanish anarchists achieved remarkable successes in their few short years of experimentation, the marginalization of the anarchists by other Republicans and the ultimate defeat of the Republican cause by the fascists put an end to the 20th century's major anarchist revolution before its trajectory of development could be discovered.

3   Haider, A., and Mohandesi, S. "Is There A Future For Socialism?" *Jacobin*. April 26th, 2012. Available at: https://www.jacobinmag.com/2012/04/is-there-a-future-for-socialism/. [accessed 7 June 2017]

4   Ibid.

5   "Manifesto of the International Socialist Congress at Basel," (1912) *Extraordinary International Socialist Congress at Basel*. Available at: https://www.marxists.org/history/international/social-democracy/1912/basel-manifesto.htm.

[accessed 7 June 2017]

6   Sewell, R. "4th August 1914: The Great Betrayal and Collapse of the Second International," *In Defense of Marxism*. August 4th, 2014. Available at: http://www.marxist.com/4th-august-1914-the-great-betrayal-and-collapse-of-the-second-international.htm. [accessed 7 June 2017]

7   Lenin, V.I. (1902) *What Is To Be Done?* "The Primitiveness of the Economists and the Organization of the Revolutionaries" and "The 'Plan' For An All-Russia Political Newspaper." Available at: https://www.marxists.org/archive/lenin/works/1901/witbd/iv.htm and https://www.marxists.org/archive/lenin/works/1901/witbd/v.htm. [accessed 7 June 2017]

8   Maoism is a revolutionary theory that drew a great deal of inspiration from Leninism. Mao argued that peasants were the key revolutionary social base in underdeveloped societies, where the industrial working class only made up a small portion of the population. After the Chinese Communist Party's victory in the Chinese Civil War, many Marxist revolutionaries in the developing world adopted Maoist theory and practice to adapt to the agrarian conditions of their own societies. Mao later developed a critique of the Soviet Union's geopolitical policy and bureaucratization during the Sino-Soviet split.

9   Rabinowitch, R. (1976) *The Bolsheviks Come to Power: The Revolution of 1917 in Petrograd*. (Chicago: Haymarket Books) p. 311. Rabinowitch's account of the crucial period in the lead-up to the October Revolution is an exceptional historical study. It is required reading for any would-be revolutionary.

10   Lenin, V.I. (September 1917) "One of the Fundamental Questions of the Revolution." Available at: https://www.marxists.org/archive/lenin/works/1917/sep/27.htm. [accessed 7 June 2017]

11   Kosman, M. "Beyond Kronstadt; the Bolsheviks in power."
     August 7th, 2005. Available at: https://libcom.org/library/
     beyond-kronstadt. [accessed 7 June 2017]
12   Deutscher, I. (2003) *The Prophet Armed: Trotsky, 1879-1921.*
     (London: Verso) p. 424. Available at: http://bit.ly/21HpMWL.
13   "Demands of the Kronstadt Insurgents, Expressed in the
     Resolution of the General Meeting of the Crews of the Ships
     of the Line," February 28th, 1921. Available at: http://isites.
     harvard.edu/fs/docs/icb.topic519973.files/Demands%20
     of%20the%20Kronstadt%20Insurgents.pdf. [accessed 7 June
     2017]
14   This is not the place for a lengthy discussion of the economic
     history of the Soviet Union. However, I think the key to
     understanding the development of the Soviet economy and
     its ultimate collapse lies in a careful study of the institution
     of one-man management, the debate over workers' control of
     production and the debate over the pace of industrialization
     from 1917 into the 1930s. I hypothesize that the perceived
     need to industrialize rapidly contradicted the original
     Bolshevik aim of workers' control. Simply put, workers
     could not reliably be expected to produce enough surplus
     value for rapid capital accumulation if they remained in
     control of production. This problem incentivized the erosion
     of workers' control in favor of a system where the state
     acted like a single capitalist, extracting surplus value for the
     purpose of developing the Soviet economy and military. We
     would benefit greatly from a careful historical study of this
     problem.
15   "Sorghum & Steel," *Chuang*, No. 1. (2016) p. 42. Available
     at: http://chuangcn.org/journal/one/sorghum-and-steel/1-
     precedents/. [accessed 7 June 2017]
16   Ibid. p. 69. Available at: http://chuangcn.org/journal/one/
     sorghum-and-steel/2-development/. [accessed 7 June 2017]
17   Ibid. pp. 76–82. Available at: http://chuangcn.org/journal/

one/sorghum-and-steel/2-development/. [accessed 7 June 2017]

18 Ibid. pp. 84–5. Available at: http://chuangcn.org/journal/one/sorghum-and-steel/2-development/. [accessed 7 June 2017]

19 Ibid. pp. 86–90. Available at: http://chuangcn.org/journal/one/sorghum-and-steel/2-development/. [accessed 7 June 2017]

20 Ibid. pp. 92–3. Available at: http://chuangcn.org/journal/one/sorghum-and-steel/2-development/. [accessed 7 June 2017]

21 Ibid. pp. 96–7. Available at: http://chuangcn.org/journal/one/sorghum-and-steel/2-development/. [accessed 7 June 2017]

22 Ibid. pp. 97–100. Available at: http://chuangcn.org/journal/one/sorghum-and-steel/2-development/. [accessed 7 June 2017]

23 Ibid. pp. 101–6. Available at: http://chuangcn.org/journal/one/sorghum-and-steel/3-ossification/. [accessed 7 June 2017]

24 As was the case during most periods of upheaval in the pre-Deng period, CCP figures attempted to direct popular anger toward the subjective failings of authority figures (for example, antiquated, improper or counterrevolutionary attitudes), and away from the material inequities and power imbalances that were largely responsible for unrest. At the same time, the CCP often placed the responsibility for unrest on privileged groups like university students, while aggressively suppressing the rebellious activity of poorer workers and peasants.

25 "Decision of the Central Committee of the Chinese Communist Party Concerning the Great Proletarian Cultural Revolution," August 8th, 1966. Available at: https://www.marxists.org/subject/china/peking-review/1966/PR1966-

33g.htm. [accessed 7 June 2017]

26   "Sorghum & Steel," *Chuang*, No. 1. (2016) p. 130. Available at: http://chuangcn.org/journal/one/sorghum-and-steel/4-ruination/. [accessed 7 June 2017]

27   Hunan Provincial Revolutionary Great Alliance Committee. (1968) "Whither China?" Available at: http://anti-imperialism.com/2012/10/17/whither-china-1968/. [accessed 7 June 2017] This little-read work is one of the most important documents to rise out of the Cultural Revolution, considering its careful analysis of the forces at work in contemporary China and its extraordinary prescience.

28   This observation is not intended to forgive the almost blind, teleological belief in "socialism as industrialization at whatever cost" that prevailed among numerous communist parties throughout the 20th century. The perceived necessity to industrialize in a manner consistent with a highly linear interpretation of Marx's theory of capitalist development certainly contributed to the development of heavy-handed, centralized states. Nevertheless, it is also impossible to ignore the fact that 20th-century "socialist" countries faced constant military pressure and competition from capitalist states, whom it would be difficult to balance against without the industrial development required to support modern military forces. This prevailing military logic further fueled state centralization and helped to erode any possibility of worker democracy. The fact that these societies were placed in such unforgiving geopolitical binds is one of the great tragedies of the 20th century's revolutions.

29   I do not place too much personal emphasis on this contradiction, since I am not a Marxist. Instead, I leave it as a challenge that requires immediate analysis for those on the anti-revisionist Left. The purpose of this challenge is not to engage in the ceaseless repetition of 20th-century debates. Rather, its purpose is to ask how our interpretations of

20th-century history impact our beliefs about revolutionary strategy in the present.

30 The persistent competition, and brief outbreak of outright hostilities, between the neighboring so-called socialist powers of the Soviet Union and the People's Republic of China is one of the best examples of this phenomenon.

31 The name attached to communalist practices is unimportant. The Zapatistas call it Zapatismo, the Kurds call it Democratic Confederalism, Bookchin called it libertarian municipalism, but all referred to similar forms of political practice and social organization.

32 "Precisely because it wants to grow, the commune can only take sustenance from what is not it. As soon as it cuts itself off from the outside, it weakens, devours itself, tears itself apart, loses it vitality, or surrenders to what the Greeks call, with their entire country in mind, 'social cannibalism,' for the very reason that they feel isolated from the rest of the world. For the commune, there is no difference between gaining in power and concerning itself essentially with what is not it." The Invisible Committee. (2014) *To Our Friends*. (Cambridge: Semiotext(e)) p. 70. Available at: http://theanarchistlibrary.org/library/the-invisible-committe-to-our-friends.pdf. [accessed 7 June 2017]

33 Democracy is not known by its process; it is known by its effects. The process reveals its character in the effects it creates. If the pursuit of absolute consensus confuses the people and robs them of their power to act, then it cannot possibly be a democratic process. Power is not just what is ideally *represented* in the laws of a society — who governs, who is the sovereign, what are the rules and prohibitions — but what is *actualized* in its practices: Who produces goods, knowledge, people and so on, and who appropriates these things? Who can change the way that people think and act in this society, and to what extent? What kind of people

is this society producing? Who is it excluding and what role does this exclusion play in the social order? Can the fundamental pillars of this society be challenged, altered or overthrown? What struggles and contradictions shape its continuous development? Democratization is not the same thing as simply saying that everyone has "the right to vote." Democratization is the extension of the power to contest, shape and alter the real facts that make a society what it is. Thus, participants in the communes must strive to make their practices democratic in fact, not simply in theory.

34 For further information on the political and social systems being developed in Rojava, see: Knapp, M., Flach, A., and Ayboga, E.. (2016) *Revolution in Rojava: Democratic Autonomy and Women's Liberation in Syria Kurdistan*. (London: Pluto Press); Strangers in a Tangled Wilderness. (2015) *A Small Key Can Open a Large Door: The Rojava Revolution*. (Chico: AK Press); Biehl, J. "Impressions of Rojava: a report from the revolution," *ROAR Magazine*. December 16, 2014. Available at: https://roarmag.org/essays/janet-biehl-report-rojava/. [accessed 7 June 2017]; Simons, P. "Lessons From Rojava: Democracy and Commune," *CrimethInc. Ex-Workers' Collective*. May 19, 2016. Available at: http://www.crimethinc.com/blog/2016/05/19/rojava-democracy-and-commune/. [accessed 7 June 2017], Saadi, S. "Rojava revolution: building autonomy in the Middle East," *ROAR Magazine*. July 25, 2014. Available at: https://roarmag.org/essays/rojava-autonomy-syrian-kurds/. [accessed 7 June 2017]

35 For a description of the practice of democratic confederalism in Turkey, particularly before the latest outbreak of civil conflict, see: TATORT Kurdistan. (2013) *Democratic Autonomy in North Kurdistan*. (Porsgrunn: New Compass Press).

Chapter 13

Why We Fight

A thousand goals have there been hitherto, for a thousand peoples have there been. Only the fetter for the thousand necks is still lacking; there is lacking the one goal. As yet humanity hath not a goal. But pray tell me, my brethren, if the goal of humanity be still lacking, is there not also still lacking—humanity itself?

Friedrich Nietzsche, *Thus Spake Zarathustra*

Ours is the struggle of life against death. This may seem like a simplistic statement, but it is true. We are fighting against an inhuman system, one that places the power of the dead god of money above all possible human considerations. We are fighting against a system that perpetuates itself by preying on the weakest parts of humanity, and by encouraging us to view one another with suspicion, distrust and hatred. We are fighting against a system that is driving us headlong toward the catastrophic destruction of whole species and ecosystems. We are fighting for the soul of the world, locked in the ceaseless battle of freedom against oppression, strength against weakness and love against hate.

It is not simply this system's irrationality, or its path to self-destruction, that makes it so detestable. It is capitalism's ugliness, brutality and barbarism that spurs us into this desperate and uncertain struggle to overthrow it. We cannot breathe in a world that tries to reduce us to mere appendages of a money-making system. We cannot tolerate a society that brutalizes us, and our brothers and sisters, because of the color of our skin, our religious beliefs, our gender or our misfortune of being born into poverty. We cannot abide the pathetic values of this system or its dull mediocrity, which threatens to drown every wonderful part of our world with consumerist trash. We love life, we love this world and we love its beauty, and because we love these things, we rage against the horrors and injustices of a system we witness daily destroying them.

Contemporary society keeps itself alive with a politics of fear and resentment. It constantly reminds us that we are disposable, that we are just one misstep away from ruin and destitution. The anxious drive to keep making money, to keep surviving, is a constant presence that slowly poisons our minds. It seeps into our relationships with each other, it saps our ability to empathize with other people and it works its terrible influence on even the most important decisions of our lives. When this poison takes over, it overwhelms our sense of humanity and consumes us with a greed that knows no limits.

Fear and greed, the two most detestable human emotions, are capitalism's lifeblood. Worst of all, this system teaches us to redirect this fear and anxiety onto the most vulnerable people in our society. It encourages us to treat ourselves as the victims of others who bear no responsibility for our pain. It tells us to let out our violent rage onto immigrants, refugees, minorities, gays, our spouses and our children. This system brings out the worst in humanity, all while telling us that we are sick, deluded and wrong for wanting a different world.

Still, we dream. We dream of a world where this brutal system is relegated to the pages of history. We dream of a world without rich or poor, ruler or subject, master or slave. We believe that a world where beauty trumps greed is not only possible, but also necessary. We believe, despite years of being beaten into submission by schooling, work and propaganda, that the future is ours to seize. We know that there is no machine, weapon or army stronger than the power of the people when we unite in a common struggle. We hope that we can overcome the fears and doubts that hold us back from building this world to come. We pray that others feel the same as we do.

The simple truth is that capitalism cannot live a single day without our consent. The worst knowledge of all is that, passively or actively, we allow these terrible things to happen to us and to those around us. How many of us confront oppression with an unyielding strength? How many of us are willing to do whatever it takes to put an end to the injustices that are simply taking place right now on our own street? To be sure, there are individuals whose passion for freedom shines through the darkness. But most of us keep our heads down, go to work and come home. We remain afraid to take the first step, afraid to talk to one another, afraid to do what has to be done.

The moments in history when this wall of fear finally breaks down are unmistakable: millions take power into their own hands, taking their rightful place as masters of their own destinies. To date, these flashes of brilliance have always subsided. We return to complacency, to passivity and to fear. If we are to fulfill the great mission of our time, we have to shatter this fear and rise up once more. We have to become better than our present selves. We have to exceed ourselves in strength, in dedication and in humanity.

The task that faces us is enormous. The bourgeoisie was a revolutionary class, because it transformed fragmentary elements within feudal society—scattered manufacturers, and the urban and rural poor—into the foundations of capitalist society. It defined itself as a class by creating another, the proletariat, which it would exploit ruthlessly in its endless drive to accumulate wealth. The challenge we face now is much more difficult than what the bourgeoisie faced under feudalism.

The working class cannot create revolutionary change in society by simply reshaping it in its own image. There is nothing dignified or noble about being forced to labor. The working class cannot change the world by making itself into a fetish. Instead, we have to lift a new system of values out of capitalism's wreckage.

Workers, students, the young, the old, the marginalized and the unemployed must band together to create a society without classes. If the working class is going to lead a revolution worth the struggle and sacrifice that any revolution demands, then it must ultimately abolish itself. Our revolution will not establish a "worker's society" or place work at the center of life. It will ask what work is necessary to secure a good and dignified life for humanity, including the time to develop as a human being.

This is why we fight—not just for material comfort for ourselves and our children, but also to place life itself at the center of our world. We have to shatter the petty values of our time—fear, greed and resentment—and replace them with values worthy of a noble existence. The liberation of humanity from labor promises not just to eliminate poverty, but also to give us the opportunity to choose our own values. We can finally have the chance, and the precious time, to choose the kind of lives that we want to live, unfettered by the need to scramble for a wage. There is greatness within us all waiting for the chance to be unleashed and in our struggle to free ourselves we can give voice to this greatness. We are simply fighting for the chance to live life the way it should be lived.

Before Fred Hampton, deputy chairman of the Black Panther Party, was assassinated, he would end speeches by leading his listeners in chanting "I am a revolutionary!" Black and white, rich and poor, student and worker alike, the assembled people would join in, rising to a mighty swell. Hampton did not ask for our submission, our loyalty or our votes. Rather, he asked us to join him in recognizing the strength within ourselves and to use that strength to make revolutionary change in society. He knew that so-called ordinary people are capable of incredible things and that history is written when that transcendent potential within us all bursts forth. Hampton posed his listeners a difficult question: Are you ready to give more than you ever thought possible? Are you ready to dedicate your life to something larger than yourself?

Today, we must ask this same question of ourselves. We are embarking on the greatest struggle in the history of humanity. We are surrounded on all sides by incredible dangers. Those who struggle for freedom face imprisonment, torture, slander and ostracism. Some of us will lose our lives. Many already have. There is no guarantee that we will succeed or that our sacrifices will be remembered by those who come after us. All we have is our hope, our love for one another, our rage against injustice and a goal to strive toward. So, ask yourself: Is that enough? Can I struggle for what I know to be right, despite all the danger that struggle entails and all the sacrifices I will have to make? Am I willing, not just to die for this struggle, but also to live for it—to give years of my life to a cause with no certainty of victory? I cannot answer this question for you. Only you can.

To struggle is to give meaning to one's life. It is our capacity to struggle, to consciously change ourselves and our world, that makes living beings unique. We are not the mere recipients of natural events, history or inherited ideas and institutions. We can change our destinies if we have the strength. For us, taking part in the revolutionary struggle is the only way to constantly ascend to new heights and fulfill our calling as living beings. To be sure, this struggle is perilous. To struggle for freedom is to risk death, but it is precisely this risk that allows us to truly live. By choosing to fight for a better world, we transcend the shackles of fear. All creation is hard, dangerous and uncertain, the creation of a new world especially so. We embrace this challenge. Were the struggle easy, it would not be a worthy task for humanity.

Let us fight for our freedom, and for equality, dignity and justice. We may be victorious and we may overcome the challenge of our era. Still, the struggle will continue. There is no end to history, or to the rise and fall of new ways of thinking and ways of life. There may come a time, many years from now, when today's problems seem quaint. But first we must do our part to ensure that our descendants can live in a world beyond poverty and tyranny, where the Earth itself is not threatened by the greed of a few. To those who are already fighting: I salute you. To those who have yet to join the struggle: I extend a hand of friendship and solidarity. I look forward to fighting together with you in the years to come.

Glossary

Automation: The replacement of human work with the work of self-governing machines.

Capital: Money, tools, buildings and so on put to work to produce a surplus. In its simplest form, capital is money used to make more money. Because someone needs to labor in order to turn money into more money, a pile of money is not capital. Capital is the social relationship that allows its owner to make a surplus out of the things that they own.

Capitalism: A system of production for profit based on the extraction of surplus value from wage laborers. Contemporary capitalism has three potentially fatal contradictions: 1. Capitalism is based on the exploitation of labor, but its development (through automation) makes labor increasingly obsolete. 2. Capitalism requires the capitalist class to have a monopoly on the means of production, but the rise of distributed production erodes that monopoly. 3. Capitalism requires infinite growth to survive, but we live on a planet with finite resources.

Capitalist: A person who owns capital and uses it to make a profit.

Class: A group of people who share a common social status because of their relationship to the productive system of their society. Classes only exist in a society where groups of people have different stratified relationships to production, such as a society where some people own the things needed to produce goods and where others work for them for a wage.

Commodity: A good with exchange value or a good produced to be traded, bought and sold.

Communism: A state of society in which wage labor and the production of value have been abolished. Each person contributes what they can according to their abilities and each person receives goods according to their needs.

Dead labor: See *Capital*.

Deflation: A rise in the value of currency relative to commodities.

Demand: An economic term for the desire and ability to purchase a commodity.

Distributed production: A production paradigm defined by the use of advanced general-purpose tools like computers and 3D printers to design goods, distribute blueprints for them across an electronic network and produce them individually.

Exchange value: The relative measure of which commodities will exchange for a particular commodity. Exchange value is a relationship between two things established by the fact that both were produced with a certain quantity of labor.

Fiat currency: A form of currency whose value is not linked to or based on that of any other commodity, such as gold. Modern fiat currency came into existence when the US left the gold standard in 1971.

Financialization: The process whereby profits increasingly accumulate through financial channels like the stock market, public and private debts, and derivatives markets rather than trade and commodity production.

General rate of profit: An expression of the rate of surplus value produced by a capitalist economy as a whole.

Good: An item or product, used in this book to refer to its value as a useful object and not as a thing for exchange.

Gross domestic product (GDP): The total value of all of the goods produced in a given economy.

Industrial production: A production paradigm based on the use of specialized machines to produce large numbers of goods in a central location, like a factory, and distribute them to consumers using an infrastructure like roads, railways, shipping lanes and airways.

Inflation: A fall in the value of currency relative to commodities.

Labor: Human work measured in the abstract terms of labor hours. In a capitalist society, labor is a commodity that serves as the source of value for all other commodities.

Labor theory of value (labor theory): The economic theory that labor creates exchange value in a capitalist economy.

Law of value: The requirement to produce an eternally rising amount of exchange value in order to keep the process of capitalist accumulation going. The law of value is the central constraint of capitalism and what drives capitalists to search endlessly for ways to keep making a profit.

Living labor: See *Labor*.

Mass production: The production of a large number of identical goods, often by using specialized machines.

Means of production: The collection of tools, machines, buildings and raw materials needed to produce a good.

Mode of production: The dominant system that a society uses to produce the goods it needs to sustain itself. A mode of production is defined by the means of production needed, the kind of labor needed, the production paradigm and social relations between the classes in that society. In short, a mode of production is a social relationship mediated by technology. Industrial capitalism and agrarian feudalism are two examples of modes of production.

Neoliberalism: Capitalism's strategy of adaptation following the serious crisis of the late 1960s and 70s. This strategy forged a true world market by assaulting the post-war accommodation between capital and labor in the developed world, and opening protected markets to international capital in the developing world.

Overaccumulation: When so much capital accumulates in a capitalist economy that there are few possible outlets for profitable investment.

Overproduction: When an industry produces more goods than can be profitably sold.

Politics. The struggle to shape and determine the power relations in a society.

Production paradigm: The general model of a process used to produce goods.

Proletariat: A class of people who work for a wage and own little more (in terms of capital) than their own labor power.

Radical automation: A long-term decline in the demand for hours of labor per worker caused by automation.

Rate of exploitation: The ratio between the value produced by workers and the wages they receive.

Rate of profit: The amount of profit that a capitalist earns relative to their investment, calculated in radical economics by dividing profit by wages and capital investment.

Socialism: A socioeconomic system where the means of production are owned by, controlled by and operated for the benefit of the working class.

Social relations: The relationships and hierarchies formed between individuals, groups, classes and institutions in a given society. The fact that capitalists have money and workers need to work for wages is an example of a hierarchical social relation, because the capitalists' ownership of the means of production allows them to force workers to work for them if the workers do not want to starve.

State: A professional body composed of bureaucrats, police, military, legislators and the like that exists as a coercive apparatus, clearly distinct from and above the people.

Surplus value: The value produced by workers laboring for longer than the time it takes for them to produce the value needed to pay their wages.

Tendency of the rate of profit to fall: The fact that the ratio of invested capital to living surplus value tends to rise over time, reducing the rate of profit.

Use value: The fact that a thing is useful to someone. Use value is subjective and not a mathematical quantity.

Value: In economics, the term "value" is a stand-in for *exchange value* (see previous).

Wage labor: A form of social organization where workers sell their ability to labor as a commodity.

Work: A human activity involving effort, ranging anywhere from farming to giving haircuts to writing code.

Zero Books

CULTURE, SOCIETY & POLITICS

Contemporary culture has eliminated the concept and public figure of the intellectual. A cretinous anti-intellectualism presides, cheer-led by hacks in the pay of multinational corporations who reassure their bored readers that there is no need to rouse themselves from their stupor. Zer0 Books knows that another kind of discourse – intellectual without being academic, popular without being populist – is not only possible: it is already flourishing. Zer0 is convinced that in the unthinking, blandly consensual culture in which we live, critical and engaged theoretical reflection is more important than ever before.

If you have enjoyed this book, why not tell other readers by posting a review on your preferred book site.

Recent bestsellers from Zero Books are:

In the Dust of This Planet
Horror of Philosophy vol. 1
Eugene Thacker
In the first of a series of three books on the Horror of
Philosophy, *In the Dust of This Planet* offers the genre of horror
as a way of thinking about the unthinkable.
Paperback: 978-1-84694-676-9 ebook: 978-1-78099-010-1

Capitalist Realism
Is there no alternative?
Mark Fisher
An analysis of the ways in which capitalism has presented itself
as the only realistic political-economic system.
Paperback: 978-1-84694-317-1 ebook: 978-1-78099-734-6

Rebel Rebel
Chris O'Leary
David Bowie: every single song. Everything you want to know,
everything you didn't know.
Paperback: 978-1-78099-244-0 ebook: 978-1-78099-713-1

Cartographies of the Absolute
Alberto Toscano, Jeff Kinkle
An aesthetics of the economy for the twenty-first century.
Paperback: 978-1-78099-275-4 ebook: 978-1-78279-973-3

Malign Velocities
Accelerationism and Capitalism
Benjamin Noys
Long listed for the Bread and Roses Prize 2015, *Malign Velocities* argues against the need for speed, tracking acceleration as the symptom of the ongoing crises of capitalism.
Paperback: 978-1-78279-300-7 ebook: 978-1-78279-299-4

Meat Market
Female flesh under Capitalism
Laurie Penny
A feminist dissection of women's bodies as the fleshy fulcrum of capitalist cannibalism, whereby women are both consumers and consumed.
Paperback: 978-1-84694-521-2 ebook: 978-1-84694-782-7

Poor but Sexy
Culture Clashes in Europe East and West
Agata Pyzik
How the East stayed East and the West stayed West.
Paperback: 978-1-78099-394-2 ebook: 978-1-78099-395-9

Romeo and Juliet in Palestine
Teaching Under Occupation
Tom Sperlinger
Life in the West Bank, the nature of pedagogy and the role of a university under occupation.
Paperback: 978-1-78279-637-4 ebook: 978-1-78279-636-7

Sweetening the Pill
or How we Got Hooked on Hormonal Birth Control
Holly Grigg-Spall
Has contraception liberated or oppressed women? *Sweetening the Pill* breaks the silence on the dark side of hormonal contraception.
Paperback: 978-1-78099-607-3 ebook: 978-1-78099-608-0

Why Are We The Good Guys?
Reclaiming your Mind from the Delusions of Propaganda
David Cromwell
A provocative challenge to the standard ideology that Western power is a benevolent force in the world.
Paperback: 978-1-78099-365-2 ebook: 978-1-78099-366-9

Readers of ebooks can buy or view any of these bestsellers by clicking on the live link in the title. Most titles are published in paperback and as an ebook. Paperbacks are available in traditional bookshops. Both print and ebook formats are available online.

Find more titles and sign up to our readers' newsletter
at http://www.johnhuntpublishing.com/culture-and-politics

Follow us on Facebook
at https://www.facebook.com/ZeroBooks

and Twitter at https://twitter.com/Zer0Books